Colonial Encounters
in the Age of
High Imperialism

IMPERIAL SOLIDARITY *This turn-of-the-century American cartoon caricatures China's plight as the Western powers and Japan confront one another and extract territorial, financial, and commercial concessions from a demoralized Quing dynasty. The various states are represented by their national symbols in the aftermath of the unsuccessful, antiforeign Boxer Rebellion: the British lion, the French cock, the Russian bear, the Japanese panther, the German and Austrian eagles (looking more like vultures), the Italian wolf, and the Chinese dragon. Note that the American eagle appears in the background, above the fray, a stance that reflected its supposedly non-Imperialist "Open Door" policy towards China.* (Reprinted by permission: American Heritage Publishing.)

LONGMAN WORLD HISTORY SERIES

Colonial Encounters in the Age of High Imperialism

SCOTT B. COOK

RHODE ISLAND SCHOOL OF DESIGN

MICHAEL ADAS
Series Editor

RUTGERS UNIVERSITY AT NEW BRUNSWICK

 LONGMAN

An imprint of Addison Wesley Longman, Inc.

New York • Reading, Massachusetts • Menlo Park, California • Harlow, England
Don Mills, Ontario • Sydney • Mexico City • Madrid • Amsterdam

For Charr and Michael

Executive Editor: Bruce Borland
Developmental Editor: Lily Eng
Project Coordination and Text Design: Ruttle Graphics, Inc.
Photo Researcher: Susan Kaprov
Cover Designer: Mary Archondes
Cover Illustration: The Second Lahore Durbar, 1846. The Granger Collection.
Electronic Production Manager: Angel Gonzalez Jr.
Manufacturing Manager: Willie Lane
Electronic Page Makeup: Ruttle Graphics, Inc.
Printer and Binder: RR Donnelley & Sons, Inc.
Cover Printer: The Lehigh Press, Inc.

For permission to use copyrighted material, grateful acknowledgment is made to the copyright holders on p. 162, which are hereby made part of this copyright page.

Colonial Encounters in the Age of High Imperialism

Library of Congress Cataloging-in-Publication Data

Cook, S. B., 1952—
Colonial encounters in the age of high imperialism/Scott B. Cook.
      p.   cm.   --(Longman world history series)
Includes biographical references and index.
ISBN 0-673-99229-2 (alk. paper)
1. Imperialism.   2. Colonies--History.   3. Civilization--History.   4. Technology transfer--History.   5. World politics--19th century.   6. World politics--20th century.   I. Title.   II. Series.
JC359.S4   1995
325'.32--dc20

                                                                    95 - 20933
                                                                    CIP

3 4 5 6 7 8-DOC-01 00 99

Contents

Maps and Illustrations

Author's Preface

Our's is a world profoundly shaped by the recent experience of imperialism. Whether we are conscious of it or not, we are all citizens of a global community that bears the unmistakable imprint of past European domination. The legacies of Western empires that once straddled the planet and occupied some three-quarters of its land surface remain long after the burst of late-nineteenth century expansion was over and some thirty years after all but a few of the colonies became independent. A quick glance around the globe confirms that we are, in fact, the world's first generation of postcolonials.

Consider the following: Cars in Nigeria are driven on the left (as they are in Britain). French is the predominant language of the Ivory Coast whose official name is the République de la Côte d'Ivoire. Many Indian railway tracks are small gauge, quaint relics of the British period. The Caribbean island of Jamaica is mostly populated by the descendants of African slaves whose white head of state (Queen Elizabeth II) is directly descended from the rulers of what once was a leading slave-trading nation. The streets of the capital of the Sudan, Khartoum, are laid out as a series of Union Jacks (courtesy of Lord Kitchener). Some 2,800 miles to the northwest, Casablanca's urban design and public architecture still contain a French colonial aesthetic that combines modernism and Orientalism. North African couscous complements Paris' cuisine, just as rijstafel (from Indonesia) enlivens the Dutch palate and (Indian) chicken tandoori enriches Britain's table fare. As recently as 1994, the president of Angola in southern Africa was a man with the un-Bantu but very Portuguese name of José Eduardo dos Santos.

Moreover, most of world has adopted the calendar that we have been using since 1752 (Japan, Egypt, China, and Turkey all added the Gregorian calendar between 1873 and 1917). One hundred years ago, timepieces throughout the world were set according to a standard fixed on Greenwich, a suburb of London, after an international assemblage of Western scientists and geographers designated it as the longitudinal prime meridian in recognition of Britain's naval supremacy and its contribution to global exploration. Approximately one third of humanity professes to be Christian, almost double that of Islam, the next largest faith. English is the second most widely spoken language in the world (Mandarin Chinese is first, Hindi is third, and Spanish is fourth). The world's loftiest peak,

Series Editor's Preface

It is fitting that Scott Cook's *Colonial Encounters in the Age of High Imperialism* is the first volume to appear in the HarperCollins World History Series. Although cross-cultural exchange has been an increasingly prominent feature of human history for millennia, the decades from the 1870s to the outbreak of World War I in 1914 marked a time of unprecedented interaction between diverse peoples and societies all across the globe. In terms of sheer numbers and the intensity of cross-cultural contacts in this period, as well as in the volume of the diffusion of ideas, institutional arrangements and material culture, no historical era had seen such a thorough closure between different regions and centers of civilization. A genuinely global civilization had been coalescing since the early decades of European overseas expansion in the fifteenth century. But its full integration and articulation occurred only in five or six decades before World War I. In those years the forces and structures emerged that would powerfully shape twentieth-century history, which can be seen as the first epoch in which global patterns and processes took precedence over regional and intra-civilizational developments.

As Scott Cook's original and provocative account of these momentous transformations makes clear, the industrial nations of Europe and North America provided much of the momentum for this process. These imperialist powers came to rule directly or dominate informally most of the globe in this era. They were also the main agents of contact between culture zones and civilizations, and the major source of the diffusion of new technologies and ways of thinking about and organizing societies and environments. Industrialization not only gave the peoples of western Europe and its North American offshoots hitherto unimaginable advantages over all other cultures and civilizations in military and communications technology, it allowed them to dominate the global market economy. Thus, Western dominance set the tone for the era, and resistance or reactions to it on the part of colonized people throughout much of the rest of the globe were emerging as preeminent features of late-nineteenth century and twentieth-century history.

Although Cook does not neglect the factors that made for the unprecedented global dominance of the West, one of the great strengths of *Colonial Encounters in the Age of High Imperialism* is the in-depth attention that he gives to the responses of colonized peoples from the Congo and Hawaii to India and South Africa. In his fine narratives of carefully chosen, illustrative case studies he brings together patterns of political interaction, resistance, and accommodation with astute analyses of resulting social and cultural transformations. In these studies Cook gives special attention to gender, race, and class issues and their cross-cultural implications. In concluding sections and separate chapters, he explores the broader dimensions of some of the key themes he weaves into the narratives. These include the impact of Western technology in different cultural contexts, the images of and actual roles played by women in colonized areas, and the patterns of migration and settlement on the part of both Europeans and colonized peoples that marked this epoch of imperialist expansion and intense cross-cultural exchange.

Like all of the volumes that will appear in the HarperCollins World History Series, *Colonial Encounters* is intended to provide comparative and global perspectives on a key phase or process in human development. These studies may be used to supplement world civilization texts or may themselves serve as texts for thematic courses with a global dimension. They are intended to provide both in-depth case narratives illustrating major global themes, and to focus student attention on central questions and patterns in cross-cultural interaction at pivotal points in human history. The volumes in the HarperCollins World History Series are also designed to provide readable and provocative syntheses that incorporate the most recent trends and findings in research and scholarship in various historical fields.

MICHAEL ADAS
Series Editor
Rutgers University at New Brunswick

towering over 29,000 ft. and located in Nepal's Himalayan range, is named for a former surveyor-general of British India (Sir George Everest). Its lowest point, the Mariana Trench, which plunges nearly 36,000 ft. below sea level, bears the name of Mariana, the seventeenth century Austrian-born Spanish queen who sent a band of Jesuits to the neighboring Mariana Islands. Africa's largest body of fresh water, Victoria Nyanza or Lake Victoria, was, along with more than 40 other prominent topographical locations, cities, and states, named for the queen whose reign was perfectly aligned with Britain's imperial heyday. And women in Hawaii wear the *muumuu*, a garment designed by nineteenth century American Protestant missionaries to cover naked Polynesians.

Yet the legacy of early modern and modern imperialism amounts to more than transported foods, place names, and Western conventions. The entire world is partitioned into nation-states, many of whose boundaries were set by European imperialists ignorant of or indifferent to existing ethnic and cultural borders. The Code Napoleon governs legal practice in Madagascar, Martinique, Mauritania, and in many other parts of the former French empire (it also influences legal procedures in Louisiana and much of Europe and Latin America). The government of India bears the stamp of bureaucratic and legislative models bequeathed by Britain. France maintains close ties with its former African colonies and has militarily intervened in them no fewer than thirteen times between 1960 and 1986. In 1982, a British force that included a contingent of Gurkhas from the former quasi-dependency of Nepal, reconquered the Falkland Islands from Argentina. In so doing, it may have fought the last old-styled colonial war, of the type it had waged since 1700. And, on a different level, the progeny of a formerly colonized world herald the arrival of a heterogeneous global culture that, despite the long reach of McDonald's, Hollywood, and Standard Oil, is not wholly Americanized. For example, many of our finest contemporary writers, such as V. S. Naipaul and Edward Said, write in the language of their ex-colonial masters. With passions and ideas forged in the crucible of their own multicultural identities and transnational experiences, they have managed to express in terms both urgent and eloquent the dawning challenges of the post-colonial era.

For many, old-fashioned imperialism remains stubbornly alive, though operating in new, less apparent, and thus more insidious, guises. Often termed "neo-colonialism" (which combines lingering European influence with overwhelming U. S. economic, cultural, and strategic might), it is said to determine global trade and investment patterns that keep much of the Third World poor and dependent on the West. It is also said to be apparent in the life chances of those now living in the former colonies. The International Monetary Fund (IMF) has used a "Physical Quality of Life Index" to gauge Third World life chances based on such statistics as the mean birthrate, life expectancy, literacy, daily caloric intakes, and infant mortality as well as on per capita gross national products.

By almost any measurement, health, education, employment, and housing conditions and opportunities in the West far eclipse those found in the Third World. In 1990 the IMF calculated that a person born in sub-Sahara Africa had less than a 90 percent chance of surviving one year, could only expect to live 57 years, had a 48 percent chance of ever becoming literate, and as an adult was likely to ingest barely 2,000 calories a day. In comparison, a person born in the West had a better than 98 percent chance of surviving one year, had a life expectancy of 75 years, had a 95 percent chance of becoming literate, and on average could expect to ingest 3,400 calories each day. The question that divides experts is whether, or to what extent, such circumstances can trace their origins to the colonial epoch and to the policies and practices of the imperialists. While such questions lurk beyond the scope of this work, it is important to note that many scholars see them as connected with the issues raised here.

This book could not have been written without the support and assistance of many persons. The manuscript was read in large part or in its entirety by Professors Michael Adas, Michael Budd, and Pamela Walker. Their generous comments and invaluable insights and corrections resulted in substantial improvements. I am also deeply grateful for the suggestions offered by the publisher's anonymous readers, most of which I have tried my best to incorporate. Of course, I alone am responsible for any errors of fact or interpretation that remain.

It goes without saying this work has drawn liberally from the wellsprings of existing studies concerning modern imperialism. Something of the great debt I owe to scholars is evident in the works I have cited in the "Further Reading" sections. I am also indebted to the staffs of the libraries of the Rhode Island School of Design and Brown University who were unfailingly helpful.

To Michael Adas—*praeceptor et amicus meus*—I owe a special thanks for suggesting that I write this book and then for continuing to back me even after he had read the early drafts. Without the steady commitment of Bruce Borland of HarperCollins and the kind help of his assistants, Chris Biscoe and Lily Eng, this book might not have seen the light of day. It certainly benefited from the editorial and production skills of Eleanor Millspaugh. Finally, I am pleased to acknowledge the support of the Rhode Island School of Design, which helped mightily with a sabbatical leave and a Faculty Development Grant. I am also indebted to a host of friends and colleagues, especially Revae Lepannen, Don Keefer, Toby Ayers, Kevin Johnson, Jessica Swedlow, Elizabeth Grossman, Baruch Kirschenbaum, Jane Adas, Heidi Saunders, Marilyn Rueschemeyer, Yuriko Saito, Howard and Mary Runkel, Suzanne Schlatter, Peter Lacovara, Patricia Mantle, M Mn, M Mj, MB, and LL. This book is appreciatively dedicated to two persons who have given me years of emotional, material, and moral sustenance: Charr Cook and Michael Budd.

Introduction

This book is an introduction to the last and most extensive phase of Western expansion that engulfed the world between 1870 and 1914. Variously called the "New Imperialism," "Classical Imperialism," or "High Imperialism," it has been the subject of countless scholarly, literary, and polemical books, articles, and tracts. Considering the prolonged impact of imperialism and of other global forces linked to it (industrial capitalism, technological diffusion, and racism), it is not surprising that interest in the subject shows no signs of abating.

Unlike most college texts that focus on modern imperialism, this book does not replicate existing critiques of the standard theories of late nineteenth century expansionism. The focus of this text is on the general and particular experiences of persons living under imperialism. This book attempts to recapture important aspects of a pivotal moment in global history when African, Asian, and Pacific Islander societies were confronted by an unprecedented combination of military aggression, technological assertiveness, cultural dissemination, and economic transformation. It tallies and assesses the impact of those encounters. Although *Colonial Encounters* balances non-Western and Western perspectives, experiences, and motives, in view of the fact that colonialism was initiated by the West, the following accounts typically begin with a presentation of Western calculations and actions.

Several features have been incorporated to enhance the book's usefulness. Illustrations and maps supplement the text. Chapter introductions and conclusions present and summarize key issues and perspectives. Three case study chapters are also highlighted by "voices from the past," statements by persons who experienced colonialism firsthand. "Further Reading" sections offer the reader a guide to more detailed and advanced literature. A final aid is a glossary of important, usually foreign, terms.

The book is designed to underscore the great variety of colonial experiences without obscuring the basic characteristics of imperialism in general. The first chapter examines the European and African scenes at the cusp of the late nineteenth century stampede for colonies. It also provides an overview of the best known feature of the time, the so-called 1880s "Scramble for Africa." Various regions of the continent—West, South, East, and Northeast—and four of the most prominent imperial powers—France, Britain, Italy, and Germany—have been included to emphasize the diverse as well as the similar patterns of coexistence, resistance, and conquest with the onset of European hegemony. All of this is succinctly analyzed in light of the principal theories of late nineteenth century expansion.

The book highlights three specific colonial encounters: King Leopold's acquisition of the Congo, the cultural-economic prelude to America's annexation of Hawaii, and the contested politics of British rule in India. Each case contains historical narratives around which interpretive analyses are woven. I have chosen these examples because each exhibits a different aspect of the imperialist phenomenon. They were also selected to encompass colonial powers with distinct national developments and imperial styles as well as colonial societies that varied greatly from each other in size, culture, and location. Thus, *Colonial Encounters* presents detailed examples of Belgian, American, and British rule in the three main theaters of modern imperialism: Africa, the Pacific, and Asia.

The Congo is a classic instance of a territory suddenly subjected to a premeditated colonialism powered by the standard incentives: a thirst for profit and prestige. Its experience is also salient because, like many colonies, its colonial administration created a native work force that supplied Europe with coveted commodities. Unlike many colonies, the conspicuously vicious system of forced labor enforced by Leopold's administration outraged Euro-American public opinion and finally compelled Leopold to relinquish his private African fiefdom (if only to the Belgian government). Lastly, Leopoldian initiatives in the Congo, in conjunction with Britain's occupation of Egypt (1882) and France's seizure of Tunisia (1881), triggered the rush to occupy the rest of Africa.

Hawaii, by contrast, is an instructive example of a gradual colonialism at work: the islands were annexed by the colonial power (the U. S.) in a jingoistic spasm following the Spanish-American War of 1898 after decades of incremental cultural domination by traders and missionaries. Hawaii also reveals something of the dramatic changes in population composition that often accompanied colonialism, especially in white settler dependencies of which Hawaii was a partial type. Finally, the Hawaiian case permits us to relate the American experience of continental and overseas expansion to better known European models of expansion.

The inclusion of British India reminds us that the era of high imperialism consisted not only of newly acquired territories but of possessions won in earlier periods. Here India is used to show how imperialists and Western-educated indigenes clashed in their views and expectations of imperial rule, of its methods and its aims. Moreover, India is simply too important to be omitted from any study of global imperialism. It was the most populous and prestigious of colonial possessions and was the place where indigenous reactions to colonial rule first cohered into political and cultural nationalism. In this, India not only "lit the way" for other colonial nationalist movements, it demonstrated that even at the height of empire the seeds of its destruction were already being sown.

These cases are supplemented and linked by three shorter chapters that explore broader imperial patterns: technological, demographic, and gender. While all three aspects naturally form an integral part of the colonial histories of the Congo, Hawaii, and India, by sifting them out, it becomes easier to grasp the essential roles played by each. In addition, these connective thematic chapters allow for a concentrated development and analysis of aspects common to imperialism around the globe. In other words, they serve as illuminations of colonizing continuities that contextualize the case study chapters with their narrower, nuanced foci fixed on particular colonial sites and moments.

Each of these phenomena—technology, colonial demographics, and gender—was directly related to the means by which imperialism was imposed and sustained. Each reveals a great deal about the pervasiveness of imperialism as a global development, an idea, and a way of life. First, without modern technological inventions and medical discoveries—such as the rifle, quinine, the shallow-draft gunboat, railways, and telegraphs—Europeans could not have overwhelmed and subjugated others as they did. Second, large population shifts not only facilitated economic exploitation by bringing workers and resources together in concert with an expanding global economy, they also fashioned a global mosaic where Africans now inhabit the New World, Indians the Caribbean, the Chinese Southeast Asia, and Europeans South Africa, North America, and Australasia. And third, the experiences, roles, and impacts of women under colonialism considerably defined the imperial era whether women acted as imperial helpmates, missionaries, or critics or as vital members of indigenous social systems and resistance efforts.

These key colonial themes have also given rise to some engrossingly productive controversies. Modern technology continues to be scrutinized as a rationale that Westerners have employed to assert their superiority over non-Westerners. The question of whether it caused or facilitated the extension of empires is also debated. The voluntarist nature of the massive flows of non-Westerners across colonial boundaries and along major sea routes continues to be questioned. Did these migrations amount to slavery in a new guise or were they an exercise of free will in the rational pursuit of better economic opportunities away from home? And what has been the legacy of immigration on host ecologies and communities? With respect to gender, were the foundations of imperial rule undermined by the presence of Western women who, with their alleged prejudice and prudery, supposedly calcified the "natural" relations between colonizing and colonized males? And what of the impact on race relations and the colonial economy exerted by colonized women whether as laborers or merchants, or as the concubines of white settlers?

Notwithstanding the variety of scholarly opinion on these and related points, what is far less disputed is that the empires could not have been maintained without the enabling and coercive powers of industrial technology. The world-wide capitalist economy to which the empires were inextricably tethered would not have functioned as efficiently or yielded as much profit to the Western industrial states without the organized distribution of cheap colonial labor, female as well as male, whether within their homelands or in distant colonial enclaves.

The reader should note that throughout the book I have used "imperialism" and "colonialism" interchangeably, taking my cue from the "book of common usage" rather than from the specialist's lexicon. Yet I must also point out that the words have been used in dissimilar ways by many scholars. "Imperialism" in particular has multiple meanings. Here imperialism/colonialism denotes formal (political and economic) or informal (economic but not political) domination by a foreign power or powers. The three cases I have explored concern *formal* dominance by an *overseas* power (though most of the Hawaiian chapter recounts the period of cultural and economic domination that led up to the assumption of political control) because this was the prevalent mode of Western expansion at that time. But these choices do not mean to imply that imperialism was entirely confined to the West (Japan embarked on imperial subjugation), that informal control was negligible (it embraced nearly all of Latin America, China, and much of the Ottoman empire), or that imperialism's sole outlet was overseas (Russia and the U. S. devoured vast contiguous territories).

Two further related points can be made. First, formal control of non-Western peoples by the West between 1870 and 1914 was preceded by and built on earlier phases of European expansionism. Second, late nineteenth century imperialism was part of a broader global hegemony composed of a burgeoning Euro-centered economic system, a chauvinistic assertion of Western culture, a rise of "scientific" political ideologies of supremacy (Social Darwinism and biological racism), and a decisive European lead in arms, machines, and other technologies. Lastly, "metropolitan" means the homelands of the Western empires (Europe and the United States) and "periphery" refers to the areas of actual or prospective colonies (Africa, Asia, and the Pacific).

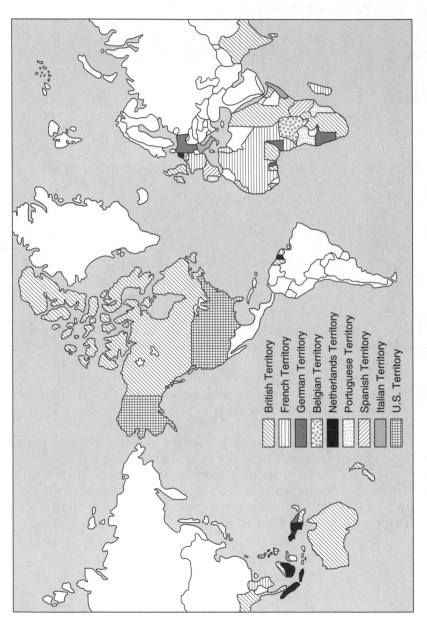

THE WORLD DIVIDED UP *By 1900 much of the world had been claimed by the European powers, even though not all lands had been effectively occupied.* (Reprinted by permission: University of Minnesota Press)

Legend:
- British Territory
- French Territory
- German Territory
- Belgian Territory
- Netherlands Territory
- Portuguese Territory
- Spanish Territory
- Italian Territory
- U.S. Territory

1

THE LAST WAVE

Europe's Conquest of Africa, 1880–1900

In little more than a generation, Europeans added 10 percent of the world's population and 20 percent of its land surface to their overseas empires. This imperial wave crested between 1880 and 1900 when virtually the whole continent of Africa, Southeast Asia, and the South Pacific were brought under the sway of Union Jacks, Stars and Stripes, and Tricolores. As the twentieth century dawned, the colonies of Britain, France, Germany, Belgium, Italy, the Netherlands, Denmark, Spain, and Portugal along with the Russian and American landmass empires accounted for nearly three-quarters of the earth's surface (Antarctica excepted) and 60 percent of its population. The lion's share was claimed by Britain, which ruled over a fourth of the world's land space and a third of humanity. Such was the grasping tenor of the times that even this did not satisfy the ultra-imperialist Cecil Rhodes who wished he could "annex the planets" for the British crown. "Where there is space," Rhodes once said, "there is hope."

When the dust had settled at the turn of the twentieth century there was not much left that could be snatched without provoking a war with rival powers. This situation especially pertained to Ottoman Turkey and Qing (Manchu) China, where multiple European interests precluded domination by any single power. In the New World, flouting the Monroe Doctrine or baiting the Royal Navy in an attempt to reconquer Latin America would have been pointless; British-led

European interests already prospered there without political control. Generally, imperial expansion paused between 1900 and 1910 as administrative occupation was consolidated in lands acquired over the previous two decades. Territorial disputes over Afghanistan, Persia, and Siam were settled peaceably with their independence left formally intact. An exception to amicable conflict resolution was the bloody collision of the Russian and Japanese empires in Korea in 1904–1905. Though few appreciated it at the time, the resounding victory of a "yellow" Asiatic power had dire implications for Europe's holdings throughout Asia. Before and after World War I imperialism resumed its forward momentum with the final dismantling of the Ottoman empire in Libya and the Middle East. Independent Morocco was dismembered by France and Spain. And in the 1930s the empires attained their maximum size as Mussolini's legions subjugated Ethiopia.

Referring to the period of 1870 to 1914 as the era of "high imperialism" (or the "new imperialism" or "classical imperialism") presumes other imperial eras and prior waves of formal European expansion. In fact, this period was the last burst of Western expansion that began with the Renaissance Iberian empires in the age of "discovery" (fifteenth and sixteenth centuries) and continued with the sea-borne empires of Holland, France, and Britain in the age of mercantilism (seventeenth and eighteenth centuries). A temporary reversal of imperial fortunes between 1775 and 1825 resulted in the loss of the thirteen British colonies, French Haiti, and Spanish America. Offsetting this, however, were notable gains by France in Algeria and Indochina and by Britain in India and South Africa.

Although certain continuities linked the era of high imperialism to previous waves of expansionism, five aspects were unique to the period of 1870–1914. First, the pace was dizzying; more land was occupied in the quarter century before the outbreak of World War I than in the previous seventy-five years. The unprecedented result was global domination by a single continent. Second, newly created or unified states (Italy, Belgium, and Germany) acquired colonies for the first time in their history. Older empires (Spain, Portugal, and the Netherlands) were revitalized. The United States, which had been expanding constantly since its inception, occupied its first major noncontiguous territory (Alaska) before 1870, but most of its overseas possessions were won between 1898 and 1900.

Third, expansion occurred in a competitive international climate as statesmen, military officers, and businessmen calculated their odds for retaining or increasing their global stature. The British feared that the next century would belong to the American and Russian continental leviathans and engaged in "pegging out claims for the future" to ensure a continuation of British transoceanic power. The French perceived the competition as a race calling it the *course contre la montre* (race against time) while the Germans expressed similar apprehensions in the term *Torschlusspanik* (fear of the closing door). Fourth, an avowedly imperialist ideology emerged for the first time in history. Small but effective propaganda groups peddled an imperialist sensibility that touched both popular and elite culture, embellishing monumental architecture, public exhibitions, art, and literature. Fifth and most vitally, imperialism occurred in conjunction with a globalizing economy whose financial and industrial centers were in Europe. A capitalistic market system began to embrace colonial and noncolonial regions alike, and colonialism itself must be seen as an integral part of a broader extension of the West's economic, cultural, and military dominance across the world.

THE EUROPEAN BACKGROUND: INDUSTRIALIZATION, IDEOLOGIES OF SUPERIORITY, AND IMPERIALISM

Most of the late nineteenth century colonizing frenzy was directed at Africa where, between 1870 and 1914, virtually the entire continent was annexed by seven European powers. To understand better the motives and the methods of the Europeans as well as the responses and initiatives of the Africans, four specific instances of colonial expansion will be briefly relayed. These will be preceded by a sketch of pertinent European and African circumstances on the eve of expansion. The chapter concludes with an extended comparative analysis where specific colonial impulses and experiences are assessed in light of some of the more influential theories advanced to explain the final wave of colonial expansion.

By 1870 the political boundaries of Western and Central Europe had been set by diplomacy and warfare. Yet the result satisfied few. France deeply resented the loss of Alsace-Lorraine in the Franco-Prussian war (1870). Accordingly, Germany feared French retaliation. Italy craved even more territory beyond what it had recently gained from Austria (1866). Britain was alarmed by the shift in the balance of power and especially by the menacing challenge posed by the industrializing German Reich. The diplomatic temperature was raised by episodic crises in Eastern Europe where Russia intervened on behalf of Balkan insurgents and against their overlords, the Ottoman Turks, and where Russian designs inevitably clashed with Austrian interests in the region. International jealousies, fears, and unquenched ambitions led to diplomatic bravura and lavish military spending. Between 1870 and 1914 much of Europe divided itself into grand alliance networks. The continent became an armed camp, with mass conscripted armies, grand steamship fleets, a wider deployment of the latest technology, and the generalized use of "scientific" military training and tactics. With little room for safe maneuvering at home, the larger world became a safer arena for pursuing dreams and compensating for weaknesses.

Periodic economic turbulence added to a mood of uncertainty fueled by rapid material and social change. Between 1873 and 1896 Europe was hit by successive boom-bust economic cycles known as the Great Depression. The continent was rocked by bankrupt businesses, panic-stricken stock exchanges, failed banks, and soaring unemployment. At the same time, growing literacy, improved standards of living for the employed, and the enfranchisement of working class adult males increased the political clout of workers that was measured as much at the ballot box as on the factory floor. Organized unions bargained for better wages, working conditions, and security. Some celebrated strikes turned ugly and ended in violence. With the "red peril" of socialism on the rise, elites reacted with defensive and deflective measures including appeals to patriotism and experiments in "state socialism" with the creation of state-funded workers' injury insurance and pension funds.

During this period Germany (1879), France (1892), and the U. S. (1896) passed high tariffs to boost their economies by shielding vulnerable industries from intensifying foreign competition. In public discussions, colonies became the logical corollary to high tariff walls. Together they would promote trade. Procolonialists—whether businessmen, military officers, churchmen, or others—organized themselves into lobbies that pressured governments and disseminated propaganda. They were joined by the jingoist mass press and a growing number of politicians. Imperialism was no monopoly of the right. Britain's "proimperial" Conservatives waged wars of conquest in South Africa, Afghanistan, and West Africa (1874–1880), but it was the supposedly anti-imperial Liberals who occupied Egypt in 1882. Germany's aristocratic chancellor, Otto von Bismarck, was virtually immune to imperialist propaganda (but seized colonies anyway between 1884–1886). In Wilhelmine Germany, colonialism was supported by the center-right whereas in republican France, the center and part of the left were more apt to back colonial ventures while the right was obsessed with *revanchism* (the policy aimed at regaining Alsace-Lorraine). Colonies were seen as both a source and proof of national greatness. Accordingly, the Germans, Italians, and even the French envied Britain its empire. The French publicist Pierre Raboisson caught the mood of the moment when he said that there never was a great power that lacked colonies.

Industrialization and unprecedented population increases in Europe made overseas expansion more likely. The most important consequence of industrialization, of course, was that it widened the technological gap between Europe and the rest of the world. By the 1870s Europe enjoyed a superiority in weaponry, medicine, manufacturing, transport, and communications technologies. This superiority provided it with the means to invade and hold Africa, something it could not otherwise have accomplished. Indeed, the new industrial system produced the standard arguments for colonial acquisition: the need for markets for manufactured goods or investments and the need for secure supplies of raw materials. It scarcely matters that little of this actually occurred in sub-Saharan Africa before 1914. It was enough that colonial publicists of the 1880s and 1890s shaped the political debate by using such rationales. Of nearly equal weight was the case for "emigrationist colonialism" whereby surfeit European populations could be shifted overseas to areas suitable for large-scale white settlement.

Significantly, late nineteenth century Europe was awash in doctrines of domination. The result was that colonialist sentiments were expressed in an ideological atmosphere of cultural and racial superiority. Nationalism became aggressive; one nation would belittle others as it worshipped itself. Outsiders became the chosen targets of the European radical right which openly embraced anti-Semitism, xenophobia, and "color" racism. But the state also nourished a more respectable mass nationalism buttressed by the creation of an acculturating national education system. It flourished icons and sponsored festivals (national holidays, heroes, monuments, jubilees, flags) that inculcated alleged national virtues. Social Darwinism seemed to validate rogue nationalism and cut-throat *caveat emptor* capitalism (expertly practiced by America's notorious robber barons). Each nation seemed to have its complement of those who anguished or exhilarated over the approaching apocalyptic "struggle for existence" where the universal laws of "natural selection" would expunge the infirm and ensure the "survival of the fittest."

Biologically defined racism, verified by "objective" and "infallible" science, edged out far older forms of prejudice based on physical appearance and cultural attributes. The new racism claimed that the intellectual and moral faculties of a particular race were inherited and fixed, quantifiably measured by racial variations in skull size and shape, facial characteristics, and body types. This racism was reinforced by a more pervasive technological ethnocentrism that argued that the industrial and scientific advances of modern Europe were absolute gauges of European superiority over such "primitives" as the Amerindians and Africans as well as over the formerly civilized but now barbarian Chinese and Indians.

THE AFRICAN BACKGROUND: STATE BUILDING, ECONOMIC CHANGES, AND ECOLOGICAL CONSTRAINTS

Certain nineteenth century developments in Africa directly (and often negatively) impinged on the Africans' ability to resist Europeans. Such was true of fluctuations in state size, composition, and strength. Where

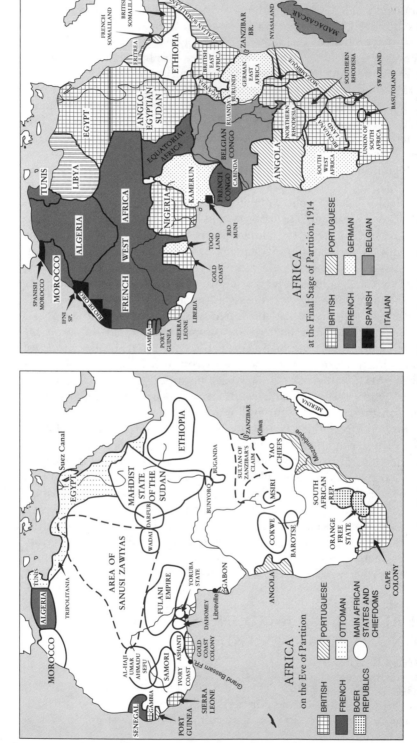

AFRICA PARTITIONED By 1914 nearly all of one continent was claimed by another. Many boundaries were arbitrarily set in the chancellories of Europe. (Reprinted by permission: John Wiley & Sons, Inc.)

AFRICA
at the Final Stage of Partition, 1914

BRITISH PORTUGUESE
FRENCH GERMAN
SPANISH BELGIAN
ITALIAN

TUNIS
LIBYA
MOROCCO
SPANISH MOROCCO
IFNI SP.
RIO DE ORO
ALGERIA
FRENCH WEST AFRICA
GAMBIA
PORT. GUINEA
SIERRA LEONE
LIBERIA
GOLD COAST
TOGO LAND
NIGERIA
KAMERUN
RIO MUNI
FRENCH CONGO
CABINDA
EQUATORIAL AFRICA
EGYPT
ANGLO-EGYPTIAN SUDAN
ETHIOPIA
ERITREA
FRENCH SOMALILAND
BRITISH SOMALILAND
ITALIAN SOMALILAND
UGANDA
BRITISH EAST AFRICA
ZANZIBAR BR.
RUANDA
BURUNDI
GERMAN EAST AFRICA
BELGIAN CONGO
ANGOLA
NORTHERN RHODESIA
NYASALAND
SOUTHERN RHODESIA
MOZAMBIQUE
MADAGASCAR
SOUTH WEST AFRICA
BECHUANA-LAND
SWAZILAND
BASUTOLAND
UNION OF SOUTH AFRICA

AFRICA
on the Eve of Partition

BRITISH PORTUGUESE
FRENCH OTTOMAN
BOER REPUBLICS MAIN AFRICAN STATES AND CHIEFDOMS

MOROCCO
ALGERIA
TUNIS
TRIPOLITANIA
Suez Canal
EGYPT
AREA OF SANUSI ZAWIYAS
MAHDIST STATE OF THE SUDAN
DARFUR
WADAI
ETHIOPIA
AL-HAJJ UMAR AHMADU SEFU
SAMORI
FULANI EMPIRE
ASHANTI
GOLD COAST COLONY
IVORY COAST
Grand Bassam Fr.
DAHOMEY
YORUBA STATE
Libreville
GABON
BUNYORO
BUGANDA
ZANZIBAR
Kilwa
SULTAN OF ZANZIBAR'S CLAIM
YAO CHIEFS
Mozambique
COKWE
MSIRI
BAROTSE
ANGOLA
SOUTH AFRICAN REP.
ORANGE FREE STATE
CAPE COLONY
MERINA
SENEGAL
GAMBIA
PORT. GUINEA
SIERRA LEONE

many newly emergent states lacked sufficient time to consolidate themselves or construct enduring loyalties among the subject and often ethnically diverse populations before being confronted by the Europeans, older declining states were incapable of mounting as vigorous a defense as they would have in their prime. Furthermore, the expansion and contraction of states also increased the incidence of invasions and raids by opportunistic marauding bands. Nevertheless, in many places the appearance of new, consolidating empires—such as the Sokoto Caliphate, Zulu, Egypt, Zanzibar, Bornu, Tukulor, and Mandinka—and the expansion of older ones—such as Ethiopia, Dahomey, Benin, and Buganda—presented Europeans with a tougher challenge than they would have met a century before.

Another important development was the rise of traders and producers of cash crops destined for Europe. European products (chiefly textiles, hardware, arms, and liquor) increased African dependence on foreigners. The increase in trade between coastal West Africa and Europe generated newly settled and more politically cohesive communities clustered around extensive kola-nut, palm, and cocoa orchards. Widening trade circuits linked to the outer world also spawned a new class of entrepreneurial merchants and middlemen like the slave-born Ja Ja, king of Opobo (Nigeria) and the East African Swahili-Arab merchant king Tippu-Tip. Links between new African products and the metropolitan-centered global economy were especially apparent in West Africa where, for instance, cultivators of vegetable oil cash crops harvested for export to Europe suffered hardship when the world price of machine lubricants plunged in the late 1860s as alternative, competitive products—especially American petroleum—became available.

The new commerce also stimulated local economies and tended to lessen the power of kings and aristocrats who exerted less control over the new trade than they previously had when slavery dominated the coastal economies. At the same time, innovative rulers and upwardly mobile traders were able to use revenues from commerce to support larger armies and administrations.

In addition, contacts with Europeans further facilitated culturally and politically charged socioreligious movements and revivals that arose in the precolonial era. Islam, partially revitalized by the massive threat posed by an assertive Western dominance, provided inspiration, an alternative to European structures of organization and development, and a cultural and intellectual homogeneity for a number of African peoples. Perhaps the most famous instance of this was the state founded by Muhammad Ahmad Ibn Abdallah (the *Mahdi*) in the Sudan that between 1882 and 1898 toppled Anglo-Egyptian rule with an extended *jihad* (holy war), and refashioned a social order based in large part on Qur'anic principles. While sometimes disruptive and unstable, emergent Islamic states, ideologically empowered and administratively complex, often proved formidable adversaries to infidels—whether European Christians or African animists—and, occasionally, even to rulers belonging to rival, "heretical" Islamic sects.

Demographic changes and natural limitations had, by the 1880s, deeply influenced political and economic developments throughout Africa. Population levels rose in West Africa and Angola following the mid-nineteenth century cessation of the transatlantic slave trade. This population boom may have increased ecological and social pressures in the region, but it also raised productivity. Possibly in tandem with this demographic change, historians have recorded greater political central-ization and societal modernization in the mid–1800s; however, it is equally possible that this reflected growing contact with Europeans. For long before the Scramble, coastal Africans had been absorbing specific Western devices and skills without having to submit to Europeans.

Still, no African polity could command the kinds of resources that were available to the European states of the 1870s. And far more impor-tantly, only one African state could match the technological and organi-zational resources of the relatively small forces and matériel that Europe actually *deployed* to Africa. Many states lacked standing armies. Others were hindered by fractious succession crises or rotating leaderships. Un-like Europe, where nation-states and dynastic empires predominated, Africa boasted a wide range of polities from the highly centralized em-pires of the West African savanna to the decentralized bands of East Africa. Power was often diffused through loose confederacies or con-fined to small geographic units such as the city states of the West African river deltas. The larger states contained heterogeneous populations, sometimes ruled over by aristocratic elites who had few, if any, linguistic or ethnic ties to the peoples beneath them.

Infertile soils cover much of the continent, limiting agrarian tech-niques to the slash and burn method and thereby inducing periodic population shifts. Such areas were equally incapable of supporting large populations or elaborate state systems. Pastoralism was impossible in much the equatorial zone where the lethal tsetse fly prevented the breed-ing of horses and livestock. Most crucially, industrialization had not oc-curred. A number of states compensated for the lack of modern military hardware by importing armaments. A few even employed craftsmen and smiths to reproduce and repair European arms. But in the end the tech-nological–economic gap was too wide to bridge and Africans either suc-cumbed to the European overlords or, in a few instances, became danger-ously dependent on European arms dealers. A final misfortune was the influx of diseases that preceded, accompanied, and intensified the Euro-pean onslaught. Much of Central and East Africa was ravaged by cholera, smallpox, rinderpest, and famine. The result was lost productivity, social turbulence, mass migrations, and decimated populations that were still recovering from the ravages of the slave trade.

THE SCRAMBLE FOR AFRICA

What triggered the Scramble for Africa in the mid to late 1880s was an unpredictable and unrelated combination of events: France's invasion of Tunisia (1881); Britain's occupation of Egypt (1882); Belgium's King Leopold's offensive in the Congo (early 1880s); and Germany's sudden taking of Cameroon, Southwest Africa, Tanganyika, and Togoland (1884–1885). The cumulative result of these developments was heightened tension and a surge of reactive and preemptive colonization. Italy, upset at losing Tunis to the French, sought consolation in the Horn of Africa (and in an alliance with Germany and Austria). Meanwhile, Britain's unilateral seizure of Egypt was an insult to French pride. (Ever since Napoleon's quixotic bid for an Asian empire, France had been the dominant power in Egypt.) Paris' endorsement of a treaty of "friendship and protection" between the explorer-adventurer Savorgnan de Brazza and Makoko, chief of the Bateke (a Congolese people), was partly influenced by Britain's precipitate action in Egypt. At the same time, Leopold's movements in the Congo raised the suspicions of Portugal, Britain, and others with interests in the region. Germany's colonial blitz in turn generated a new flurry of commercial and consular activity by France and Britain, especially in West Africa where the precipitate German action had suddenly barred their merchants from familiar markets.

Between November 1884 and February 1885 the West African Conference was held in Berlin to alleviate or at least address the problems raised by this initial round of activity. Jointly sponsored by France and Germany (in itself a triumph of Bismarck's policy of détente with France), it was attended by delegates from fourteen nations including the United States. Bismarck's real intent was to fan Anglo-French discord and prise France away from its preoccupation with regaining Alsace. But the Berlin conference accomplished rather more than that. It sanctioned free trade in the Congo and freedom of navigation on the Niger and Congo rivers. It also set the ground rules for European colonization by establishing the doctrine of *effective occupation:* to receive international recognition of a claim to a territory, effective occupation had to be demonstrated. With this doctrine delegates hoped to end the indiscriminate practice of simply asserting a "degree of influence" over a large interior space by establishing a toehold in an adjoining coastal strip. Yet the wholesale partition of Africa did not result from the Conference but from a series of bilateral agreements between 1884 and 1890 and incremental occupation.

The African land rush was underway, intermittently halted by metropolitan distractions and African resistance. Between 1885 and 1900 nearly the entire continent fell to European rule. The most important elements of this process were: Britain's decision to remain in Egypt more or less permanently; France's sprint through Western and equatorial

Africa cheered on by the Undersecretary for the Colonies, Eugene Éti-
enne; and Leopold's bold bid for a Nilotic empire. The following examples reveal continuities and dissimilarities in the Scramble. They cover
four different parts of Africa and four different colonizing powers: the
French in the West, the British in the South, the Italians in the Northeast,
and the Germans in the East.

CASE 1: FRANCE AND THE WESTERN SUDAN

The French first arrived in West Africa in the 1520s. Apart from Senegal,
they barely ventured inland despite occasional dreams of forging a vast
empire in the interior. The first move in that direction occurred in the
1850s under Senegal's industrious and influential governor Louis Faid-
herbe. This was followed up twenty years later when French officials on
the spot systematically began the conquest of the region. Often they
waged their campaigns without support from Paris. Those officers in the
Western Sudan (*officiers soudanais*) were the real instigators, propelled by
visions of a Niger River bustling with French steamers and a Sahara criss-
crossed by French railways and dotted with tricolor-masted forts. Some
even hatched a bizarre scheme to create a huge desert lake fed by a canal
from the Mediterranean (it came to nothing).

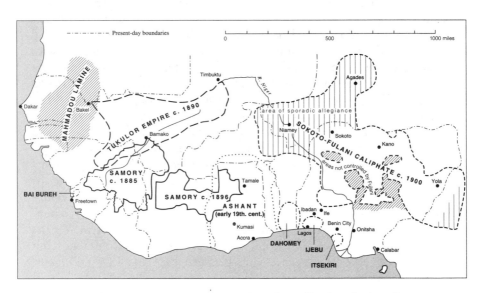

SUDANIC WEST AFRICA   *In the initial phase of colonialism, stiff resistance
was mounted by Lamine, Ahmadu (Tukulor), and Samory (Samori) Ture. The
French proceeded east and southeast from their base at Dakar (Senegal).*
(Reprinted by permission: Africana Publishing Corp.)

In France such schemes were rendered somewhat less implausible by the propaganda machines of such groups as the *Comité de l'Afrique française* which claimed that the area (containing some 1.8 million square miles occupied by present-day Mali, Burkina Faso, Niger, Mauritania, and part of Guinea) had enough wealth to rival India's. The minister of public works, Charles de Freycinet, dramatized the region's economic appeal by alleging that it was peopled with 100 million potential consumers of French goods and willing producers for the French markets (the actual population was around 11 million). Colonial sympathizers argued that a French Western Sudan would raise French prestige, brace a shaky Third Republic at home, upstage England, and help to avenge the ignoble defeat by Prussia in 1870.

On the threshold of European occupation, West Africa underwent notable state expansion, religious revitalization, and economic transformation. A number of Western Sudanic states that were eventually overtaken by the French (Tukulor, Cayor, Mandinka, and Lamine's empire noted below) were of fairly recent origin and were often ethnically mixed, administratively elaborate, and militarily adaptive. Each was constructed with the aid of Islam. At once reformist and fundamentalist, Western Sudanic Islam (like its Islamic counterparts elsewhere in the continent) supplied an inspiration (often redemptive in purpose and millenarian in outlook) for the mobilized masses and their self-made leaders. Conquests by *jihads* were the customary means of gaining and retaining empires. The appearance of centralized polities was also encouraged by important economic changes, particularly in agriculture. As stated above, the expansion and diversification of cash crops and raw materials for the European market—especially peanuts, cocoa, and palm oil—reflected a growing impingement of the global economy on African societies and had critical consequences for the development of new elites with expanded systems of coercion and governance. It was these developments that created a band of rivals to French hegemony, most notably Samori Ture, ruler of the Mandinka empire.

French expansion throughout Africa between 1870 and 1900 was largely military in impetus. The *officiers soudanais* who seized the initiative in the Western Sudan did so for personal glory and national grandeur. They were ambitious, aggressive, and Anglophobic. Typical was Captain Jean-Baptiste Marchand, whose brazen exploits were animated by a "love of our nation" complemented by a "hatred of Albion" (England). And though they often acted without prior authorization from Paris or St. Louis (the capital of Senegal), Captain Galliéni, Colonel Archinard, Colonel Borgnis-Desbordes, and their fellow officers were never countermanded or repudiated. As the French colonial theorist and official Jules Harmond explained, conquest "is immoral . . . but it is a forced immorality," an inexorable part of the "struggle for existence."

It took France over twenty years to wrest control of the Western Sudan where the determined resistance of African leaders and peoples was a direct response to the military nature of French expansion and was sustained by strong indigenous political entities. In almost each case, the French were met by a combination of cooperation, diplomatic delaying tactics, and warfare. Yet the Cayor state (Senegal), the Tukulor empire of Ahmadu (Mali), the polity of Mahmadu Lamine (Senegambia), and the Mandinka empire of Samori Ture (Guinea and Burkina Faso) were constrained from offering coordinated or persistent resistance to the French. They initially misjudged the strength and intentions of the intruders who feigned interest only in trade. They were also deceived by treaties the French never intended to honor. Some were beset with domestic unrest. Tukulor was at times unwieldy; its provinces were under the control of Ahmadu's wayward relatives. Both Tukulor and the Mandinka state strove to govern ethnically diverse peoples. The empires of Lamine and Samori were still expanding and Tukulor was of recent origin. Hence none was able to exploit well-established traditions and loyalties; they had to inculcate new ones. Local enemies abounded and these often seemed more threatening than the French newcomers. Not surprisingly, initial French offers of guns, friendship, and protection were frequently accepted.

Until the French mounted a direct assault against them, local rulers avoided open conflict. Even minor territorial infractions and diplomatic affronts were overlooked. But after repeated and flagrant transgressions and the onset of railway construction, the African rulers could no longer ignore the imminent peril to their regimes. To diplomacy and evasion they now added open and guerrilla warfare. At the same time, they appealed to personal loyalty, ethnic solidarity, and Islam to win support among their people.

Of these leaders, Samori Ture is the best known. Born around 1830, the son of a farmer, Samori ventured into trade primarily in livestock, kola nuts, and weapons but also in slaves. He then switched to soldiering and soon amassed a band of loyal followers thanks to his forceful personality, leadership skills, and vision of a Mandinka state united under the banner of Islam. More than half of his life was spent in empire building (1852–1882) and the remainder of it in defending what he had created. In the last years of his life as a free man (1882—1898), he thwarted the French with an exceptionally efficient military state. He fashioned an army with modern weapons (except artillery) and solid unit *esprit*. He sponsored new technologies and his smiths could manufacture near replicas of modern rifles. His own military skills were legendary even to the French who admired the audacity and tenacity of the "Bonaparte of the Soudan." As the French closed in on three sides he appealed (unsuccessfully) for British protection. When his position became untenable, he shifted his empire several hundred miles to the East, leaving a razed countryside in his wake.

THE FALL OF TURE *After years of confrontation and evasion, Ture was cornered and captured by the French in 1898.* (Reprinted by permission: Archives Roger-Voillet)

    In this new location Samori carried on the struggle and tried to form an alliance with neighboring states. But distrust and resentment precluded any enduring coordinated effort. Yet in 1897 he scored against the French in the North and, to the East, against the British who were completing their conquest of Ashanti (Ghana). The following year his forces were mauled by the French at Sikasso. Shortly thereafter, Samori, along with 100,000 starving followers, was captured. He was exiled to Gabon where he died in 1900. In the end, Samori and the other Sudanese leaders were unable to withstand the deadly mixture of divide and conquer tactics, modern weaponry, and French military organization. But the victory was bittersweet. The campaign took far longer than expected and the French failed to develop what Faidherbe had hoped would be a second India.

CASE 2:   BRITONS AND BOERS IN SOUTH AFRICA

Although British imperialism subjugated both Africans and Boers (or Afrikaners, mostly descended from post–1652 Dutch settlers), the struggle for South Africa between the two white communities (Boers and Britons) will be the focus here. This focus demonstrates that empire showed little regard for race or color: even other *whites* could become its prey. The Anglo-Boer conflict also involved the most intractable and the costliest imperial war in the era of high imperialism. Still, it should not be overlooked that some 5 million *black* South Africans were also forcibly brought within the imperial ambit between 1870 and 1914.

Britain had seized the Cape from their Dutch adversaries during the Napoleonic wars (first, temporarily, in 1795 and then, permanently, after 1806) because it offered an ideal harbor and provisioning station for naval and commercial vessels destined for the East. Relations between indigenous Africans, the long domiciled Boers, and recent British arrivals were shaped by an intensifying contest for control over land, labor, resources, and culture. Throughout the 1800s whites gained at the expense of blacks, as frontier raids and skirmishes flared into open warfare. The usual outcome was a victory for British arms and an incremental extension of colonial boundaries. At the same time, the British on the Cape wrestled with the Afrikaners, a number of whom trekked North in the 1830s to escape British interference and cultural domination. There they founded two landlocked republics: the Orange Free State and Transvaal (the South African Republic). From the 1830s to around 1870, land-hungry Boers were little disturbed by London in their expansionist dispossession of the largely Bantu-speaking Africans in their midst.

Relative neglect by Britain ended with the discovery of the world's largest mineral deposits, diamonds in 1867 and gold in 1886. At about the same time, South Africa's strategic role as a way station to India was diminished with the opening of the Suez Canal (1869) and overshadowed by the transformation of a modest provisions economy (mostly meat and grain) into a wealthy producer of precious metals and gems. By the end of the century, Transvaal mines alone produced more than one quarter of the world's output of gold. Most of this was mined with British capital and was distributed through London-based consortiums. In 1895–1896 diamond production, controlled by the monopolistic De Beers Consolidated Mines Company, earned some £5.4 million for London investors. In addition, the gold rush unleashed a flood of British and European immigrants.

These economic and demographic developments affected British policy. As most of the wealth was located on Boer lands, Britain found it harder to tolerate the fiercely independent and now wealthy republics. In 1871 Britain annexed diamond-rich Griqualand West. Thereafter the British exerted considerable pressure to amalgamate the Boers and the two

British colonies, Cape and Natal. In 1877 the colonial secretary, Lord Carnarvon, flushed with success over welding Canadians into a confederation and eager to apply the federal principle to a new heterogeneous European population in South Africa, sanctioned the annexation of the Transvaal. Tied to this was the elimination of the greatest Bantu threats to white settlerdom. Between 1878 and 1880 the British defeated the Xhosa, contained the Sotho, and vanquished the fearsome Zulus. But these feats backfired. With their foes removed, the Transvaalers had no need of the imperial shield of protection. Declaiming "Africa for the Afrikaners," they resorted to a surprising show of arms. In 1881, following a few Boer victories, London restored virtual independence to the Transvaal republic.

Over a decade later, the Colonial Office under the avowed imperialist Joseph Chamberlain (1895–1900) adopted a more aggressive stance. Expansionist proconsuls were appointed and new pressure was applied to the Transvaal. In 1895 Chamberlain tacitly approved the ill-famed Jameson Raid, a dismally flawed putsch against the Transvaal government. Now fully convinced of the sinister designs of the British, Boer opposition stiffened. In 1898 Paul Kruger, the embodiment of the loutish backcountry farmer (who believed the world was flat) to the British press and a shrewd, independence-loving leader to his people, was re-elected president of the Transvaal with a huge mandate. Britain's response was that if left unchecked, Afrikaner nationalism would demoralize anti-Boer Africans and overwhelm the less prosperous Cape and Natal provinces.

London was also distracted by friendly overtures between the Boers and the nearby German colony of Southwest Africa (Namibia). The German threat was local as well as global, entailing a direct challenge to Britain's industrial and naval leadership. In 1894–1895 a German firm built a railway linking Transvaal to the seaport of Lorenço Marques in Portuguese Mozambique without passing through any British territory. This gave the Boers an opportunity to regain control over their foreign trade. It also thwarted Cecil Rhodes' plan to corral the Boers within surrounding British territory (the protectorates of Bechuanaland (Botswana) and Zambesia (Matabeleland and Mashonaland, now Zimbabwe)).

At the same time, local elements worked on behalf of the empire. European, British, and American investors and merchants who grew disenchanted with the economic regulations of the Transvaal state agitated for British rule. The most important of these was the mineral magnate and rabid imperialist Cecil Rhodes. Rhodes was an English immigrant, a notorious mysogynist who had made a fortune in diamonds, an unabashed patriot who fervently hoped that America would admit the error of 1776 and rejoin the British empire, and a philanthropist who founded the famous Rhodes scholarships for Anglo-Saxon youths throughout the world to attend Oxford University. As chairman of De Beers and prime minister of the Cape (1890–1895), Rhodes used his considerable influence and wealth to promote British power. His treaties with African rulers in Bechuanaland and Zambesia (Zimbabwe; known as Rhodesia until 1979), laid the foundation in those places for British rule. The Jameson Raid was his brainchild, one that cost him his political career.

From his appointment in 1897 as Britain's High Commissioner and governor of the Cape, Alfred Milner soon became a key player. He quickly surmised that Boer resistance could not be eroded by coercion or conciliation and believed that the Afrikaners posed a genuine threat to the empire. Aware of the possibility of Germany resuming its 1894–1896 "alliance" with Transvaal, Milner concluded that war was the only way to end the impasse. His pretext was a demand that Transvaal extend the vote to recently arrived immigrants known as *Uitlanders* (foreigners). Transvaal refused, fearful that such a concession would undermine its pastoral way of life. It offered an ultimatum of its own: that Britain send its recent reinforcements back home. This, in turn, was dismissed by the British. The war was on as whites fought against whites.

It is impossible to exaggerate the significance of the Boer War of 1899–1902. It was a ferocious affair (it cost British taxpayers some £200 million) and it took overwhelming numbers and severe measures to quell the Afrikaner commandos, a militia of farmers turned guerrilla irregulars. It created an anti-imperialist faction in British politics and prompted the publication of the first radical, theoretical critique of British imperialism by the noted Liberal journalist, John A. Hobson.

Yet as far as the imperialists were concerned, the war's legacy proved exceedingly brief. They fashioned the Union of South Africa by fusing Boer states with British colonies into a unitary state with the hope of creating a white settler state dominated by British colonists. But despite Milner's best laid emigrationist schemes, Afrikaners continued to outnumber Britons. With the replacement of the imperialist Unionists with the more sympathetic Liberals in Britain in 1905, the road to self-rule by white South Africans was paved. Five years later the new union was officially proclaimed and effective political control shifted to the Afrikaners by virtue of their numerical dominance within a preponderantly white franchise. Thus, in an ironical twist of events, the Boers had lost the war but won the peace.

CASE 3:   *ITALY IN ETHIOPIA*

As the British tightened their grip on South Africa, the Italian government embarked on a reckless imperial adventure of its own in Ethiopia. It began quietly enough with a small bridgehead at Assab on the Red Sea (1882) and expanded to include the nearby port of Massawa in 1885. However, probes beyond the coast were seldom tried and were usually met with spirited resistance. In 1887 a small Italian contingent (500 men) was surprised and destroyed at Dogali in the Northern Ethiopian province of Eritrea by a larger, well-equipped force under *Ras* (duke)

Alula. The Italians stumbled back towards their coastal enclave where they fortified themselves with fresh reinforcements from Italy. Instead of mounting a punitive expedition, they opted for a policy of destabilizing Ethiopia by subsidizing restive vassals of the emperor Yohannes IV, especially the king of Shoa province, Menelik.

With Menelik's ascension to the Ethiopian throne on the battlefield death of Yohannes in 1889, the Italians became hopeful that their strategy was about to pay off even though Menelik had never taken up arms against his emperor. Italy hoped that their client would now become their puppet. Ethiopia seemed theirs for the taking. But Menelik II (as he now was styled) had no intention of becoming the tool of foreigners. He turned the guns, money, and advice the Italians had lavished on him against them. In 1889 relations began to sour in the aftermath of the Treaty of Wichale (Ucciali). Under the terms of the Italian version of the treaty, Italy acquired Eritrea, declared a protectorate over Ethiopia, and gave Menelik additional arms, funds, and loans. The emperor accepted the gifts and conceded Eritrea but would not agree to the protectorate, which was not part of the Ethiopian version of the treaty.

Fortunately for Menelik, war could be postponed partly because Francesco Crispi, Italy's imperialist prime minister, was out of office between 1891 and 1893. He used the period to stockpile an impressive arsenal with the latest arms including artillery and a consignment of repeater rifles from the Tsar of Russia that were actually superior to anything the Italians had. When war finally came (1895) it turned out to be a brief contest. For Italy it ended ingloriously. The decisive battle was fought in March 1896 at Adwa (Adowa) where 100,000 Ethiopians routed 20,000 Italians and *askaris* (European-led African infantry). Losing over 40 percent of their men, the Italians fled to Eritrea, sued for peace, and revoked the protectorate. Much to Italy's chagrin, the new realities were instantly confirmed when the latest European-made maps of Africa replaced "Italian Abyssinia" with independent "Ethiopia."

As might be expected, Adwa was greeted in Italy with disbelieving shock. After all, Europeans had defeated Africans against greater odds. In Ethiopia itself, a British-Indian force one-fourth the size of the Italian army at Adwa had seized the imperial capital in 1868 and defeated the emperor Tewodros II who committed suicide shortly afterwards. (But the Italians had overlooked the fact that Tewodros had alienated many of his nobles who, in turn, had assisted the British.) Hence, news of the Adwa disaster reverberated throughout Italy. Crispi's government fell, riots broke out in Milan, Naples, and other cities, and General Baratieri, the hapless Italian commander, was arrested. Profoundly embarrassing, Adwa seared the Italian conscience. When the fascist dictator Benito Mussolini resumed the offensive against Ethiopia in 1935, he would be content with nothing less than unconditional capitulation. "Even if I am given everything," he swore, "I prefer to avenge Adowa."

To outsiders, Ethiopian linguistic, religious, and regional divisions appeared far stronger than loyalty to nation and emperor. The imperial unity forged by emperor Tewodros II (1855–1868) and delicately preserved by Yohannes IV (1872–1889) was supposed to crumble as disgruntled vassals rose up in the wake of an easy Italian victory. But the Italians had badly misread the situation. They had anticipated an easy victory over a people they considered to be savages who were ruled by feudal, semi-barbaric chiefs. The slightest exhibition of force was thought to be sufficient to cause Ethiopia to fracture into particles. Italians had also failed to appreciate the zeal and stamina which Christian Ethiopians had displayed in their protracted war with Muslim Mahdist Sudan during the 1880s. They discounted the difficulties the terrain posed to invading forces and had underestimated Ethiopia's cultural vitality as well as its resolve to resist foreign incursions.

They did not believe that patriotic and religious appeals to "motherland, emperor, and faith" could rally scores of thousands to Menelik's banners from all across the country. Finally and most strangely, they had reckoned without Ethiopian arms and generalship. This, in part, explains Baratieri's foolish behavior at Adwa where, against his better instincts, he allowed himself to be prodded into battle by Crispi's urgent telegrams, and where he blundered by dividing his outnumbered forces and marching them across unfamiliar ground at night using inaccurate maps. And he did all this despite the last-minute defection of Ethiopian allies who knew what his exact battle plans were.

By contrast, the Ethiopians had assessed their Italian foes with uncanny insight. Eleven years before Adwa, Yohannes reflected with prophetic accuracy: "The Italians have come here . . . from ambition to better themselves . . . With the help of God they will depart again, humiliated and disgraced in the eyes of the world." Or, as Bismarck indelicately put it, Italy had a big appetite but very bad teeth. Ethiopia was fortunate in its enemy. The feeblest of the imperial powers had taken on the strongest of the African states.

From Italy's standpoint, the entire episode had been propelled by national pride, domestic anxieties, and the Great Power ambitions of its leaders. An empire had not been demanded by people or parliament. It was the obsession of a few, especially Crispi (premier, 1887–1891, 1893–1896). Recalling the radiant dominions of ancient Rome and the Mediterranean sway of Italian Renaissance city-states, Crispi and likeminded others mapped out a new destiny for Italy around *mare nostrum* ("our sea," the imperialist designation for the Mediterranean). Unfortunately for Italy, North African prospects were currently blocked by France's preclusive strike into Tunis, Britain's occupation of Egypt, and Britain's support of Ottoman hegemony over Libya. Unwilling to antagonize England and seeking revenge against the French for grabbing Tunisia with its sizable Italian population, Italy turned to the Horn of

AN AFRICAN VICTORY   This Ethiopian picture depicts the rout of Italian forces by Ethiopia at Adwa in 1896. Note the weapons wielded by each side. (Reprinted by permission: African Museum of Natural History)

Africa with the initial blessing of the British who saw Italy as a useful counterbalance to a small but active French presence in the area.

In Ethiopia Menelik II (1889–1913) made certain that neither Italy nor any other power would be in a position to reverse what had been achieved at Adwa. Disarmingly duplicitous, he devised a successful foreign policy based on contradictory treaties: with France against Britain; with Britain promising neutrality in the event of a Franco-British conflict; and with the Mahdists against France, Britain, and Leopold of the Belgians. Domestically, he accelerated the modernizing and centralizing processes begun by Tewodros and Yohannes. He strengthened the monarchy and extended Ethiopia's borders. He began to construct a modern infrastructure and built state schools and hospitals. One French newspaper boisterously declared Menelik's state "the Japan of Africa." Ethiopia had not merely weathered the Scramble, it emerged larger and stronger.

CASE 4:   GERMANY AND EAST AFRICA

The colony of German East Africa or Tanganyika (Tanzania) was the handiwork of one man, the noted explorer and colonial publicist Karl Peters. In clear disregard of the stated wishes of the German government, Peters journeyed from Zanzibar well into the Tanganyikan interior where he signed a number of treaties with local rulers. But such was his popularity with the German public that when he returned home in 1885 Bismarck had little choice but to recognize the treaties. In 1886 an Anglo-German accord fixed the boundary between German and British territory and affirmed the Sultan of Zanzibar's nominal authority over Tanganyika's coast.

But the commitment to restrict German activities to the interior was soon violated when the German East Africa Company (DOAG) set up commercial and consular offices in several coastal cities (1887—1888) where a Swahili-speaking Afro-Arab mercantile elite had ruled for centuries. The German action instantly provoked an uprising led by a prominent Arab ivory and slave merchant, Abushiri ibn Salim al-Harthi. Within weeks the Germans were ejected by tens of thousands of Africans and Afro-Arabs under the loose leadership of Abushiri, the "springing panther."

In 1889, Abushiri, overconfident after his successes, entrenched his forces in inadequate bulwarks and agreed to a truce that the Germans used to organize a punitive expedition. In the interim, Italian, Portuguese, British, and German naval vessels blockaded the coast and prevented the Arabs from obtaining more arms. Months later, German marines and warships returned. Artillery and naval bombardments blasted Arab forts apart and German-officered *askaris* pursued Africans who were equipped with spears, arrows, and shields. Eventually, Abushiri was captured and hanged. With the surrender of other Arab leaders in 1890, the uprising all but collapsed. That same year Germany replaced the DOAG with direct rule and began the struggle to subdue the Chagga, Nyamwezi, Hehe, and other interior peoples.

What induced Bismarck to sanction colonies in East Africa, Southwest Africa, West Africa, and the South Pacific? The shrewd chancellor who, apart from the period 1884–1886, consistently rejected colonialism ("I am no colonial man") seems to have been influenced by three considerations. The first was diplomatic. Colonies next to British and French possessions would elevate Anglo-French tension, annoy Britain, and divert French attention away from Alsace. The second consideration concerned the possibility of social upheaval in Germany. The current cycle of economic depression (1882–1886) coupled with agrarian unemployment seemed likely to result in social unrest. As protectionism and "state socialism" failed to cushion the impact of the present economic downturn, it was argued that colonies might help by boosting overseas trade and reviving local industry. They could also bring class-divided Germans together in a common endeavor.

The third and most important reason involved domestic politics. Bismarck could not disregard the growing popularity of colonialism, reflected in the recent formation of the powerful lobby the *Kolonialverein*. In the midst of the 1884 election he co-opted the colonial issue so as to lure pro-colonialist voters away from opposition parties and increase support for his programs in the Reichstag (the German parliament's lower chamber). It was a short-lived strategy and, with Germany's economic revival, Bismarck's older view that colonies were humbug soon reasserted itself.

For its part, the Abushiri revolt is best explained as a response to German insults and to the loss of autonomy. Peters and his cohorts held Arabs and Africans in open contempt. By lowering the sultan's flag and raising their own they not only contravened the Anglo-German pact, they deeply enraged Arabs. The Germans seem to have been exceptionally tactless, terrorizing local inhabitants with impunity. They invaded mosques and disrupted prayers, burst into harems and assaulted women, and broke into houses and arrested leading citizens. They struck at the heart of village life with taxes on burials, inheritances, and roads. Most egregiously, they confiscated the lands of persons who had failed to produce deeds that the Germans were prepared to acknowledge (few owners possessed such deeds).

German success over Abushiri was the result of German strengths and indigenous deficiencies. The Germans had been as ruthless in suppressing Abushiri as the British had been in eradicating Boer commandos (whom the British systematically placed in the world's first concentration camps). They executed suspected rebels, indiscriminately leveled coastal villages, looted, and razed crops and houses. They also had a decided advantage in weapons and tactics. German technology demoralized African warriors who attributed magical powers to those in command of thunder-like cannon and bullets that rained havoc from the skies. After Abushiri's execution, the Germans coaxed Afro-Arab leaders to their side with promises to restore trade privileges, reinstate slave labor (though the Germans claimed to be anti-slavery), compensate creditors, and, for a select few, provide salaried posts in the new regime.

On the other side, Abushiri can be faulted for waging war by besiegement and pitched battles instead of resorting to guerrilla tactics (the most effective means of resisting Europeans). Moreover, Abushiri's brutal ways drove many Africans to side with the Germans. With tragic consequences for his supporters, Abushiri underestimated the Germans, declaring that "The English are surely wealthy and powerful, but the Germans seem to be very weak people." Finally, internal schisms and the lack of a central organization or a unifying purpose beyond a shared revulsion of the Germans were serious defects. Among the resisters, mutual suspicions divided town dwellers from rural warriors and both from Arab notables throughout the rebellion. These schisms finally proved catastrophic as defeat and failing health overtook Abushiri. That the "springing panther" was betrayed and handed over to the Germans by an ally is, perhaps, only the most dramatic example of the internal ruptures that crippled the rebel forces.

CONCLUSION

Historians and other scholars have devoted considerable time and effort to understand the primary motives and impulses behind European expansion. Since 1900, a number of grand, sweeping, monocausal theories have appeared, each of which has offered a particular explanation. For the purposes of this brief survey, these can be grouped into three categories: economic, political, and excentric. (For more information, see Further Reading at the end of this chapter.)

Economic theories argue that changes in European economic conditions in the latter half of the 1800s contributed to empire building largely in order to safeguard overseas sources of raw materials and to establish safe and profitable havens for the export of European goods and capital. Of these particular economic aims, the theoretical emphasis has focused on the need to find secure outlets for surplus European capital in an era of industrial, commercial, and agrarian competition. Indeed, many of the leading economic theorists have been Marxists who have muddied the conceptual waters by linking imperialism not with empires but by defining it as a stage in the development of advanced capitalism. Thus, imperialism for Marxists is a term that describes an economic phenomenon (they use "colonialism" to describe European territorial rule).

Political theories actually include a number of loosely affiliated propositions. One set theorizes imperialism as a transoceanic extension of nationalism. Another stresses overseas conquest as an outgrowth of nation-state building that, in Central and Western Europe, had reached its ultimate geographical limits short of a large-scale war. Consequently, states that could not expand at home turned abroad to satisfy their unsatiated territorial appetites. Yet another theory interprets African, Asian, and Pacific Island colonies as badges of national pride at a time of acute national chauvinism. A "social imperialist" subset of political theories highlights the sociopsychic benefits of colonies for a growing mass electorate at home and, more importantly, the political benefits for the governing regime that can claim credit for upstaging a European rival or that can distract citizens from their own domestic woes. A final set of political theories stresses the strategic (military) importance of particular lands and sea lanes. All of these theories emphasize politics and accord little or no importance to economics.

Both economic and political theories focus on the European propellants of expansionism. A third set, excentric, deliberately shifts attention to the periphery. As originally formulated, the excentric theory argues that Europeans preferred to pursue wealth and greatness informally, without incurring the direct costs of governing indigenous societies. Thus, formal conquest only became necessary when the bonds of European–non-European economic collaboration collapsed. For a multiplicity of reasons, collapses occurred repeatedly after 1870 when European demands exceeded the collaborative capabilities of various indigenous sociopolitical institutions and arrangements. One variant excentric theory underscores the friction that arose between European settlers and indigenous societies; this friction resulted in periodic frontier clashes that were effectively resolved when metropolitan troops defended settler interests. The inevitable result was colonial growth at the native peoples' expense. Another excentric hypothesis revolves around the "man on the spot," the local imperialist who applied pressure on the metropole to expand a small colonial holding into a larger one.

None of these theories has proved singularly conclusive or permanently silenced its critics. Even from the four cases cited above, it is clear that monocausal theories of imperialism can not do justice to the multitude of factors that contributed to European expansion in Africa or elsewhere. As of this moment, a perhaps unsavory explanatory goulash that contains a number of factors seems the only tenable option. In most instances of formal colonialism both economics (trade, the domestic socioeconomic climate, and overseas investment, production, and development prospects) and what might be termed "state politics" (global strategy, military power, nationalism, international standing, and domestic politics) interacted as traders, producers, financiers, prospectors, and speculators combined with military officers, colonial officials, missionaries, and politicians to shape key events and conditions. Inasmuch as state-political and economic considerations were joined in actuality, it makes little sense to divorce them in theory.

Thus, many apparently pure cases of economic or "state-political" imperialism seem less so on closer inspection. This is true even of Ethiopia, the clearest of the above examples of imperialism as an overseas extension of nationalist politics. But Italian colonial advocates, drawing on explorers' claims of ample commercial potential in Ethiopia, argued that the colony could support 300,000 resettled peasants who would help relieve population pressures and supply Italy with much-coveted coffee and grains. Such arguments did not move Crispi who was determined to secure continued power for himself and Great Power status for Italy. But for others, promised economic dividends made a suspect colonial enterprise more respectable. And in any event, Eritrea was only a stepping stone to a North African empire where both prestige and profit supposedly awaited Italy. (Italy invaded Libya in 1911.)

Conversely, historians have treated West Africa as a simple case of commercial imperialism. But jealousies among local European traders were balanced by larger interstate rivalries as was evident in the convening of the West African conference of 1884. Also, Germany's seizure of Togo and Cameroon set off a regional colonial scramble that was almost as much about German military prowess and European diplomatic circumvention as about West African palm tree products and groundnuts. With India, historians have tended to take the opposite view: in India everything could be attributed to strategy. Thus Britain's occupation of Egypt was based on the presumption that the Suez Canal was the lifeline to India. If the Suez was vital, it seemed to follow that Egypt must be held and the Nile secured to its source. Therefore, a "domino-theory" rationale justified a string of British dependencies stretching from Egypt to the Sudan, Uganda, and Kenya. But, in fact, economic considerations were just as important as strategic ones for safeguarding India. After all, India's unrivaled importance derived largely from trade and from revenues that covered the costs of British rule as well as from Indian troops that fought in numerous imperial locales.

Economic and "state-political" impulses also meshed in individual personalities. Rhodes the imperialist ideologue cannot be evaluated independently of Rhodes the savvy self-promoting tycoon. On a smaller scale, Karl Peters was similarly motivated by personal vanity, national chauvinism, and a search for greater wealth. The *officiers soudanais*, though primarily on a crusade for national redemption and personal advancement, were partly responsible for creating the fantasy that the Western Sudan was an undiscovered El Dorado. In the metropole, Bismarck's foray into colonialism is best explained by a mingling of "state politics" and economics. Colonialist propaganda persistently balanced the two, sometimes cynically so. It has been argued that the imperialist French prime minister Jules Ferry made what he knew were unrealistic claims of untapped African and Asian wealth to gain support for his overseas ventures. Certainly his assertion that "colonial policy is the daughter of industrial policy" was a rhetorical stretch. But whether such statements were extravagant, unfounded, or legitimate, they reveal the niche occupied by economic arguments within a larger French colonial debate that oozed with Gallic pride and envy of the English.

In reality, military capability, domestic tranquillity, and international influence were not sustainable for any length of time without wealth and productivity. In the competitively fevered *fin de siècle,* states had to balance all of these. Each state operated within economic frameworks that were "nationalized" in the sense that financial, industrial, and commercial markets were nationally integrated (or were well on their way to becoming so). Moreover, firms and investors with international dealings were nationally chartered and affiliated. The loyalty of such tradesmen and financiers may have been conditional but few hesitated to enlist the resources of the state to safeguard their interests. Even statesmen such as Britain's aristocratic Lord Salisbury who were contemptuous of moneyed and commercial men went to war (1899–1902) in part to secure vital South African resources.

Once begun, territorial aggrandizement acquired a momentum of its own. Policy makers and army officers typically felt that halting any advance would result in stagnation and decline. At the same time, the haphazard and episodic manner of imperial expansion suggests an absence of premeditation. This is not to say that empires were acquired unconsciously or, as Sir John Seeley coyly put it, in "a fit of absence of mind," but that there was no single mastermind or grandiose blueprint in London, Paris, or Berlin. Of the metropolitan statesmen surveyed here, only Crispi seems to have known what he was after from the outset. But even his general plans had to be scrapped and redrafted as changes in local circumstances warranted.

Having said this, the methods of European expansion in Africa reveal several patterns of similarity. The most obvious pattern was that a formal takeover was actually preceded by some prior activity in the area, whether mercantile, missionary, or military. By 1880, the French, British, Portuguese, and Spanish had maintained a continuous presence at select points along the African coastline for decades (or even centuries). As Europeans ventured inland, so-called "treaties of friendship" were signed between African leaders and European traders, missionaries, or explorers. These treaties paved the way for protectorates or annexations proclaimed by European governors, consuls, or army officers based in neighboring enclaves. Imperial troops or company police were then deployed to enforce the new order and African military resistance was gradually extinguished. At some point, Paris, Berlin, or London sanctioned expansion with vital reinforcements and matériel. In each case a limited number of European troops was supplemented by much larger European-led African mercenary forces.

Accordingly, peripheral factors, including the deeds of the "men on the spot," were pivotal. A dramatic illustration was Peters' unilateral plunge into East Africa. Furthermore, local European initiatives were seldom reversed by the metropole. Indeed, they were often incorporated into a more elaborate imperial vision as happened when the exploits of the *officiers soudanais* were placed within the larger idea of creating an unbroken swath of French Sudanic territory from the Atlantic Ocean to the Red Sea. This response was the French counterthrust to Rhodes' notion of a string of British African possessions from (South Africa's) "Cape to Cairo." (All became expressed as colorful cartographic splashes: red for Britain, purple for France, and blue for Germany. Hence, Rhodes' famous obsession with "painting the map red.") In South Africa, Rhodes' schemes, Milner's determinations, and Uitlander grievances on the one side and Kruger's defiance and German intrigue on the other spawned a profusion of British anxieties concerning India, mineral wealth, German ambitions, and Britain's international reputation. Apart from Carnarvon's federalist initiative and Chamberlain's direct interference, a South African–based subimperialism played the decisive role in the region, conditioned by the magnetizing pull of a turbulent frontier, a destabilizing influx of immigrants, and unparalleled mineral discoveries. Oftentimes, London was a reactive, almost reluctant, participant.

Local European initiatives were also remarkably varied. In Southern, Central, and East Africa evangelizing missionaries introduced new schools, hospitals, and trade networks. They also brought African clients into European cultural and diplomatic orbits, thus naively or intentionally serving as the forerunners of empire. In the case of Britain, formal control was often preceded by what might be termed corporate imperialism. This control began when the British state granted chartered companies trade privileges and administrative powers, hoping to spare taxpayers the costs of colonization. But such companies usually ran at a loss leading to direct British intervention. This happened with Rhodes' British South Africa Company (Rhodesia), William Mackinnon's Imperial British East Africa Company (IBEA, Kenya), and George Goldie's Royal Niger Company (Nigeria). (The pattern of private company ventures leading to direct crown rule was even more pronounced in the German empire.) Of course, private and state officials often worked in tandem. For instance, Britain's protectorate over Uganda (1894) reflected the complex conjunction of marauding IBEA company troops, Protestant missionary activity in Buganda, Anglican church agitation in England, a government inquiry headed by the British consul of Zanzibar, and a conniving foreign secretary (Lord Rosebery).

Ultimately, the continent succumbed to superior European forces wielding divide and conquer tactics. Europeans advanced by a formidable combination of bravado and stealth, complex aspirations and impromptu maneuvers, diplomacy and warfare, modern transport and, of course, lethal firepower. France's conspicuous reliance on military means throughout the Western Sudan was necessitated by the absence of French missionary and mercantile agents and by the prevalence of stiff African resistance. In Tanganyika, the Germans first tried "friendship and protection" treaties but quickly resorted to guns and shells. In Eritrea, Rome alternated between diplomacy and military operations. In South Africa, where the British were long established, recognized as powerful, or regarded as preferable to the roughhewn Afrikaners, several Bantu states chose cooperation. But the British did resort to brute force when necessary and both Zulus (1879) and Boers (1902) were ultimately bested in battle. In any case, differences in expansionist styles—French state militarism versus British private entrepreneurship should not be allowed to obscure more fundamental similarities.

Colonies had to be won and maintained by force simply because Africans everywhere resisted the Europeans. Although armed resistance was highlighted in the preceding cases, other modes of confrontation were also widely employed. (Furthermore, initial forms of resistance were succeeded by ones conditioned by the colonial context: tradition-based rebellions, peasant uprisings, labor strikes, passive resistance, and nationalism.) Many states opted for accommodation or European alliances perhaps because they were weak, unprepared, had misdiagnosed European intentions, or perhaps because they perceived in the changing situation an opportunity to exact privileges, protection, or revenge against a neighboring enemy. It is important to remember that Europe intruded on existing interstate dynamics and that African reactions and perceptions were influenced by local circumstances. For many interior peoples Europeans posed an unexpected and overwhelming challenge.

In the end, African resistance could only delay, not halt, the colonial juggernaut. Even temporary success was dependent on several factors: access to modern technology; able leadership; a unifying identity or sense of purpose; and an early, correct appraisal of European aims. Common purpose often arose out of shared cultural values and political traditions. The Mahdist Sudanese possessed these and kept the British at bay for the better part of two decades. But, as we have seen, some of these components were all too often lacking. In East Africa Islam might have provided an ideological impetus for revolt but neither Abushiri nor other Arab notables invoked it. Indeed, as Abushiri's rebellion showed, anti-Europeanism was by itself insufficient to weld disparate peoples together. Samori possessed many of these advantages but he ultimately lost access to vital gun supplies and was unable to inspire patriotic or religious unity among his new subjects.

Africans frequently used diplomacy to confront and impede Europeans. But as Europeans increasingly supported one another, it was difficult for African rulers to counter with a strategy of divide and resist. When European statesmen fully perceived the danger posed by their own gun merchants, they moved to cut off the supply of arms to their African adversaries with the Brussels Treaty of 1890. Indigenous diplomatic and military options were further curtailed by internal socioethnic divisions. Even in West Africa, where states were comparatively large and strong, embittered rivalries between expanding and contracting states often prevented anti-European alliances from forming until a very late stage. Nevertheless, as we have seen, under the right circumstances African resistance could prevail. Ethiopia demonstrated that it was possible to surmount the numerous obstacles that blocked the way to African military success. By combining remarkable leadership, unshakable cultural unity, an overriding political loyalty, and an uninterrupted supply of Western arms, the Ethiopians staved off Italian colonization for nearly fifty years.

FURTHER READING

The late-nineteenth century explosion of colonies has been matched by a late-twentieth century proliferation of colonial studies. Then, as now, there is no end in sight to the bustle of empire-related activity. And just as the post–1870 imperialists trod new geographical terrain, so recent scholars have broken much important new ground. Information, perspectives, and debates are constantly expanding, straining our ability to keep abreast of the latest discoveries and reformulations. Works falling under the imperial rubric are no longer congregated under three or four Library of Congress call number headings but are dispersed throughout the library. Scholars from many nations, wielding diverse methodologies, and based in several disciplines have joined traditional political, constitutional, and economic histories with literary criticism, sport, medicine, popular culture, sexuality, environmental and development studies, feminism, and a cache of national and regional studies covering the entire former colonial landscape.

What follows in this and subsequent "Further Reading" sections, is, therefore, a highly selective guide to a voluminous pertinent scholarship. It is weighted towards introductory books and confined to works in English that are widely available. Preference is given to recent publications concentrating on the 1870–1914 era.

GENERAL WORKS

A number of useful surveys of modern European imperialism have appeared in the last two decades. An explicitly comparative study of European empires from the 1700s to decolonization is D. K. Fieldhouse's forthright *The Colonial Empires* (London: Macmillan, 1982). Shorter and more interpretive is Woodruff D. Smith's, *European Imperialism in the Nineteenth and Twentieth Centuries* (New York: Nelson-Hall, 1982). More challenging is Raymond F. Betts' finely layered essay *The False Dawn: European Imperialism in the Nineteenth Century* (Minneapolis: University of Minnesota Press, 1975). Eric Wolf's original *Europe and the People Without History* (Berkeley: University of California Press, 1982) incorporates non-European perspectives in a Marxist critique of early modern and modern expansion within a developing global economy.

Other works focus on a single empire. The liveliest account of the British Empire is Bernard Porter's idiosyncratic *The Lion's Share* (London: Longman, 1984). More evocative and less critical is James Morris' *Pax Britannica* trilogy (New York: Harcourt Brace, 1968, 1973, 1978). The classic interpretation of French late nineteenth century expansion is still Henri Brunschwig's *French Colonialism, 1871–1914: Myths and Realities* (New York: Praeger, 1966). Winfried Baumgart examines the experience of empire in light of standard theories of imperialism in *Imperialism: The Idea and Reality of British and French Colonial Expansion, 1880–1914* (Oxford: Oxford University Press, 1989). The best short survey of German imperialism is Woodruff Smith's lucid *The German Colonial Empire* (Chapel Hill: University of North Carolina Press, 1978). A useful introductory anthology on American imperialism is Thomas G. Paterson and Stephen G. Rabe, eds., *Imperial Surge* (Lexington, Mass.: D.C. Heath, 1992).

Also worthy of mention are three works that deal with the culture of imperialism. For an eclectic overview see Heinz Gollwitzer, *Europe in the Age of Imperialism, 1880–1914* (New York: Harcourt, Brace & World, Inc., 1969). Edward Said, *Culture and Imperialism* (New York: Vintage Books, 1993) excavates the impact of empire on "high" art and literature and a lot more besides. For empire in English music halls, classrooms, cinemas, and touring extravaganzas, see John M. MacKenzie, ed., *Imperialism and Popular Culture* (Manchester: Manchester University Press, 1992).

THEORIES OF IMPERIALISM

The best introductions to the debate are: Harrison M. Wright, ed., *The 'New Imperialism': Analysis of Late Nineteenth-Century Expansion* (Lexington, Mass.: D. C. Heath, 1976); and William B. Cohen, ed., *European Empire Building* (St. Louis, Mo.: Forum Press, 1980). Both works allow theorists to speak for themselves as does D. K. Fieldhouse's abridgment of economic theories, *The Theory of Capitalist Imperialism* (London: Longman, 1967). J. A. Hobson's *Imperialism: A Study* (Ann

Arbor: University of Michigan Press, 1972) remains the most seminal work, written during the Boer War (1902) by a British journalist who criticized colonial expansion but was sympathetic to capitalism. The most famous Marxist analysis of imperialism as a fundamentally economic phenomenon was the Russian revolutionary V. I. Lenin's *Imperialism: The Highest Stage of Capitalism* (New York: International Publishers, 1979, first written in 1916), which drew heavily on Hobson as well as earlier Marxist critiques. D. C. M. Platt has subjected economic theories to rigorous, sometimes demolishing, scrutiny. See his *Finance, Trade, and Politics in British Foreign Policy, 1815–1914* (London: Oxford University Press, 1968).

A notable variation on economic theories is Joseph Schumpeter's idea that imperialism was a "social atavism," a relic from the feudal past. Composed in the immediate aftermath of World War I, his theory focused on militarism and pre-war "objectless" colonial aggrandizement. Though problematic, his interpretation offered some key insights into the anxious responses of traditional elites to socioeconomic changes introduced by rapid industrialization that others such as Hans-Ulrich Wehler have developed in profitable ways (Schumpeter, *Imperialism and the Social Classes* (New York: Augustus M. Kelly, Inc., 1951); and Wehler, "Bismarck's Imperialism, 1862–1890," *Past and Present* (1970), pp. 119–155).

For more recent interpretations of theories of imperialism, see Wolfgang Mommsen's *Theories of Imperialism* (New York: Random House, 1980) and Roger Owen and Bob Sutcliffe, eds., *Studies in the Theory of Imperialism* (London: Longman, 1980). Wm. Roger Louis' *The Robinson and Gallagher Controversy* (New York: Franklin Watts, 1976) presents the debate surrounding the seminal works of two historians who argued for the primacy of peripheral as against metropolitan causative agents.

INDUSTRIALIZATION, IDEOLOGIES OF SUPERIORITY, AND IMPERIALISM

Daniel Headrick has written two books that trace the imperial consequences of technological and scientific developments. The stronger narrative is *The Tools of Empire* (Oxford: Oxford University Press, 1981), which contains engaging accounts of steam-powered gunboats, quinine, and rifled guns. *The Tentacles of Progress: Technology Transfer in the Age of Imperialism, 1850–1940* (Oxford: Oxford University Press, 1988) is a less wieldy, if instructive, digest of trains and drains, ships and cables, and metals and crops.

The nexus between nationalism and imperialism is stressed by Brunschwig (cited above); Carlton J. H. Hayes, *A Generation of Materi-*

alism, 1870–1900 (New York: Harper and Row, 1963); and William L. Langer, *The Diplomacy of Imperialism 1890–1902* (New York: Knopf, 1951). A different sort of book is Benedict Anderson's extended essay *Imagined Communities: Reflections on the Origin and Spread of Nationalism* (London: Verso, 1991) part of which covers the extension of European ideas of nations and nationalism to the colonial world.

European conceit was laid bare in Edward Said's classic *Orientalism* (New York: Vintage Books, 1978), a work that has spawned a generation of scholarship, whether emulative or reactive. A broad glance at European attitudes and their consequences is V. G. Kiernan's *The Lords of Human Kind* (New York: Columbia University Press, 1986). A more analytical study is Philip Mason's appraisal of the function of colonial ideologies in *Patterns of Dominance* (London: Oxford University Press, 1970). Still useful for the post–1870 period despite their titles are Philip D. Curtin's *The Image of Africa: British Ideas and Action, 1780–1850* (Madison: University of Wisconsin Press, 1964) and George D. Bearce's *British Attitudes towards India, 1784–1858* (Oxford: Oxford University Press, 1961). The same is true of William B. Cohen's *The French Encounter with Africans, White Responses to Blacks, 1530–1880* (Bloomington: Indiana University Press, 1980), which contains two chapters on French racism and empire in the 1800s.

Three works from among the vast literature concerning scientific racism that deal specifically with modern imperialism are R. Horsman, *Race and Manifest Destiny: The Origins of American Racial Anglo-Saxonism* (Cambridge Mass.: Harvard University Press, 1981); R. A. Huttenback, *Racism and Empire* (Ithaca, N.Y.: Cornell University Press, 1976); and Christine Bolt, "Race and the Victorians" in C. C. Eldridge, ed., *British Imperialism in the Nineteenth Century* (London: Macmillan, 1984). From the perspective of the colonized, see Frantz Fanon's *The Wretched of the Earth* (New York: Grove Press, 1968) and *Black Skin, White Masks* (New York: Grove Weidenfeld, 1991); and Octave Mannoni's *Prospero and Caliban* (New York: Praeger, 1964). The intellectual dimension of Western technological and scientific superiority as it related to non-Europeans was barely traversed until the publication of Michael Adas' illuminating synthesis, *Machines as the Measure of Man* (Ithaca, N.Y.: Cornell University Press, 1989). For an exploration of social Darwinian ideas as they related to imperialism in Britain, see Bernard Semmel's *Imperialism and Social Reform* (Garden City, N.Y.: Anchor Books, 1968).

THE SCRAMBLE FOR AFRICA

M. E. Chamberlain's, *The Scramble for Africa* (London: Longman, 1989) is a concise reading of the diplomatic background to the Scramble. Two panoramic introductory histories of Africa during this period are the short *The Making of Modern Africa Vol. I* (London: Longman, 1988) by a consortium of Commonwealth historians (A. E. Afigbo, E. A. Ayandele, R. J. Gavin, J. D. Omer-Cooper, and Robin Palmer), and the more exhaustive *General History of Africa Vol. VII: Africa Under Colonial Domination, 1880–1935* edited by A. Adu-Boahen (London: Heinemann Educational Books, 1985). Outstanding compilations can be found in the following: Michael Crowder, ed., *West African Resistance* (London: Hutchinson, 1971); Prosser Gifford and Wm. Roger Louis, eds., *Britain and Germany in Africa* (New Haven, Conn.: Yale University Press, 1967); idem., *France and Britain in Africa* (New Haven, Conn.: Yale University Press, 1971); Robert O. Collins, ed., *The Partition of Africa, Illusion or Necessity* (New York: John Wiley & Sons, 1969); and the first two sections of Robert I. Rotberg and Ali A. Mazrui, eds., *Protest and Power in Black Africa* (New York: Oxford University Press, 1970). In addition to the incisive chapter by Donald A. Limoli in Collins, Italy's Ethiopian debâcle is covered in Glen St. J. Barclay, *The Rise and Fall of the New Roman Empire* (London: Sidgwick & Jackson, 1973). By far the largest literature relates to South Africa. Good introductory surveys are: Leonard Thompson, *A History of South Africa* (New Haven, Conn.: Yale University Press, 1990); and Donald Denoon and Balam Nyeko, eds., *Southern Africa Since 1800* (London: Longman, 1989). D. M. Schreuder, *The Scramble for Southern Africa, 1877–1895* (Cambridge: Cambridge University Press, 1980) is a nuanced revisionist study of late-nineteenth century British imperialism in South Africa that stresses the role of local factors.

2

THE HEART
OF IMPERIAL DARKNESS

King Leopold's Congo

Under Belgium's king Leopold II, the Congo was subjected to the worst excesses of modern European colonialism. Beginning in the 1870s and 1880s, Leopold schemed his way to dominance over the Congo basin through a maze of European challenges and Central African uncertainties. He secured his tropical holding by a combination of diplomacy, warfare, and sheer skulduggery. Between 1885 and 1908 he governed the Congo as a private fiefdom known as the Congo Free State. During those years, he stripped the area of much of its exposed natural resources and conscripted scores of thousands of Africans into a monstrous system of forced labor. For more than two decades Leopold's rule over the Congo unleashed a nightmarish deterioration in the conditions of daily life, leading to the deaths of hundreds of thousands, possibly millions. Under Leopold, the Congo became the heart of imperial darkness.

This chapter will explore that calamitous encounter. It describes how conditions in the Congo on the eve of colonialism helped the Belgian king to gain a foothold. Leopold employed his expansive talent, energy, and imperial ambition to win support from rival European powers who could have thwarted his Central African quest. The focus will then shift to the Congo where the systematic conquest culminated in the early 1890s in the armed contest between the Congo Free State and the state of Manyema (run by a Swahili-speaking Arab-Bantu elite). A final section shows how European control was extended over

33

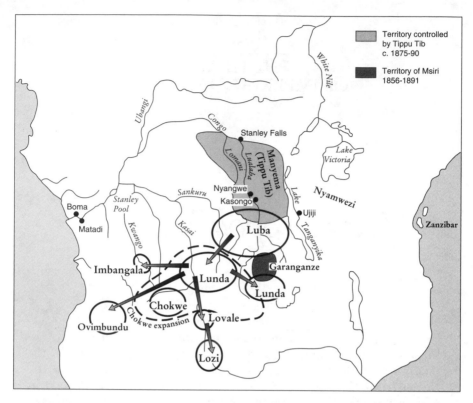

THE CONGO ON THE EVE OF COLONIZATION *Between the 1870s and 1890s, Leopold's expeditions entered from the West (at Boma and Matadi) and ventured North, East, and South using the rivers as highways.* (Reprinted by permission: Cambridge University Press)

subjugated peoples in areas severely scarred by a ravenous rubber industry. It ends by assessing the impact on the Congolese, Leopold, and European public opinion.

THE RISE OF TIPPU-TIP

Western imperialists frequently justified empire on the spurious grounds that the annexed territory was either empty or populated by "primitive" peoples. Such assertions were as erroneous with respect to the Congo as they were to other places and peoples. In fact, the history of precolonial Congo, intricate and dynamic, is still being compiled. The unavoidably brief account that follows can only hint at it.

The Congo—now the independent republic of Zaire—occupies the center of sub-Saharan Africa. It is home to hundreds of distinct societies and cultures representing the cumulative legacy of centuries of population influx and internal migration. At a little less than a million square miles—about one-third the size of the continental United States—the Congo was historically sparsely inhabited; the population densities were lower than those of Eastern and Western Africa. This lower density was a product of the Congo's challenging topography and flora. Parts of the great Northern swath of dense tropical forests were virtually impenetrable and poor, latosolic soil covered much of the gigantic river basin. Until the introduction of such high-yielding crops as cassava from America, much of the Congo produced little if any food surpluses. Large sections of the country were only capable of supporting small hunting, fishing, and gathering bands; scattered pastoralist populations; and limited agrarian settlements that practiced shifting cultivation to prevent permanent soil erosion.

By contrast, the broad savannas and high plateaus of Southern and Eastern Congo sustained more diverse economies based on settled cultivation and textile, iron, and craft production. These economies not only encompassed fairly extensive trade networks, but also supplied the material foundation for the growth of political and religious elites. The Congo basin was thus a mosaic of centralized monarchies, sprawling confederations, and smaller, loosely structured societies. Aggressive and despotic regimes coexisted with peaceful and egalitarian ones. Despite the patchwork of polities and economies, there was a cultural unity among the Bantu who by far comprised the largest linguistic group. This unity characterized the social and economic life of communities based on networks of kinship and patronage and preserved by a flourishing oral tradition. This unity was also reinforced by widespread religious beliefs, magico-spiritual practices, and symbolic systems.

Immediately prior to Leopold's arrival on the scene, key political and economic transformations made European penetration easier. Large established states like Luba and Lunda that had occupied or dominated Central and Southern Congo for some time suddenly crumbled under the convergence of dynastic, economic, and military crises. In both states long-reigning and able monarchs died in the 1870s. The lack of undisputed lines of succession produced a scramble among rival contenders for the thrones. The resulting turmoil exposed the states to domestic and external dangers. Succession crises had not wrecked the indigenous states in the past, but on this occasion political instability was aggravated by economic and demographic distress. Ivory, the principal source of wealth, virtually disappeared from the Luba heartland of Northern Katanga and Eastern Kasai. At the same time, a drop in population occurred due to a spate of new lethal diseases and an intrusive slave trade controlled by Arabs based in the Western Indian Ocean. These developments were closely related to the advances of three devastating military intruders. First, the Cokwe (Chokwe) collided with the Lunda in the West. Second, the Swahili-Arabs assaulted the Northern and Eastern provinces of the Luba states. Third, in Southern Katanga a warrior-trader named Msiri (the "Mosquito") quashed local Luba satellites and replaced them with his own conquest state of Garenganze.

These coinciding events hastened the collapse of the Luba and Lunda empires. The invading forces wielded firearms purchased from Europeans on the coasts and, as such, enjoyed an immense advantage over the older states, which had few such weapons. When the Luba attempted to rescue their economy by extending their ivory raids into new territories, they were blocked by gun-toting Swahili-Arabs. Even the inaccurate flintlocks used by the Cokwe reaped a deadly harvest of Lunda warriors whose tightly massed ranks presented ideal targets.

The largest of the new successor states was Swahili-Arab Manyema, centered in East central Congo. Its triumph over established polities proved short lived, however, and, like Msiri's Garenganze, it was vanquished by Leopold's troops. Manyema and Leopold's colony shared similar features. Both were plundering, predatory states. The Manyema economy rested on the Arab slave and ivory trades while Leopold's Congo Free State depended on ivory, rubber, and, later, copper. Both were governed wholly or partially by foreign elites. Leopold's was staffed by Europeans with Belgians predominating while Manyema was ruled by men who were partly Arab in ethnicity, religion, and culture. Both were extensions of larger military, economic, and political complexes whose origins lay beyond the Congo: Belgium in the case of Leopold's state, Zanzibar and the East African coast in the case of Manyema.

In an even broader sense, both states were provincial offshoots of vast cosmopolitan systems. Where Leopold's Congo was part of a globalizing Western imperialism powered by industrial capitalism, the Swahili-Arab domain was joined to an urbanized, Islamicized, and commercialized Arab hegemony—intercontinental and often informal—that stretched from North West Africa to the islands of the Indian Ocean. Given its size and wealth as well as its critical relationship with Leopold's colony, a brief look at the origins and political and economic development of the Swahili-Arab state of Manyema will help us to understand how it fell prey to Leopold's agents and soldiers.

The Swahili-Arabs were an ethnocultural mix of Persian Gulf Arabs and East African Bantu who inhabited the coastal towns of Tanganyika (Tanzania), Kenya, and Somalia as well as the major offshore islands of Zanzibar and Pemba. Swahili-Arabs developed a syncretist brand of Islamic faith as well as a distinct language, Kiswahili, widely spoken throughout East Africa today. The Arab presence in East Africa dates from the first century A.D. when mariner-merchants from Oman on the Arabian peninsula began plying their trade in the Indian Ocean. Over the following millennium they settled in the area in significant numbers. By the end of the eighteenth century, a considerable population of prospering Arabs was trafficking in cowries (sea shells used as currency), cloth, muskets, and gunpowder in exchange for African ivory, gold, gum, and slaves. In the mid-nineteenth century the ruler (sultan) of Muscat on the Arabian Peninsula transferred his capital to Zanzibar. There he boosted the island economy by introducing Indian moneylenders and clove cultivation and by asserting his grip on Swahili-Arab enclaves on the mainland. At the same time, Swahili-Arab influence radiated out from its coastal and island fastnesses, slowly extending a vibrant commercial empire into the hinterland. Trade was based on two principal staples: slaves, most of whom were used in East Africa, and elephant ivory, which ended up in America, Europe, and India as piano keys, billiard balls, combs, jewelry, and furniture decoration.

The Manyema state was the result of the Swahili-Arab quest for ivory and slaves. It was also the creation of the able and enterprising Hamid bin Muhammad al Murjebi, better known as Tippu Tip or Tippu Tib. This remarkable individual was a successful military commander, skillful ruler, shrewd negotiator, and consummate entrepreneur. He was born around 1835 of African-Arab parentage and reared in the interior region of Tanganyika where he learned Kiswahili and was schooled in the Qur'an. At an early age he displayed a great interest in his father's ivory business and mounted his own long-distance caravans before he was twenty. Eventually he surpassed not only his father but all his competitors in wealth and influence. By the 1870s he had become the greatest of the Swahili-Arab merchant princes in Central Africa. By tenacity, charm, and guile as well as nimble diplomacy, he increased his commercial sway over areas previously untapped by Arab merchants.

When persuasive methods failed, Tip relied on crushing force, earning the legendary name *Mkangwansara* ("he who is fearless"). According to Hamid bin Muhammad the name Tippu Tip was an African reference to the rapid fire sound of his fearsome guns that went "tip-tip-tip." His martial reputation was confirmed in 1867 when he defeated the warriors of the fierce and seasoned fighter, King Nsama III. Something of Tip's talents are revealed by the incident. Tippu Tip and Nsama were bargaining over the latter's enormous stocks of ivory, which Tip desperately wanted. When the talks broke down, Tip charged the ruler with bad faith after Nsama had accepted the trader's glittering bribes. By Tippu Tip's own account, the merchant was summoned to the royal court to explain his insolent behavior. En route, he and his escorts were ambushed. Arrows pierced the flesh of Tip and two of his attendants, but Tip's men promptly recovered, took the offensive and, with negligible losses to themselves, rained bullets on a phalanx of Nsama's men. A thousand warriors were said to have fallen within an hour. The king fled in terror. His stores of ivory were impounded and Tip's fame as the brave vanquisher of the "Napoleon" of central Tanganyika spread far and wide.

"TIPPU TIP" (Hamid Bin Muhammad al Murjebi)   The famed Swahili-Arab merchant founded the Eastern Congo state of Manyema. (Reprinted by permission: The Illustrated London News)

With his giant caravansaries and armed porters Tip ventured West, beyond Lake Tanganyika and into the Congo. He journeyed both as merchant and as prince brandishing his military might with European guns and impressive discipline all in order to protect a trade that often aroused opposition. Bit by bit he disposed of resistance and removed local dynasts, occasionally assuming for himself the title of the deposed ruler in a bid for legitimacy. With the Luba on the verge of total collapse, Tippu Tip encountered little additional resistance in the Eastern Congo. By 1875, he had established his Manyema state with a capital at Kasongo and another large city, Nyangwe (with more than 30,000 inhabitants), situated a few miles down the Lualaba.

Manyema was a part of a constellation of Swahili-Arab commercial states centered on Zanzibar. Tippu Tip's title of *liwali* (governor) symbolized his official subordination to the sultan of Zanzibar. In fact, he ruled mostly on his own, levying taxes, regulating trade, directing raids, organizing more substantial campaigns, and conducting relations with neighboring states. Moreover, his rule was flexible and locally based. Some African and Swahili-Arab subordinates wielded so much day-to-day power they became the near equals of the *liwali*. Tip's rule was also indirect and contact between the top Swahili-Arab echelon and the general

---

KASONGO

*The following description comes from S. L. Hinde, a captain in
Leopold's Congo forces at the time of the conquest of Manyema in the
early 1890s.*

Kasongo was built in the corner of a virgin forest . . . in the forest clearing
splendid crops of sugar-cane, rice, maize, and fruits grew; and some idea of
the extent of this cultivation may be gathered from the fact that I have ridden
through a single rice-field for an hour and a half. . . . [it] was a much finer town
than even the grand old slave capital Nyangwe . . . [At Kasongo] our whole
force found new outfits, and even the common soldiers slept on silk and satin
mattresses, in carved beds with silk mosquito curtains. The room I took possession of was eighty feet long and fifteen feet wide, with a door leading into
an orange garden . . . It was hard, on waking, to realise that I was in Central
Africa . . . Here we found many European luxuries, the use of which we had
almost forgotten: candles, sugar, matches, silver and glass goblets and de-
canters were in profusion. We also took about twenty-five tons of ivory . . .
The granaries throughout the town were stocked with enormous quantities
of rice, coffee, maize, and other food; the gardens were luxurious and well
planted . . . Both in Kasongo and Nyangwe every large house was fitted with
one or more bathrooms [and] . . . Every house or hut, however small, had an
enclosure attached to it containing the same arrangement for cleanliness . . .

Source: Stanley Longford Hinde, *The Fall of the Congo Arabs* (London:
Methuen & Co., 1897), pp. 183–185, 187–188, 200–201.

---

population was often mediated by an administrative cadre of partly Islamicized, Swahili-speaking local Africans.

The Manyema state produced some constructive changes. Select
elements of the population prospered. New urban centers generated
economic activity in which African craftsmen and traders could gainfully participate. According to various accounts, Tippu Tip's rule was
acceptable to some Africans precisely because it was milder by comparison with that of other, less scrupulous Arab leaders in the area (here-
after, Arab and Swahili-Arab are used synonymously). For those few
who actually came into contact with him, his charm, lack of condescen-
sion, and his African appearance and mannerisms won cooperation if
not loyalty. This last point bears emphasis because in some respects
Manyema was an *African* state that amalgamated indigenous and alien
(Arab) influences. So, as the language of the overlords—Kiswahili—became the *lingua franca* of the area, the overlords in turn embraced some
of the customs of the locals. This was fairly effortlessly accomplished
by Swahili-Arabs who, after all, were already largely Bantu in ethnicity
and culture. Accordingly, the gap between the Swahili-Arab rulers and
the Bantu ruled was never so great as that which divided Belgians from
Congolese.

Nonetheless, in other respects Manyema was highly destructive. It was preeminently a conquest state. It had been imposed by outsiders, was shaped by warfare, and held by force. It was also a slaving state whose perennial raids upset whole societies and slapped able-bodied men and women into permanent bondage. This situation worsened during Tippu Tip's regime (1875–1894) with the elastic rise in demand for ivory and slaves and the increasing efficiency of Tip's methods of extraction. Dismayed Africans often attempted to resist the despoliation of the Arabs, but efforts to halt the forcible removal of thousands were futile. It is therefore hardly surprising that some Africans greeted the first European forces as potential deliverers while others more cautiously waited to see what would unfold.

TIPPU-TIP'S SLAVE CARAVANS

This excerpt comes from an account by an agent of the London Missionary Society during his 1882 tour of Central Africa.

. . . We met the notorious Tip-pu-Tib's annual caravan, which had been resting after the long march . . . as they filed past we noticed many [slaves] chained together by the neck. Others had their necks fastened into the forks of poles six feet long, the ends of which were supported by the men who preceded them . . . It is difficult to describe the filthy state of their bodies; in many instances not only scarred by the cut of the *"chicote"* . . . but feet and shoulders were a mass of open sores, made more painful by the swarms of flies which followed the march and lived on the flowing blood. One could not help wondering how many of them had survived the long tramp from the Upper Congo, at least 1,000 miles distant.

Source: Leon E. Clark, ed., *Through African Eyes: Cultures in Change* (New York: Praeger, 1971), p. 333. Reprinted by permission of the author.

KING LEOPOLD'S DREAM

Nothing as complex as the subjugation of one country by another is ever the handiwork of a single individual, but the Congo is exceptional because both the form and timing of colonization were significantly determined by one man. In fact, the history of late nineteenth century Congo cannot be evaluated without taking Leopold II (king of the Belgians, 1865–1909) into consideration. The colonizing initiative rested entirely with him. Alone, he deployed private agents to carve out an African estate without the support of the Belgian government or people. He worked harder than anyone else to secure diplomatic recognition for his project, which assumed a fully political form in 1885 with the founding of *l'État Independant du Congo* (the Congo Free State). In this he seems to have been motivated by a desire to add wealth and luster to Belgium's humble dynasty and, by extension, to Belgium itself.

Leopold's colonial ambition was best summed up in a short inscription he had placed on a marble block that had once been part of Athens' Acropolis: *"Il faut a la Belgique une Colonie"*—"Belgium must have a colony." He regarded colonies as essential for three reasons. First, colonies would be a source of cheap raw materials that would lower the costs of production and make Belgian industry more competitive. Second, along with empire-generated wealth and international prestige, friction between French- and Flemish-speaking Belgians would lessen. And third, colonies could support middle class investments and careers in the form of clerks, administrators, and military officers. For Leopold, these were not idle whims but pragmatic if somewhat fantastic goals based on copious detailed notes he amassed over several visits to various European possessions in Africa and Asia. But because his people evinced little stomach for empire, Leopold had to abandon his public crusade; henceforth he hatched his colonial schemes in private.

LEOPOLD'S PROPHECY

The following excerpt is an early statement of Belgium's "needs" and prospects by Leopold, then heir to the Belgian throne.

Surrounded by the sea, Holland, Prussia and France, our frontiers can never be extended in Europe . . . [But] the universe lies in front of us, steam and electricity have made distances disappear, all the unappropriated lands on the surface of the globe may become the field of our operations and of our resources . . . Since history teaches that colonies are useful, that they play a great part in that which makes up the power and prosperity of states, let us strive to get one in our turn . . . let us see where there are unoccupied lands . . . where are to be found peoples to civilize, to lead to progress in every sense, meanwhile assuring ourselves . . . the opportunity to prove to the world that it [Belgium] also is an imperial people capable of dominating and enlightening others.

Source: George Martelli, *Leopold to Lumumba: A History of the Belgian Congo, 1877–1960* (London: Chapman & Hall Ltd., 1962), pp. 15–16.

Armed with a rationale for colonial acquisition and a blueprint for colonial exploitation, Leopold scanned the horizons for over thirty years, careening from prospect to prospect. He weighed several possibilities from China to Uruguay, from Angola to the Philippines. He was particularly enthralled by the idea of becoming a Belgian pharaoh and repeatedly strove to establish an empire on the Nile. (Leopold once scolded a skeptical minister with the retort: "You think that it is nothing to be a Pharaoh!") In the 1890s he even suggested that he would back a British occupation of China if Britain first evacuated Egypt and left it to Leopold. And when the Italians were routed at Adwa, he eagerly offered to salvage the white man's honor by seizing Ethiopia on his own. Neither proposal was taken seriously. It was only in the Congo that Leopold was allowed to put his colonial plans into practice.

Between 1867 and 1885 Leopold's interest in Central Africa evolved from a vague fascination to an informed knowledge of its human and natural properties. As a *terra incognita* suddenly "discovered" by Europeans, Central Africa received growing coverage in European and American newspapers in the 1870s. Returning explorers and missionaries recalled extraordinary landscapes and inhabitants and alluded to bountiful reserves of game, plants, and minerals. With the promise of riches before him, Leopold needed little prompting to strike out for the Congo, or, as he colorfully put it, help himself to a "slice of this magnificent African cake."

But first he had to allay suspicions that he was about to seize an area in which other European states had interests. He set out to do this in 1876 by hosting the International Geographical Conference in Brussels. His aim was to assemble Central African "experts" and establish a number of international committees, all designed to continue and coordinate geographical and commercial exploration. All operated under the supposedly impartial umbrella of the International African Association (better known by its French initials, AIA). Leopold greeted the delegates with the disarming assurance that he "was in no way motivated by selfish designs," that "if Belgium is small, she is also happy and contented with her lot." To underscore the point, the AIA's successor organization would operate under its own "international" flag, not the Belgian tricolor. The AIA was, in fact, the first of a confusing assortment of associations, foundations, and companies—some real, others sham—which Leopold devised to cloak his own private interests.

Leopold's cautious and duplicitous maneuverings deceived many. He painstakingly cultivated a reputation as a philanthropist that camouflaged his interests for several years. No less respected a figure than the builder of the Suez Canal, Ferdinand de Lesseps, had buoyantly exclaimed that Leopold's aims were scientific and "the most humanitarian of our century." The king repeatedly protested his concern for the welfare of Africans. He vowed to eliminate slavery and the slave and liquor trades, thereby pleasing enlightened segments of European opinion. In these instances, his intentions were sincere and, strictly speaking, he succeeded in realizing them. But other promises he failed to keep and probably never intended to. Final judgment must remain speculative, however, since his views changed over time and because Leopold burned many of the pertinent papers.

In the early 1880s Leopold's agents were steaming up the Congo river, laying the foundation of a colonial state. These efforts raised the suspicions of a number of European powers which, however, were too distracted to intervene against him. The result was that during the Berlin West African Conference of 1884–1885, his *Association Internationale du Congo* (AIC, the successor association to the AIA) received formal recognition by thirteen European powers and the United States on the following conditions. First, that the Congo basin remain a free trade area, with the river open to equal and unhindered international navigation. Second, that import duties could not be imposed on non-Belgian firms in the region for twenty years. Third, that the slave trade be eradicated and freedom of religion protected. And fourth, that the welfare of the indigenous peoples be promoted. The Conference explicitly stated that there was to be no repetition of the enslavement and decimation of the native populations of the Americas that had occurred in the wake of European conquest three centuries before. But within ten years Leopold had flagrantly violated nearly all of these prescriptions and prohibitions. He disingenuously named the new state the Congo Free (or Independent) State and proclaimed himself "king-sovereign," an apt title for what was in fact an absolute ruler unanswerable to the Belgian parliament.

The person most responsible for acquiring the Congo for Leopold was the famous explorer, Henry Morton Stanley. Stanley was a hero adventurer of almost epic stature who preferred the open bush to the drawing room. His bold deeds quickened the pulses of a public weaned on tales of close escapes in exotic locales. Recent Stanley biographies have unearthed an ego burdened by the weight of psychological complexes. But in his day, he was lionized as a brave and honest man who revealed "Darkest (Unknown) Africa" to an enthralled Western audience.

Stanley was born John Rowlands, an abandoned illegitimate son of Welsh parents. As a young man he emigrated to the United States where he fought for the Confederacy. After the Civil War, newspaperman Stanley covered the defeat of the Great Plains Amerindians, learning important lessons about non-Europeans that he claimed later served him in Africa. His "African period" began when he agreed to be sent by the *New York Herald* to get the scoop of the century: find the sainted Scottish missionary-explorer Dr. David Livingstone, then missing in Central Africa. In 1871, the self-conscious Stanley approached Livingstone with the perfect head-line salute "Dr. Livingstone, I presume?" The question delighted the press which understood the news worthiness of the hugely admired Livingstone. Stanley may have been privately embarrassed at the insipid greeting (after all, Livingstone was the only white man within countless miles), but it won him a secure place in the better books of quotations.

Stanley's explorer reputation was sealed on a subsequent cross-continent journey from Zanzibar to the mouth of the Congo. It was an arduous and perilous trek. At one point he tried to purchase the assistance of Tippu Tip, who reneged on his agreement when it seemed that Stanley was bent on disaster. Against Tip's advice, he rejected an easier route and insisted on clawing his way through thickets and dense forest. Miraculously he survived, sick and starving. But sixty percent of his force perished and the remainder was, like himself, ailing or emaciated. When he arrived in Europe, however, it was to the clamor of ecstatic cheers. Stanley was feted everywhere. It was then that Leopold decided that the intrepid celebrity would make the perfect agent.

Leopold did not snare Stanley immediately—Stanley wanted to explore and conquer for Britain—but the king's persistence and Britain's indifference finally wore him down. So when the author of the bestselling *Through the Dark Continent* returned to the Congo in 1879, he did so in the Belgian monarch's pay. For the next five years, Stanley probed the great basin from West to East. He set up fortified stations and laid the groundwork for a commercial state. With wagons, barter ware, and prefabricated houses, Stanley's first cavalcade (1879–1882) steamed up river wherever possible. Where cataracts and rapids impeded river travel, he lumbered through luxuriant forest and rugged terrain chiseling out a road as he went. He used every available means, including dynamite, as he blasted away whole mountainsides. His pulverizing devices were so impressive they earned him the local nickname "Bula Matari," the crusher of rocks. In 1882, struck by fever, he returned to Europe where Leopold testily reminded him that his contract had not expired. He badgered the convalescing Stanley until he left earlier than was prudent, preferring the dangers and hardships of the Congo to the king's incessant scoldings.

During Stanley's second expedition (1882–1884), economic control and military conquest were more openly pushed. This time Stanley journeyed with a portable arsenal composed of eight river steamers, two million rounds of ammunition, one thousand repeating rifles, twelve artillery pieces, and four machine guns. This equipment enabled him to establish an effective presence at the magnificent Stanley Falls on the upper Congo even though this area was well within Manyema's sphere of influence. To consolidate his gains, he erected twenty-two armed stations, formed a flotilla of steamboats, and built more roads where the river was impassable.

Just as importantly, he signed unequal treaties with some 300 African rulers. Usually he ventured unmolested but occasionally he met headmen and chiefs who were reluctant to deal on his terms. Bula Matari bullied them into submission or tricked them into believing he could manipulate the forces of nature with such dazzling gimmicks as starting a fire with dry tinder, sunlight, and eyeglasses. In this manner, European liquor, beads, cloth, and old uniforms were swapped for African lands, labor, sovereignty, and commercial privileges. As if to advertise his success and proclaim the new Congo, he dotted the area with place names honoring himself, his patron, and the Belgian royal family: Leopoldville, Lake Leopold II, Stephanieville (after the king's daughter), Rudolph-

MAKING TREATIES

Two accounts give different slants on the means by which Africans lost their land and sovereignty to Leopold's agents. The first is a treaty signed between an AIA official (E. Spenser Burns) and an unidentified king in the Lower Congo. The second is from a letter written by George Washington Williams, an African-American critic of the Congo Free State.

Art. I. The King and Chiefs of M . . . recognize that it is highly desirable that the *"Association Internationale Africaine"* should for the advancement of civilization and trade be firmly established in their country. They therefore now freely . . . give up to the said Association the Sovereignty and all sovereign and governing rights to all their territories. They promise to do all in their power to assist the said Association in its work of governing and civilizing this country . . . Art. IV. The *"Association Internationale Africaine"* agree to pay to the King and Chiefs of M . . . the following viz. 2 longs [illegible] and 8 longs cloth, and the said King and Chiefs acknowledge having received this in full settlement of all their claims against the said Association. Art. V. The *"Association Internationale Africaine"* promises: 1. To take from the inhabitants of the ceded countries, no occupied or cultivated lands, except by mutual agreement. 2. To promote to its utmost the prosperity of this country, and 3. To protect its inhabitants from all oppression or foreign intrusion . . . . Agreed to, signed and witnessed this 27th day of March 1884.

An Open Letter to His Serene Majesty Leopold II, King of the Belgians and Sovereign of the Independent State of Congo

[Stanley Falls, July 18, 1890]

Great and Good Friend,
I have the honour to submit for your Majesty's consideration some reflections respecting the Independant State of Congo . . . There were instances in which Mr. HENRY M. STANLEY sent one white man, with four or five Zanzibar soldiers, to make treaties with native chiefs. The staple argument was that the white man's heart had grown sick of the wars and rumours of war between one chief and another . . . that the white man was at peace with his black brother, and desired to "confederate all African tribes" for the general defense and public welfare. All the sleight-of-hand tricks had been carefully rehearsed, and he was now ready for his work. A number of electric batteries had been purchased in London, and when attached to the arm under the coat, communicated with a band of ribbon which passed over the palm of the white brother's hand, and when he gave the black brother a cordial grasp of the hand the black brother was greatly surprised to find his white brother so strong, that he nearly knocked him off his feet in giving him the hand of fellowship. When the native inquired about the disparity of strength between himself and his white brother, he was told that the white man could pull up trees and perform the most prodigious feats of strength . . . By such means as these . . . and a few boxes of gin, whole villages have been signed away to your Majesty.

Sources: William J. Samarin, *The Black Man's Burden: African Colonial Labor on the Congo and Ubangi Rivers, 1880–1900* (Boulder, Colo.: Westview Press, 1989), pp. 239–240; and John Hope Franklin, *George Washington Williams: A Biography* (Chicago: University of Chicago Press, 1985), p. 243–254. The excerpt from *The Black Man's Burden* reprinted by permission of the author.

stadt (after Stephanie's' husband, the heir to the Austrian throne), Baudouinville (after Leopold's son) and Stanleyville, Stanley Pool, and Stanley Falls.

THE CONGO CONQUERED

With Europeans forced to watch from the sidelines, some still trusting in Leopold's better intentions, the king of the Belgians set out to exploit his new possession. The garrisoned commercial infrastructure and treaty alliances established by Stanley were a good start but two serious problems remained: money and Congolese opposition. Throughout the 1880s the Congo venture was plagued by inadequate funds. Stanley's expeditions had consumed heavy outlays and Leopold's impressive private resources were not infinite. He invested some $5,000,000 of his own money into the Congo between 1879 and 1890, and yet it was not enough. The king-sovereign found it more difficult to attract large amounts of capital from the financial markets of Europe than he had anticipated. A fresh infusion of cash in 1890 in the form of a loan from the Belgian government was a temporary godsend and helped Leopold to extend his occupation and defeat several states in Central, Southern, and Eastern Congo. But these contests, especially the war between the Congo State and the Swahili-Arab domains (1892–1894), left the colonial state once again on the brink of insolvency.

A war that nobody wanted was the result of repeated European infractions and colliding commercial interests. The frugal Leopold dreaded the expense of a direct confrontation with the Arabs, preferring a piecemeal expansion on the cheap. For his part, Tippu Tip avoided war for years, knowing that it disrupted trade and decimated profits. For a time cooperation suited both sides and in 1887 Tip was appointed Leopold's governor at Stanley Falls, a frank admission that the Arabs were still the dominant force in Eastern Congo. It was not a happy partnership. Leopold was rebuked in Europe for hiring a notorious slaver and Tip was criticized by fellow Swahili-Arabs for not attacking the Congo State when it was undeveloped. Nevertheless, Leopold bought time to pursue other ambitions and Tip hoped to gain the new rifles and salary that came with the post. (Leopold reneged on the guns.)

For the next four years, the Arab-Leopoldian détente was sorely tested. A restless imperialist, Leopold decided to establish a new colony Northeast of Manyema in the Bahr-al-Ghazal area of Southern Sudan. He hoped to accomplish several aims: destroy the thriving slave center there and win the gratitude of Europe; establish a foothold on the Nile, the first step towards realizing his pharaonic pretensions; and counter two regional threats, Ethiopia and the Mahdist Sudan. Although he was able to erect a few small forts in a remote area adjacent to the Bahr-al-Ghazal, Leopold was not allowed even a token presence in the face of Anglo-French opposition. He was forced to withdraw his tiny contingent.

Another part of Leopold's Sudanic venture ended in tragedy that further soured relations between Leopold and Tippu Tip. Leopold had decided to rescue Emin Pasha, the European governor of the nominally Egyptian province of Equatoria besieged by the Mahdist army in Southern Sudan. In the aftermath of the stunning Mahdist victories over British-led Egyptian forces in 1883 and, two years later, the fall of Khartoum and the destruction of the "martyred" British hero, Gordon Pasha, Emin's plight became a European obsession. (Emin Effendi Hakim—born Eduard Schnitzer—was an Austrian of Jewish parentage who later adopted Turkish customs, changed his name, and may have converted to Islam.) To bolster the rescue expedition, its leader, Stanley, negotiated with Tip for aid. In exchange for 200,000 rifles, Tip agreed to supply Stanley with several hundred porters and escorts. But the rifles never came and Tip's aid was tentative. In his haste to reach Emin first, Stanley made the fatal error of dividing his force on the Aruwimi River and forged ahead with a small, swift advance column.

The larger rear party got bogged down in a densely forested area enveloped by wary peoples. Major Edmund Bartellot—dashing, egotistical, and unbalanced—was in charge. As heat, humidity, and mosquitoes intensified and as the aid promised by Tip failed to materialize, the group was convulsed by fever, disease, and panic. Supplies gave out, local bands became unfriendly, and some of the porters deserted. The sadistic and overbearing Bartellot then brought the episode to a bloody climax by browbeating local headmen into replenishing his depleted stock of porters and escorts. The resulting mêlée ended in the massacre of Bartellot and other Europeans. The shocking news was subsequently made more horrific by accounts of Tip's treachery and cruelty in connection with the relief expedition. Foremost among these was the story of an African girl who, on Tip's orders, was coldly butchered and then eaten before a group of spectators including an urbane Anglo-Irish naturalist. The Irishman, who believed that Tip performed this inhuman act to extract money from him (which he was not about to part with), watched in appalled but riveted silence, calmly retired to his hut to draw sketches of the incident, and then had an amiable chat with Tip in which the girl was never mentioned. The whole grisly episode nearly degenerated into farce when Stanley succeeded in reaching Emin (1889) only to discover that the latter had no wish to be rescued. In the end, Stanley had to abduct Emin and forcibly remove him to Zanzibar. Emin later escaped and went to the Congo where he was killed by Arab slavers (1892).

STANLEY TRAMPS THROUGH THE CONGO

An African King, Mojimba, recounted how he first met the famous explorer on one of his earliest expeditions.

When we heard that the man with the white flesh was journeying down the Lualaba (Lualaba-Congo) we were open-mouthed with astonishment. We stood still. All night long the drums announced the strange news—a man with white flesh! That man . . . must have got that from the river-kingdom. He will be one of our brothers who were drowned in the river. All life comes from the water, and in the water he has found life. Now he is coming back to us, he is coming home . . . We will prepare a feast, I ordered, we will go to meet our brother . . . He is approaching the Lohali! Now he enters the river! . . . But as we drew near his canoes there were loud reports, bang! bang! and fire-staves spat bits of iron at us. We were paralyzed with fright; our mouths hung wide open and we could not shut them. Things such as we had never seen, never heard of, never dreamed of—they were the work of evil spirits! Several of my men plunged into the water . . . What for? Did they fly to safety? No— for others fell down also, in the canoes. Some screamed dreadfully, others were silent—they were dead, and blood flowed from little holes in their bodies. "War! that is war!" I yelled . . . That was no brother! That was the worst enemy our country had ever seen.

Source: Heinrich Schiffers, *The Quest for Africa* (New York: G. P. Putnam's Sons, 1957), pp. 196–197.

The Emin Pasha Relief Expedition disaster damaged Manyema-Congo State relations almost beyond repair. What finally destroyed them was the aggressive activities of Leopold's agents in Central and Southern Congo and a growing number of raids mounted by the paramilitary colonial police force known as the *Force Publique*. In 1890, the autocratic Msiri was killed and his Garenganze state displaced by a private European company. Another contributing factor was the departure in 1890 of the astute Tippu Tip for Zanzibar to tend to private matters. Too old and pessimistic to resist the Belgians any further, he never returned to his Congo province and died in Zanzibar in 1905. In the meantime, the Congo State interrupted Arab trade and the *Force Publique* stepped up its raids on Arab outposts. In 1892 border skirmishes burst into warfare.

Detachments of the *Force Publique* led by the energetic and belligerent Captain Francis Dhanis won a string of impressive victories. By the outset of 1894 Arab resistance was effectively broken. Manyema's major cities were overrun and with that Manyema—once dubbed Tippootibia—was annexed to the Congo State. Thousands of lives were lost, perhaps as many as 70,000 on the Arab side alone. Most of these were Congolese Africans who comprised the bulk of both forces. Brussels was jubilant and the Congo became an object of popular interest at last. A grateful Leopold showered Dhanis with medals and a barony.

The details of the victory of the Congo Free State over Manyema were roughly similar to those that characterized the unequal contests that comprised the Scramble for Africa (analyzed in the previous chapter). Superior Arab numbers, ample but outmoded dry powder percussion cap guns, and the leadership of able but conspicuous commanders who were slain in battle were more than offset by modern European transport, reconnaissance, and communications as well as significantly more advanced weaponry, especially repeating rifles, 75-mm Krupp artillery pieces, and machine guns. The European forces had the advantage of a tighter and more disciplined command structure. They also benefited from defections from the Arab side as the *Force Publique's* victories mounted.

Finally, Manyema had been weakened by years of destructive warfare and slave raids before 1892. The marked deterioration in many sections of Tip's state was darkly noted by a number of Europeans. The best known was recorded by Stanley himself in 1879 in which he cited dispossessed lands, depleted livestock, untended fields, riversides clogged with old debris, pervasive famine and disease, shattered customs and institutions, and an outbreak of cannibalism (presumably resulting from the breakdown of customary taboos). The social degradation, the collapse of formerly autonomous village economies, and the infestation of deadly pests and protozoa were made more insupportable by such Swahili-Arab lapses into wanton cruelty as scorched earth razing and the use of captives for target practice. Needless to say, this both dissipated precious defensive resources and in all likelihood made many Congolese less disposed to come to Manyema's aid.

In the summer of 1890 three foreigners ventured into the Congo. One was an African-American lawyer and historian. Another was a naturalized British subject who was contracted to captain a steamer for the Congo State. The third was an Irish manager of a railway construction project. All were initially enthused about the Congo State and its civilizing mission. Two wanted to be a part of the drama, one wished simply to record its successes and assess its prospects. All three were sensitive and perceptive men who soon found their Congo experiences difficult to reconcile with their preexisting optimism. Within months of their arrivals two left disillusioned, their health ruined, never to return. One died within a year. All three were severely affected by the Congo and each wrote a critical account based on his impressions. One of them eventually played an important part in the downfall of Leopold's Congo autocracy.

George Washington Williams' journey to the Congo reflected his diverse interests and abilities. Pastor, journalist, first black member of his state's legislature, and author of two histories of black colonial and independent America, Williams went to the Congo to ascertain the financial viability of a railroad for Collis P. Huntington, his railroad-king patron. He also went to see if the Congo might be suitable for African-American settlement and to gather material for a book on Africa. What he saw converted him into an implacable critic of the Congo State. Africans he met along the way told him they despised the new state. He noted that contact with Europeans had turned once proud and self-reliant peoples into caricatures of dependency: fawning, devious, and "unmanly." The real, uncontaminated African by contrast was strong, vigorous, prospering, and satisfied. But as European sway was everywhere expanding, the outlook was grim.

Williams blamed European liquor in part, but he also was sharply critical of the servile status Europeans had reserved for Africans. He came upon officials who had abused their privileges, exercised power licentiously, neglected the people's welfare, and freed slaves only to use them as indentured servants. All this he enumerated in two diplomatic open letters, one to the president of the United States, another to the Belgian king (partially cited on page 45). He had the beginnings of an incriminating book that his untimely death in 1891 prevented him from completing. However, the letters did put Leopold on notice and alerted a tiny group of concerned Europeans and Americans. But the overall impact of the letters was negligible and Leopold's reputation was not yet damaged.

Williams had acted impassionedly and without delay. By contrast, the response of Joseph Conrad, the Polish-born British novelist, took years to germinate. It was Conrad's mariner skills and childhood fascination with African adventures that led to the captaincy of a Congo river steamer. Disillusionment set in when the company denied him command of a vessel. He was racked with fever, dysentery, and a gnawing sense of isolation. Conrad's image of the Congo soon became one of death and decay, a place rife with pests, heat, and disease. This was an environment that seemed to debase everything. There, Africans were already savage and Europeans were rapidly slipping into barbarism.

All these impressions were presented in his famous novella *Heart of Darkness* in which the maverick genius, company agent Mr. Kurtz, degenerated into madness after serving on the upper Congo. His collapse was the moral unraveling of a civilization. The hasty abandonment of the civilizing mission by Leopold appalled Conrad, but he seems to have been hounded by a question he could not answer: could more conscientious efforts have triumphed in such a place? Could civilization survive there? Whether yes or no, Conrad felt the effort should be made and his disenchantment with the Congo Free State for failing to sustain that effort was total and unremitting.

The third man was the Ulsterman Roger Casement whose involvement with the Congo was the longest. It began as an employee of a private company and the Congo State in the 1880s and ended in 1903 as the British consul of Boma (the Congo's primary port). In his official capacity he investigated incidents of labor abuse and became an arch critic of Leopold's regime. Casement's service on behalf of the British government in no way diluted his devotion to the cause of Irish freedom or softened his resentment of what he came to see as British oppression. His life ended in tragic irony. The man whose official career had been capped with a knighthood from the crown was later summarily executed by the British for participating in a revolt against that crown (the Easter Rebellion of 1916). With respect to the Congo, Casement's role in galvanizing British public opinion in 1904 against the depredations of the Congo State was instrumental in increasing international pressure on Leopold. Eventually such agitation helped to force the monarch to transfer control to the Belgian government.

Ironically, these men had experienced only the incipient stages of colonial exploitation in 1890. The economic infrastructure was in its infancy and work on the transport linchpin, the railway from Matadi to Stanley Pool, had commenced only that year. The chief export commodity was still ivory, which at that point involved relatively few Africans under the Congo State's jurisdiction. Manyema was still intact. Williams, Conrad, and Casement arrived on the threshold of a major transformation that took two decades to complete. It was during and after that crucial phase that the exploitative capabilities of the colonial state and private companies fully manifested themselves.

LATEX IMPERIALISM

With the onset of the Congo State's direct involvement in the ivory and rubber trades after 1889, exploitation began in earnest. This involvement was achieved with the state operating either as a company or through private companies that were awarded exclusive rights in specified zones. Leopold was forced to adopt this arrangement because the Congo State (Leopold) lacked the capital to develop the entire colony on its own. His difficulties in attracting capital, temporarily remedied by the Belgian state loan of 1890, persuaded Leopold of the necessity of making the colony pay for itself as quickly as possible. It must be made to export enough resources to pay the salaries of administrators, soldiers, traders, and businessmen; secure the profits of investors; and reap sufficient revenues for the colonial state. Another impetus for the joint state-private enterprise venture was the booming demand for rubber and the consequent soaring rubber prices on the world market. Joint enterprise would enable Leopold to grab as much rubber as possible. Rubber's versatility was well known and with the invention of the pneumatic tire, a host of industrial uses appeared, including bicycle and automobile tires, hoses, washers, and other products. Europe would consume all the Congo could produce and at a prodigious rate of profit to the colonial state and the concessionary companies.

The colonial state was resourceful and diligent in extracting the region's natural resources. As happened to varying degrees in other colonies, the state asserted a paramount right to the land and its products.

Some of the Congo was reserved as the personal domain of the king-sovereign, some was earmarked for development by private corporations, and the rest was assigned to the Congo State. The state based its claims on the treaties Stanley had made with various chiefs in which lands and sovereignty were supposedly transferred to Leopold. In 1885 it went further and declared outright ownership of all vacant lands in the Congo basin. It defined vacant lands as those not in current productive use nor in the immediate vicinity of a village.

Five years later another decree awarded all natural products of the forests to the state, paving the way for its entry into the rubber business. To acquire satisfactory amounts of labor, a general tax had to be imposed since slavery was by now outlawed. Lacking money, most adults paid in in-kind labor or goods. Of course, the tax was deeply resented and often evaded. This provoked a harsh response from local administrators who received premiums on the amount of revenue they collected. The more labor they could harness, the more revenues they raised and the greater the salaries they received. Some exceeded even the onerous official labor tax rate in order to maximize those salaries. In 1903 the state attempted to curb excessive demands and limited the general tax to 40 hours of labor per month per adult male. But even so, administrative abuses and corrupt practices persisted.

In addition to the general tax, the state also conscripted labor for special projects such as road building and maintenance. Often these taxes were levied on chiefs or village headmen who supplied slaves to the state. This, of course, put it in the embarrassing position of perpetuating the very institution it was supposed to eliminate. When the state purchased slaves outright, it required them to earn their freedom or "redemption" by seven years of indentured servitude. This was achieved in a variety of ways: harvesting copal or ivory, portage, chopping wood for river steamers, and paddling and canoeing in shallow waterways. Women were compelled to clean, cook, and perform other menial and sexual chores. In addition, Europeans requisitioned African possessions on demand, most commonly groundnuts or peanuts, cassava bread, and domestic animals. The last major source of colonial state revenues came from the exports of the major private companies. In exchange for exclusive rubber (or mineral) concessions in specified areas, companies paid taxes on their profits, customs duties, and dividends to the state as a major shareholder (the state owned fully 50 percent of the shares in the two largest rubber concerns). As long as the rubber boom lasted (to 1905), the state received a steady flow of income and Leopold II a handsome pile of profits.

Armed with police powers and zealously pursuing profits, the rubber companies lost no time in getting down to business. Workers were rounded up and transported to rubber vine regions. Agents were hired to set collection quotas for the village communities within their jurisdiction. Armed sentries were posted throughout the area to protect agents from reprisals and to enforce the quotas. These were typically hard to meet. At one point each man was expected to collect almost nine pounds of dry latex every two weeks. The prescribed method was to place pots beneath shallow cuts in the snaking vine to collect the dripping latex. But as companies pressed their agents to maximize output, workers became careless, slashing the fragile vines and killing them.

Little thought was given to the finite quantity of vine rubber, its perishability, or its inability to regenerate. The companies stubbornly ignored claims that rubber stocks were disappearing and were becoming endangered. Instead, they resorted to increasingly harsh methods to meet impossible quotas. Men were forced to bring their women and children to work alongside them. Failure to meet the quota meant flogging, jail or, in extreme cases, execution. Inexplicably, the alternative of planting rubber was only very belatedly attempted. After 1905 the Congo, which had been a major world supplier of wild rubber, was eclipsed by Southeast Asia and other areas that had turned to cultivated rubber.

THE HORRORS OF RUBBER HARVESTING

The following excerpt is the testimony of a Congolese refugee presented in 1903 to Roger Casement, British Consul, as he conducted an official investigation of alleged brutalities connected with the rubber industry.

It used to take ten days to get the twenty baskets of rubber—we were always in the forest to find the rubber vines, to go without food, and our women had to give up cultivating the fields and gardens. Then we starved. Wild beasts—the leopards killed some of us while we were working away in the forest and others got lost or died from exposure and starvation and we begged the white men to leave us alone, saying we could get no more rubber, but the white men and their soldiers said: 'Go. You are only beasts yourselves, you are only *nyama* (meat).' We tried, always going further into the forest, and when we failed and our rubber was short, the soldiers came to our towns and killed us. Many were shot, some had their ears cut off; others were tied up with ropes round their necks and bodies and taken away.

Source: "Correspondence and Report from His Majesty's Consul at Boma respecting the Administration of the Independent State of the Congo," *British Parliamentary Papers, Accounts and Papers*, 1904 (Cd. 1933), lxii, 357.

FROM INDIGENE TO COLONIZED

The most urgent problem facing rubber companies and the colonial state was the creation of a disciplined and responsive labor force. Between 1890 and 1914 a reluctant population of hunters, gatherers, and subsistence farmers was coerced and molded into a rural proletariat. Yet the drawbacks were considerable and apparent to officials: coerced labor was discontented labor and discontented labor was not as productive as

LEOPOLD, ROI DE *LATEX*   *This cartoon from the British satirical magazine*
Punch, *shows the rubber industry, headed by King Leopold, strangling Congolese
labor (1906).* (Reprinted by permission: The Mansell Collection.)

willing labor. To rectify this, the state hoped to fashion a pliant work
force by nourishing positive obedience to the new employer and a work
ethic more compatible with capitalist requirements.

The colonialists began with the presumption that there was no
African work ethic. Africans were depicted as unenterprising, brutish,
and enslaved by their sensual urges. Colonizers were quick to point out
that Congolese material culture was devoid of industry, lacking in mech-
anized technology, and deficient in monumental public works. A French
cleric summed up the popular view when he censured the African male

AFRICANS AND MISSIONARIES

A Belgian, Alphonse De Haulleville, expressed the standard view of the undisciplined, ignorant, and willful African and an interesting view of the missionaries' role in colonization. In the second selection, a Congolese chief made a similar comment regarding missionaries.

The idea of respect, of obedience, of the sanctity of work, of the obligation to earn one's bread by the sweat of one's brow, of the existence of duties to perform unselfishly and without remuneration, this profoundly moralizing and redemptive code of ethics can enter the heart of the savage only by means of the preaching of the Gospel. The missionary is a valuable aid to the State, whose work without him will remain precarious and without a future.

Oh, they don't buy ivory! What do they want, then? Teach us about God! Something about dying, indeed! There is far too much of that now . . . They are not coming here. If we let the white men into the country, they will soon make an end of us . . .

Sources: William J. Samarin, *The Black Man's Burden: African Colonial Labor on the Congo and Ubangi Rivers, 1880–1900* (Boulder, Colo.: Westview Press, 1989), p. 184 (de Haulleville's account as translated by Professor Samarin); and Ruth Slade, *King Leopold's Congo* (London: Oxford University Press, 1962), p. 29. Reprinted by permission.

who "smokes his pipe, belly to the sun and deigns from time to time to go hunting or fishing." At best Africans were likened to children who needed guidance, authority, firmness, and, occasionally, indulgence. At worst, they were seen as trainable dogs or imitative monkeys. Properly schooled it was hoped that they might become appreciative colonial subjects and apprenticed as manual workers, clerks, soldiers, and, in a few cases, professionals.

The state adopted as its credo *"Travail et Progrès"* (Work and Progress), which it prominently inscribed on the necklace medallions that adorned state-appointed chiefs. The colonial state also lured Africans into working for payment or gifts. Perhaps the most notable example of this was the Bangalas who gradually adopted a new identity based on their comparatively privileged socioeconomic status as servants of the colonial system. Intensely proud, they adopted European dress and headgear, a development the Belgians had cultivated and joyfully publicized. The Bangalas were thus exempted from African stereotypes and were prized precisely for their "un-African" athleticism, industriousness, and initiative. With their new status the ethnic meaning of Bangala began to fade and the name came to stand for a class of colonial intermediaries. As other peoples were absorbed into their ranks they abandoned their own ethnic identities and adopted the name of Bangala.

Another group earmarked for their approved work habits was women. The French cleric quoted earlier had pointedly contrasted the idleness of the male with the purposeful energy of the female. Consistent with this perception, women were recruited under the Congo Free State, usually involuntarily, in numbers equal to or exceeding the number of men. Their roles varied from road maintenance, portage, and agricultural labor to brickmaking and domestic service for Europeans and their subordinates. Women were valued for their strength, skill, and endurance, and proved invaluable to the new economic order. Working them alongside men did much to muddy the customary distinctions based on gender specialization even though colonizers justified the large scale employment of women by pointing out that they had done much of the work in their communities. Such assertions were self-serving and it was convenient for white men to ground their rationalization of a female work force in a racially textured ideological framework. Back home, such men were opposed to paid work for their own wives even though many European women had engaged in a variety of remunerated work outside the home.

In contrast to private companies where men and women were subjected to the harshest of conditions and where nothing more than outward conformity was required, the state showed some interest in the attitude of the worker. To enhance their willingness to work, it relied greatly on Christian missions, which had a monopoly on Western education. It was primarily in the missions that a European work ethic was instilled in the young. Work was described as divine redemption and as a vehicle for self-improvement and self-regulation. Workers were steeped in an ideology of unquestioning subservience and a belief in the wisdom and goodness of their European overlords. Lastly, work was claimed to be the catalyst of general development, or as the Congo State chiefs' medallions proclaimed in a language not many comprehended: *Travail et Progrès!* In private, Leopold thought forced labor an ideal method of keeping the population under surveillance and of preventing it from mounting an insurrection.

In creating a disciplined rural work force, the Europeans had proceeded under a number of misapprehensions. For instance, European presumptions of African laziness reflected a bias that accorded high value to Christian sobriety, Western technology, and modern science and simultaneously blinded them to the mass of visible evidence that the Congolese had already created a fully supportive community, economy, and culture. Systems of social and political organization were everywhere evident in local houses, tools, adornments, clothing, transport, goods for trade and barter, and agriculture. In particular, early Europeans failed to credit such established indigenous pursuits as hunting, fishing, livestock herding, land clearing, and metal working. And despite the fact that Europeans routinely conceded that women were productive and active, the overall racial typecasting remained intact.

Europeans further miscalculated by relying on environmental determinism to explain the alleged lack of African civilization. In its crudest form, the environmental argument claimed that the Congolese saw little need for exertion in the midst of such a generous nature which had supplied an abundance of hardy soil, nourishing game and plants, resources for basic goods, and materials for light garments. But as the Europeans later learned, much of the soil of the tropical forest regions was subfertile, thus limiting inhabitants to shifting or nonintensive cultivation. Further restrictions were imposed by encumbering vegetation, predatory animals, heat, humidity, and epidemics. Combined, these prevented the large agricultural surpluses that were necessary for population expansion and empire formation on the order of those that emerged in West Africa.

If the Europeans did not infuse Africans with a value for work because they already had one, the colonialists did import a bourgeois work ethic with strong Christian overtones. Patron, kinship, and community ties that were integral to established work patterns were ruptured or manipulated by European employers and state officials. The new waged work was performed for a prescribed number of hours in the day or numbers of days in the month. It was closely supervised and both the working conditions and the production targets were set by the employer. Concentrating work at specific sites determined by the location of raw materials meant mass migrations of laborers under the colonial system. Most importantly, production was no longer for their own tangible benefit but for export to unknown factories and shops. Beyond this, the new ethic was introduced in a spirit of European paternalism designed to elevate Africans from their "primitive and arrested" circumstances. In this way a new work ethic was incorporated into an ideology that justified European dominance through the good and necessary work white men were performing (the oft-touted *mission civilisatrice*).

If anything, the justification became greater in the face of African hesitation and resistance, which increased with the imposition of the new economic order. Earlier Central African responses to the Europeans had been cautious but seldom unfriendly. In many instances, the generation that encountered Leopold's police was the first to have direct contact with whites. Some considered the Europeans to possess special, beneficent powers. Others, associating their white complexions with death and ancestral spirits, kept a safe distance with the warning cry "Bedimo! Bedimo!" (Ghosts! Ghosts!). One leader, Ngo-Ibila, argued that the Europeans were like cows, worth keeping and milking from time to time. But as the political, economic, and cultural intentions of the Belgians became clear, cooperation was succeeded by confrontation. For many, the easiest and best response was to flee beyond the reach of the companies and state officials. Flight only increased as rubber stocks dwindled and agents deployed increasingly desperate measures. Other rubber workers resorted to sabotage, violently slicing the vines in the hopes that the company would have to go elsewhere or shut down altogether. At higher levels of African society, many chiefs and notables bargained with the Europeans offering limited amounts of labor and supplies on the condition that they be allowed to retain their autonomy and authority.

The most visible form of resistance was armed revolt. Here the situation was often confused because violent reactions to economic practices often blended with resistance to the Congo State by local rulers attempting to preserve their own power. A rising by workers might trigger a revolt by an independent chief or vice versa. Such a situation arose simply because the colonial state had engaged in massive economic expropriation before it had fully consolidated its political control over the area. In any event, a wave of revolts engulfed Northern, Southern, and Eastern districts between 1899 and 1902. State posts were overrun and their supplies confiscated. Mining camps were burned and, in one instance, a European official was killed and allegedly eaten. Between 1897 and 1905 the Batetela of Eastern Kasai waged a fairly continuous rebellion. And from 1904 to 1906 as the number of rubber vines decreased and working conditions became ever more brutal, laborers were pushed beyond endurance and exploded in murderous assaults on company sentries.

State reprisals were severe. Armed raiding parties stormed marginal areas for labor "recruits." Expeditions pursued fleeing villagers deep into forests sometimes scorching hamlets and woods as they went. By 1906 the state confidently proclaimed a *Pax Belgica* throughout its realm

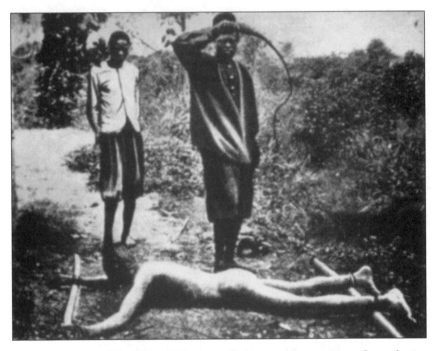

THE PRICE OF LABOR   *Whippings, slashings, amputations, and murder inflicted on the Congolese outraged Europe and America. The ensuing scandal forced Leopold to relinquish the colony to the Belgian state.* (Reprinted by permission: The British Museum)

with the collapse of warring states and with the *Force Publique* numbering almost 20,000 men and nearly 500 officers. Most reprisals took the form of lesser penalties. Resisting chiefs were degraded, divested of their offices, and either thrown in jail or forced to join a labor gang. Surveillance and confinement were common. During his 1903 investigations, Casement had stumbled upon a detention compound where abducted village women had been confined in dreadful conditions, watched over by soldiers, and painfully tied together into bunches at night. The purpose was to compel their reluctant menfolk to collect rubber. The claim was that compliance would be rewarded with the release of the female hostages.

Probably the most scandalous practices were the corporal punishments of limb amputations and whippings. In 1896 a Swedish Baptist missionary reported that body parts of African resisters had been hacked off by sentinels and soldiers. He contended that mutilation and disfigurement were sanctioned punitive policies. The state replied that these were rare incidents that were either the result of overzealous and undisciplined black sentinels or an attempt to conserve bullets in battles. The idea was that bringing back a severed hand or foot from the battlefield, preserved by smoking, would be proof that the men had used their ammunition properly, that is to kill an opponent. But when people without hands or feet began to appear that argument was discredited. Very soon evidence that body slashing was in actuality a punishment for failing to meet rubber quotas or committing other infractions became incontestable. Even more common was the application of the fearsome *chicotte*, a thick whip made of hippopotamus hide fashioned into a corkscrew shape with edges as hard as wood and as sharp as knives. The pain was excruciating and *chicotte* lashings could be fatal.

LEOPOLD'S WATERLOO

Missionaries, dependent on private companies' goodwill and tied to the colonial state, had much to lose from speaking out against atrocities. Gradually, however, missionary reports of maltreatment began to surface as the Swedish Baptist's testimony shows. Public opinion became aroused, especially in Britain and the United States where the conscience of the literary classes was pricked. A number of articles and books appeared by Conrad, Arthur Conan Doyle (the creator of Sherlock Holmes), Mark Twain, and by such respected educators as Booker T. Washington and Robert Parks. In 1903 the British government sent Casement into the interior. There he saw enough to validate missionary allegations. He wrote what by diplomatic standards was a scalding report. Published in the following year, it added vital bureaucratic ballast to Conrad's 1902 literary *tour de force*, *Heart of Darkness*.

CASEMENT'S BOMBSHELL

After a detailed documented account of the impact of Leopold's system of forced labor, Roger Casement concluded with a severe indictment.

A careful investigation of the conditions of native life around the lake [Mantumba] confirmed . . . that the great decrease in population, the dirty and ill-kept towns, and the complete absence of goats, sheep, or fowls—once very plentiful in this country—were to be attributed above all else to the continued effort made during many years to compel the natives to work india-rubber . . . acts of persistent mutilation . . . was not a native custom prior to the coming of the white man; it was not the outcome of the primitive instinct of savages... it was the deliberate act of the soldiers of a European administration . . .

Source: "Correspondence and Report from His Majesty's Consul at Boma respecting the Administration of the Independent State of the Congo," *British Parliamentary Papers, Accounts and Papers,* 1904 (Cd. 1933), lxii, 357.

As a government official Casement was barred from politics, but behind the scenes he helped to establish the Congo Reform Association (CRA) in Britain in 1904. Within months, the CRA matured into a national movement with thousands of members led by the energetic firebrand E. D. Morel. Morel, a Parisian-born British journalist with a background in the Liverpool shipping trade and a long-standing interest in African issues, supplied the talents of a skilled publicist and an able organizer. His pamphlets and books, especially *Red Rubber* (1906), electrified the British public and embarrassed Leopold and the Belgian government. His searing prose and shocking accusations were made even more credible by the naked avarice of Leopold, which made it relatively easy to cast him as a villain.

An organization that decried the excesses of imperialism, the CRA was an anomaly at the height of empire building. In the eyes of CRA members, Leopold's African realm was doubly damned because it was both brutal and because it had failed to adhere to the high-minded principles that had launched it. Morel fanned British outrage and appealed to British self-interest and idealism. Neither was hard to tap. British shipping firms, substantial merchants, and chambers of commerce resented the loss of income with the strangulation of free trade in the Congo basin. In fact, the largest contributions to the CRA's coffers were made by a shipping magnate (John Holt) and a chocolate manufacturer (William Cadbury), both of whom had extensive mercantile interests in Africa. Alongside secular outrage over Leopoldian injustices was a pricked Christian conscience that unholy acts were committed under the rule of a Christian king. For some months English church congregations heard sermons on "Congo Sundays" and sang "Congo Hymns."

It proved a combustible blend of moral ire and monetary calculation. It led many, Morel included, to concoct sweeping, unsubstantiated charges. Such attacks did not accurately reflect the complexity of the situation in the Congo. True, the king-sovereign bore ultimate responsibility for policies and deeds carried out in his name. He single-mindedly pursued profits and prestige both for himself and for a Belgium that did not seek them. The newly styled "King of Beasts" seemed an ideal candidate for demonization.

But it was less a question of whether Leopold deliberately intended to enslave than of the oppressing consequences of profiteering capitalism, Leopold's greed, and his delusionary bid for a pharaonic state on the Nile. He could not know about everything that went on in the Congo and was himself sometimes shocked by reports of atrocities. When a Swedish missionary testified to mutilated bodies, Leopold appointed a "Commission for the Protection of Natives." In the late 1890s, pained by press attacks, he dramatically ordered the terrors to end, threatening to abandon the Congo if they did not cease. The threat was idle but he was concerned with his public image and wanted to cultivate a paternalistic reputation.

Later, when Casement's report was issued, Leopold responded with a commission of inquiry consisting of three European jurists who toured the Congo, issued a report that largely concurred with Casement, and proposed several reforms (1904–1905). Leopold endorsed some of these and dispatched a personal representative to monitor their implementation. But as the media criticism mounted, Leopold withdrew into a cocoon, insisting that the whole furor was engineered by greedy British traders.

Yet the abysmal record of the Congo Free State was no illusion and despite his extravagant claims and occasional factual errors, Morel was largely correct. There were many malevolent officers such as the district commissioner who terrorized his charges and was known by the eerie epithet "Widjima" ("Darkness"). Another example was two officers whose corruption was so blatant even a derelict administration had to remove them, carefully portraying them as rare exceptions within a benevolent and diligent service corps. The root of the problem went much deeper. Combining administrative and exploitative functions in the same hands led to corruption and arbitrary despotism, especially when officials had to rely on bonuses based on agricultural and rubber output for the better part of their incomes. Moreover, brutal behavior was seldom censured by superiors. The engine that powered imperialism in the Congo was the unrestrained pursuit of wealth.

Against this, benign impulses working within the system could do little. The first commission established by Leopold was hamstrung and ineffectual. The 1904–1905 commission's recommendations were loosely interpreted. Reforms were laxly imposed if at all. Even Leopold's personal representative was thwarted when a company director bluntly told him that he would not comply with the reforms. The king's man was powerless to compel him to do so. Missionaries who bravely broke the code of silence were harassed by the companies and risked other hard-ships and dangers. One of them was singled out for assassination by a company agent. With its transparent inability to reform itself, the Congo Free State was doomed. Its patron, Leopold, was too implicated in its policies and transgressions. By 1906 even he realized that he could not hold onto the Congo much longer. Belgian opinion, initially behind its beleaguered king, began to desert him and urged the transfer of the Congo to the national government, which occurred in 1908.

CONCLUSION

Leopold II bequeathed to Belgium a colony seventy-five times its size and with a population two to three times that of Belgium's. The transfer of control did not immediately end the abuses or reform the political and economic structure in the Congo, but steps were taken to abolish forced labor altogether. Also, the demise of the rubber industry (due to shortsighted over-harvesting techniques) at least ended the atrocities connected with that dismal trade. By 1913 signs of improvement were sufficient for Morel to dissolve the CRA, satisfied that it had achieved its aims and optimistic that Belgium would look after the welfare of its colonial charges. In the view of some Europeans, the Belgian Congo eventually became a model of colonial compassion and efficiency, build-ing the schools and hospitals George Washington Williams had looked for in vain, and inviting the Congolese into more responsible positions in the colonial economy and state.

　　Other features of colonialism were too fundamental to be affected by the shift from king-sovereign to parliament. The colonial economy became even more tethered to global capitalism as the Congo became a major exporter of copper and other minerals, palm oil, cotton, and coffee. Investments in banking, transport, mining, agriculture, and forestry grew. The process of converting the population into a rural work force by coercive "recruitments" and relocations proceeded without hindrance. State capitalism attained new heights when the colonial government as-sumed control over agricultural production in the 1930s. In the aftermath of the First World War Belgium's colonial minister reaffirmed his coun-try's interest in the Congo. It was, he said, to extend civilization, create openings for Belgians and Belgian enterprise, and to promote Belgium's national economy. One does not have to strain to hear in these pro-nouncements echoes of Leopold's colonial vision formulated nearly three-quarters of a century earlier.

　　The Congo Free State had a short life (1885–1908) but it had made a notable impact on Leopold, on Belgian enterprise and, most of all, on the Congo itself. Thanks in large part to the rubber boom, Leopold had found his El Dorado. By 1900 he had recouped his earlier outlays. The exact amounts are disputed but at the very least he received several million dollars in profits and sales. As these monies were mostly spent on the Belgian royal family and nation, Leopold claimed (absurdly) that he had never made a penny out of the Congo. With the wealth yielded by rubber, he decreased the royal family's financial dependence on parliament. And he demonstrated to a people who were exceedingly slow to warm to imperialism the value and grandeur of empire. He did this in the most concrete way imaginable. He beautified Brussels and Ostend. He refurbished parks and palaces, built monuments and museums, exhibition halls and hotels, streets and pagodas, arcades, race courses, and casinos. He even began to erect the World School of Colonialism to train future colonial officials but construction on that was halted after his death in 1909. His efforts to enrich the architectural heritage of Belgium with the proceeds of African labor and products may be seen by any tourist today. Private companies also made princely profits and one rubber titan earned more than £700,000 in six years. As export values rose, revenues to the colonial state also increased which meant that the Congolese were helping to pay for the salaries of officials and the maintenance of the *Force Publique*.

Africans had little if any share in this undertaking. The virtues of a missionary education that included instruction in French, minimal technical skills, and Christian tenets were not always apparent to Congolese pupils. Sanitation management was not applied to the Congo apart from administrative stations and, possibly, army barracks. On the other hand, Western medical practices were introduced to combat the early twentieth century epidemic of sleeping sickness. Cordoning off contaminated areas and placing the infected in quarantine stemmed the decimation of the indigenous labor force. Leopold hoped that it would show the international community that he cared about his African subjects.

In fact, the Congolese population declined appreciably during Leopold's rule. Some contemporaries estimated a drop of 60 percent or more in certain areas, but reliable statistics are not available and the actual extent of depopulation is disputed. Some loss resulted directly from colonial policies but more was caused by famine, pestilence, and infectious diseases which were tied to village and crop destruction, overwork, hunger, and living in unsanitary work compounds. All of these conditions made the colonized extremely vulnerable to pestilence, crop failures, and diseases. And all of these the colonial state had either caused or contributed to to some degree. Given the absence of immunological resistance to many of the new disease strains (especially venereal disease, malaria, and smallpox) and a traditionally low birth rate, population levels only very slowly recovered after the epidemic onslaughts of the early colonial period. In view of all of this, it is reasonable to conclude that Leopold's Congo Free State amassed arguably the worst record of colonial exploitation in the modern era.

FURTHER READING

The standard history of the Congo between 1885 and 1908 in English is Ruth Slade's dated but still useful *King Leopold's Congo* (London: Oxford University Press, 1962). For a similar narrative-based analysis of the post–1908 period with a retrospective summation of the Congo Free State, see Roger Anstey, *King Leopold's Legacy* (London: Oxford University Press, 1966). The foremost scholar of Leopold's Congo is Jean Stengers most of whose work is in French. But his "The Congo Free State and the Belgian Congo before 1914" in L. H. Gann and Peter Duignan, eds., *Colonialism in Africa, 1870–1960 Vol. 1* (Cambridge: Cambridge University Press, 1969) remains tenable. For Stengers' appraisal of Leopold as a singularly old-fashioned plunderer, see "King Leopold's Imperialism" in Roger Owen and Bob Sutcliffe, eds., *Studies in the Theory of Imperialism* (London: Longman, 1980). Given the exceptional role played by Leopold, biographies are valuable for grounding his Congo exploits in the framework of a conniving personality (Barbara Emerson, *Leopold II of the Belgians* (New York: St. Martin's Press, 1979)) and an acquisitive capitalist striving to prop up a precarious dynasty (Neal Ascherson, *The King Incorporated* (London: Allen and Unwin, 1963)). Tippu Tip still awaits his biographer, but aspects of the Swahili-Arab–Leopoldian encounter that highlight Tip's involvement can be found in Norman R. Bennett's *Arab versus European* (New York: Africana Publishing Company, 1986) and Leda Farrant, *Tippu Tip and the East African Slave Trade* (London: Hamish Hamilton, 1975). David Levering Lewis's *The Race to Fashoda* (New York: Weidenfeld and Nicolson, 1987) is an exuberant account of the adventures of Stanley, Tip, and others against the background of the Scramble for Africa.

For the precolonial background, the leading work is Jan Vansina's *Kingdoms of the Savanna* (Madison: University of Wisconsin Press, 1966). This text should be supplemented by David Birmingham's survey *Central Africa to 1870* (Cambridge: Cambridge University Press, 1981). For a treatment of the Congo Free State within a broader Central African context, see David Birmingham and Phyllis Martin, eds., *History of Central Africa* (London: Longman, 1983). On Leopold's notorious forced labor regime, it is worthwhile to begin with the 1906 sensational polemic of the British journalist E. D. Morel: *Red Rubber* (New York: The Nassau Print, 1969). A more contemporary and scholarly—but no less indicting—work is William J. Samarin's excellent *The Black Man's Burden: African Colonial Labor on the Congo and Ubangi Rivers, 1880–1900* (Boulder, Colo.: Westview Press, 1989).

3

PATTERNS AND CONTEXTS

Colonizing Technologies

As the previous chapters have indicated, without the vital aid of technological implements and scientific knowledge, vast areas of the world would not have yielded so easily to European conquest and control. Equipped with rifles and quinine tablets, steamboats and railroads, Westerners could venture just about anywhere they liked with impunity. Tools of dominance proved decisive in subduing areas where local diseases, topographical inaccessibility, and the military capabilities of indigenous states had hitherto proved insurmountable.

Before looking more closely at how political control and military conquest were achieved, the more general issue of the overall relationship between technology and late nineteenth century imperialism needs to be addressed. While the relationship was a complex one and continues to be debated, what can be asserted is that technology was not a *cause* but a *facilitator* of imperialism. For centuries, Europeans had journeyed out *for* wealth and goods, adventure and curiosity, glory and Christ. They did so using the products of technology, *with* caravels and stern rudders, cannons and flintlocks, astrolabes and magnetic compasses. By 1900, technology, especially in the areas of weaponry and transportation, had enabled a very small number of Europeans to subjugate vast populations and exploit huge territories cheaply and systematically.

If technological developments and scientific progress were not a motivation for imperialism, neither were they prompted by imperialism (with a few notable exceptions, including tropical medicine). For the most part those developments were responses to challenges within a

Western industrializing culture. Of course, whatever the reasons for particular inventions, their applications were often extended to the arena of empire building. Just as the steam pump, which had been designed to remove seepage from mine shafts, was adapted to engines that drove textile looms and locomotives, so killing projectiles developed to render European conflicts deadlier could be used to maim, kill, and cow the African, Asian, and Pacific Islander. The following discussion will stress medicine and weaponry as two vital instruments of conquest and occupation.

For centuries Europeans had wished to pierce the interior of West and Central Africa in search of gold, slaves, and religious converts. Time and time again they failed, sometimes stopped by armies sometimes by fatal infectious diseases. Even as late as the 1840s European treks into West Africa were costly affairs. In the 1790s as much as 70 percent of British troops posted in West Africa died within their first year. The famous 1805 Niger river expedition by the Scottish explorer Mungo Park ended in total catastrophe: every white man died. In a repeat performance nearly thirty years later, 40 out of 49 white venturers succumbed to disease. For those lacking immunities to yellow fever, dysentery, and, above all, malaria, sub-Saharan Africa was indeed a "White Man's Grave." In fact, the equatorial African strain of malaria (*Plasmodium falciparum*) was the most virulent in the world.

For years French and British military physicians had tried to combat malaria without knowing exactly what it was or how it was transmitted. Through trial and error, they discovered that an extract made from the cinchona bark, known as quinine, was effective either as a treatment or, more importantly, as a prophylaxis. Beginning in the 1850s significant numbers of Europeans began to survive in the formerly inhospitable climate, many because they took quinine tablets prior to and during their postings to Africa. Laboratory medicine seems not to have contributed much to this advance. In fact, the increase in the general health of Europeans in tropical latitudes was the result of pragmatic applications of treatments devised after years of experience whether in Europe or overseas. The most useful measures centered on sanitation and relocation. Water supplies were cleansed and sanitary engineering helped to keep refuse from contaminating consumable air and water. Moving to higher, cooler ground and siting military barracks away from tropical population centers kept European soldiers removed from many infectious diseases and the habitats of many pathogenic microbes.

It wasn't until the advent of the germ theory of disease transmission and the related increase in epidemiological microbiology that *Plasmodium falciparum* was identified as the cause of malaria (1880), and the vector, the anopheles mosquito, was not determined until 1898. So Europeans had not understood exactly why their measures had worked. They only knew that men must be moved away from moist still air because it was thought to be insalubrious (malaria means "bad air" in Italian) and from low altitudes because malaria was more prevalent there. At the same time, the link between water and diseases like dysentery had been posited for some time and in the 1850s a contaminated water pump was demonstrated to have been the source of a cholera outbreak. These observations led to efforts to purify water supplies and improve sewage disposal. In the process, the scourge of waterborne diseases was being eliminated. As we now know, these measures helped because the removal of stagnant and contaminated water killed the mosquitoes who used these environments as breeding and larvae depositing pools. Similarly, the move to the highlands was often efficacious because mosquitoes did not inhabit high regions. And we know also that those anopheles mosquitoes carried the deadly *Plasmodium falciparum* and transmitted it to anyone who, apart from the indigenous population, had no acquired immunity to it.

The contest between armies was also decided in the European's favor in the nineteenth century. Of course, the role of weapons had been a constant in the centuries-long struggle for overseas supremacy between Europeans and others. Well before the nineteenth century a combination of factors enabled Europeans to gain a foothold or more in various transoceanic regions. Technology helped them to overpower the Aztecs and Incas, but in Africa and Asia they were confined to islands and coastlines where their superior seapower was effectively brought to bear. However, ventures further inland were often repulsed. But gradually the scales tipped in favor of the Europeans. A key factor was a steady improvement in weaponry. By the late eighteenth and early nineteenth centuries, Europeans began to penetrate Afro-Asian interiors, but their military dominance was far from assured and reverses at the hands of indigenous forces were common. By 1870, however, Europeans expected to win any military contest with non-Europeans and customarily did.

The military capacities of Westerners had developed astoundingly during the 1800s, especially with the revolution in firearms design and manufacture. In 1815, the European infantryman had to ram his powder and ball down the long chamber of his smooth-bore barrel musket. He then pressed a flint lock to detonate the gunpowder through a hole in the breech. (Rain was a dreaded hazard as damp gunpowder would seldom ignite). Ignition of the gunpowder would send the round ball down the barrel, bouncing off the sides of the chamber as it went, before exiting along an uncertain trajectory. This entire process took upwards of a minute and was best done standing up. The shot might hit a target at 80–100 yards (about the effective range of a good bow and arrow).

By the commencement of the war between the Congo State and the Swahili-Arabs (1892), the *Force Publique* was using bullet cartridges in small-bore barrel chambers whose interiors were cut with spiraled (rifled) grooves. These grooves were designed to catch the flat end of a conical bullet and propel it out in a straight trajectory. The rifles could be loaded lying down, which meant a soldier did not have to present himself as an easy target. They were also smokeless, which meant that the soldier's exact position would not be given away by telltale smoke. With such guns an infantryman could fire off 20 to 30 rounds per minute with an effective range of up to 1,000 yards. The machine gun was even more devastating. The first prototype had appeared in the 1860s when the ungainly and not always dependable Gatling gun debuted in the American Civil War. But improvements followed rapidly and by the 1880s the light, transportable, recoil-loading Maxim gun was spewing 11 bullets per second at astonished Africans.

The combination of rapid-fire repeating rifles and machine guns rained misery down on the victims of imperialism. The result was the effective European occupation of Africa between 1890 and 1914. In the Congo the new Albini rifles played the decisive role. In Chad in French West Africa, a 320 man French force defeated 12,000 Chadian warriors wielding 2,500 guns of their own (1899). And, in a definitive clash at Omdurman in 1898, the British utterly destroyed the Mahdist Sudanese. There, twenty Maxims (along with good luck and skillful generalship) had enabled the British to slaughter 11,000 out of some 52,000 charging Sudanese in a few hours. (British losses were 48.) The Mahdist losses were staggering both in absolute numbers and in casualty rates which, at 20% killed, outdistanced all major colonial encounters and rivaled those of the Franco-Prussian War. So effective were the latest killing machines and so confident had Europeans become that defeat at the hands of Africans and Asians was seldom contemplated. When, in 1879, the Zulus surprised and nearly wiped out a British invasion force of 1,800 men at Isandhlwana, a numbed Queen Victoria could only wonder "How this could happen we cannot yet imagine."

But as the Ethiopian rout of Italian forces at Adwa (1896), the Mahdi's cleansing of the Sudan of Anglo-Egyptian forces between 1883 and 1898, and the masterfully elusive Samori Ture (1882–1898) all demonstrate, weaponry did not render the Europeans invincible. Put another way, technology was no respecter of race. It responded equally well to any skilled person, irrespective of skin color. This was a truth the British painfully learned in 1857 when the northern regions of "their" India erupted into revolt. One reason for the early success of the rebellion was that Indian troops had been well trained in artillery use. In the course of the insurrection, they displayed their proficiency by bombarding their besieged British officers. Consequently, after 1857, Indians were never again entrusted with artillery pieces. But the lessons of 1857 did not end there and the uprising underscored the ambivalent role that arms technology was capable of playing. In fact, the revolt was triggered by the issuing of the new Enfield rifle bullets whose casings were greased in animal fat. Orthodox Hindu and Muslim soldiers, instructed to bite off the casings with their teeth, considered this defiling. Accordingly, they refused to use the guns, setting off a chain reaction that culminated in wide-spread revolt. But this innovation was not only instrumental in inciting the mutiny, it was partly responsible for ending it. For as historians have observed, the new Enfield rifle with its offending greased cartridges enabled the British to quash the mutineers who had deprived themselves of a very superior weapon indeed.

In other instances, Africans and Asians lacked the wherewithal to produce for themselves weapons capable of withstanding the imperialists' murderous firepower. To the extent that they survived bloody engagements, they often did so using European guns supplied by independent gun dealers. When this supply dried up, as it finally did for Samori Ture (though not for Menelik II), catastrophe promptly ensued. A few African communities had possessed the capacity to manufacture and repair guns in the past, but they lacked the heat blast furnaces capable of forging iron that was needed by the mid–1800s. Some modernizing states—Meiji Japan by 1900 and Ranjit Singh's Punjab in the 1830s—acquired the industrial capacity for modern gun and artillery manufacture but, as the eventual occupation of the Punjab by British forces in the 1840s demonstrates, even these were no guarantors of independence. In any event, more than iron-smelting furnaces was required for the post–1870 generations of rifles, machine guns, and artillery.

The imperial applications of Western military capabilities and medical breakthroughs were matched in other areas of applied science and technology. The age of high imperialism, in fact, corresponded with the age of widespread technology transfer from the West to the rest of the world. The Old World "technology highway" of antiquity and medieval times that had conveyed a number of inventions (e.g., paper, gunpowder, and the stirrup) from the East to the West was long abandoned, but it had not been replaced by a comparable flow in the opposite direction until the 1800s. Now Western engineers proceeded to alter the landscape of the imperialized world with bridges, roads, tunnels, irrigation systems, harbors, and such modern wonders as the Suez Canal. Telegraph lines and submarine cables connected the continents and laced the oceans enabling nearly instantaneous communications that lessened isolation, permitted the timely deployment of troops to quell colonial uprisings, and increased interaction between colonies and the metropolitan states.

Returning once more to the Congo as a microcosm of a globalized technology circuit, some of the more important developments and their impacts may be cited. Steamships made contacts between Europe and the Congo cheaper, more frequent, and reliable. Steam-propelled river boats performed the same function inland but they also had the offensive capability of mounted guns. The development of reliable batteries was used to supply electrical power to telegraphs that sped vital news of wars and commercial dealings, giving Europeans a tremendous edge. The establishment of railroads completed the transportation infrastructure of domination and exploitation. Generally railroad layouts conformed to the Matadi-Leopoldville pattern with one terminus located at an ocean port and the other placed at a major site of resource extraction or processing. A secondary use of colonial railways was to transport troops in an emergency, a consideration that influenced the design of British India's sprawling railroad network.

Sometimes terrain had to be leveled before roads and railroads could be built. In this endeavor dynamite proved invaluable. The Swedish chemist Alfred Nobel invented dynamite when he discovered that combining diatomaceous earth with highly volatile nitroglycerin eliminated the latter's notorious instability without diminishing its potency. Stanley burrowed through hillsides and blasted away natural impediments to his mighty roadways using dynamite. These were mostly designed for commercial traffic and by the 1890s much of that was in rubber. Two unrelated inventions sent the value of rubber soaring by the end of the nineteenth century. The first invention stemmed from mixing and heating latex with sulfur (vulcanization), which strengthened and increased the plasticity of rubber, making it far more useful (1840s). The second, as we have seen, was the invention of the pneumatic tire (1888) which was perfectly suited to the new mass-produced bicycle and automobile. By the first decade of this century the Congo became the rubber capital of the Old World, exporting 20 percent of the world's rubber output, second only to that of the Amazon basin. It was thus with fitting irony that Prince Albert, Leopold's son and heir, once entered the Congo riding a bicycle that was equipped with vulcanized pneumatic rubber tires.

As these incidents suggest, technology served ideological as well as physical purposes. It was directed at the colonizers as an objective proof of superiority and a justification for white domination. Some Europeans engaged in a breathtaking circular logic by reasoning that a society that had produced advanced technology was generally advanced because it had produced advanced technology. The West's ability to make chemical compounds, produce hard and durable metals, identify microbes, and substitute electrical power and internal combustion engines for human and animal brawn and wind and water power, signified to Westerners and some others besides that they were more developed in other spheres of human thought and action: in governance, religion, ethics, social customs, and philosophy. Such attitudes could and did promote a kind of imperial welfarism, a program of development and uplift that, however ethhnocentric and patronizing, was nonetheless well-intended. They also played a role in erecting inhuman systems of domination and control that wreaked havoc with local (and global) ecologies. Both were at work in the Congo and elsewhere where colonial organization and exploitation were inseparable from social, cultural, and material change.

FURTHER READINGS

The most readable single-authored volume on the role of technology and anti-malarial medicine is Daniel Headrick's *The Tools of Empire* (New York: Oxford University Press, 1981). Also see *The Tentacles of Progress: Technology Transfer in the Age of Imperialism, 1850–1940* (New York: Oxford University Press, 1988) by the same author. For a wide-ranging exploration of the role of the railways as instruments of imperial control, colonial development, and global economic integration in both formal and informal colonial settings, see Clarence B. Davis and Kenneth W. Wilburn, Jr., eds. with Ronald E. Robinson, *Railway Imperialism* (Westport, Conn.: Greenwood Press, 1991). The best synthesis of the cultural and ideological impact of Western science and technology on colonial policy and the colonized is Michael Adas, *Machines as the Measure of Man* (Ithaca, N.Y.: Cornell University Press, 1989).

Quite recently, a number of works have examined the environmental legacy of the applied technologies of modern imperialism. Especially for the British empire see: Alfred Crosby, *Ecological Imperialism: The Biological Expansion of Europe, 900–1900* (Cambridge: Cambridge University Press, 1986) and J. M. MacKenzie, ed., *Imperialism and the Natural World* (Manchester: Manchester University Press, 1990). On the role of human disease and colonialism as well as comparative investigations of Western science and medicine as forms of cultural imperialism, see: Philip D. Curtin, *Death By Migration: Europe's Encounter with the Tropical World in the Nineteenth Century* (Cambridge: Cambridge University Press, 1989); Roy MacLeod and Milton Lewis, eds., *Disease, Medicine, and Empire: Perspectives on Western Medicine and the Experience of Western Expansion* (New York: Routledge & Kegan Paul, 1988); David Arnold, ed., *Imperial Medicine and Indigenous Societies* (Delhi: Oxford University Press, 1989); Teresa Meade and Mark Walker, eds., *Science, Medicine and Cultural Imperialism* (New York: St. Martin's Press, 1991); and selections from Terence Ranger and Paul Slack, eds., *Epidemics and Ideas* (Cambridge: Cambridge University Press, 1992).

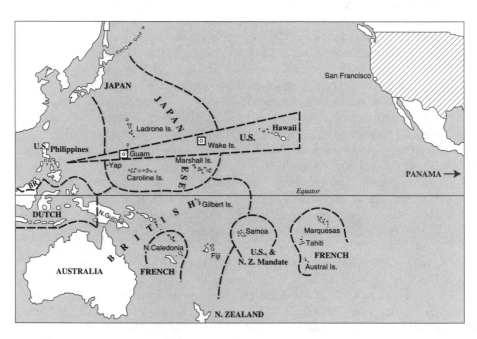

OCEANIA IMPERIALIZED *The Pacific was the last region to be incorporated into the Western empires. This post-World War I map does not show Germany's prewar colonies–the Carolines, Ladrones, Marshalls, part of Samoa, and the Northeast quadrant of New Guinea. (Reprinted by permission: The Hawaiian State Archives)*

4

ISLANDS OF MANIFEST DESTINY

America in Hawaii

The colonization of Hawaii by the United States stands in marked contrast to that of Leopold's conquest of the Congo. First, Western control was not imposed abruptly: it occurred over the span of three quarters of a century. Second, there was no single mastermind at work. Third, economic interests were ultimately tied to strategic considerations that in the Congo were negligible. Fourth, where Leopold's seizure of the Congo contributed to the colonial stampede of Africa, Hawaii was acquired at the end of the Partition of the Pacific. And fifth, where the Congo was a textbook example of a tropical colony of resource extraction undertaken by a handful of Europeans, Hawaii was a hybrid tropical-settler dependency where Westerners and East Asians overwhelmed and displaced the native population. In brief, larger historical forces and structures—the intrusion of a Western-led international economy, the transmission of Western culture particularly Christianity, and the modern Western propensity for exerting proprietorial control over people, resources, and nature—are even more striking in the Hawaiian case though this does not mean that individuals or groups lost their capacity to shape events and influence circumstances.

This chapter charts Hawaii's loss of control over its culture, economy, and polity. It begins with the transformative cultural influences originating in the West and focuses on a key agent of change, the New England Protestant missionaries. Hawaiian receptivity to alien customs and beliefs facilitated the spread of Westernization in education, religion, government, land, production, and labor. The missionaries, their ethnocentrism, and their impact on the native community were

73

*critical. Attention then shifts to foreign, particularly American, mer-
chants and businessmen who succeeded in molding an economy compatible with and more responsive to the capitalist requirements of the
age. This change had profound political repercussions and the chapter
concludes with an assessment of the most critical of these, the revolution of 1893 and the annexation of Hawaii by America in 1898.*

KAPUS AND TABUS: OLD AND NEW

The cultural contest between Hawaiians and Westerners began with the
visit of the renowned English naval explorer Captain James Cook in
1778–1779. His arrival happened to coincide with the start of an annual
festival customarily inaugurated by the appearance of *Lono*, the Hawaiian
god of peace, fertility, and prosperity. By tradition, *Lono* reigned for three
or four months as the dominant deity while the war god *Ku* temporarily
relinquished that position. Tabus that normally regulated social and physical interactions between nobles and commoners and men and women
were relaxed or suspended during "*Lono's*" festival. Cook's timing, the
shape and dimensions of his ship, and certain of his acts, such as circum-
navigating the island of Maui prior to landfall, might have been interpreted as signs of the appearance of *Lono* or one of his emissaries.
Whether regarded as the deity himself or an exalted person embodying the
divine force (*mana*), Cook was revered and feted until, again according to
tradition, it was time for him to leave and for *Ku* to resume his place.

   As survivors of Cook's voyage recounted, Cook departed on a date
that, quite by chance, conformed to the prescribed moment of *Lono's*
withdrawal. But as ill-luck would have it, a broken mast forced him to return a few days later and the mythical spell was ruptured. Cook's acci-
dental slaying could therefore be interpreted as consistent with Hawaiian
beliefs. It is also possible that the scores of Hawaiians who plunged their
spears into Cook's body did so to acquire some of his *mana*. Because his
men also possessed *mana* (albeit in lesser amounts), consorting with them
and acquiring their artifacts became the means by which Hawaiians could
enhance their own status. Female commoners sometimes defied the authority of chiefs and husbands, sexually availing themselves to the British
in order to invest their offspring with greater *mana*. The accomplished
warrior, Kamehameha the Great (1758–1819), used his position to obtain
a European bed, knives, forks, and plates and, because food possessed
and transmitted spiritual qualities, instructed a servant to cook in the
English style. He even hoisted the British ensign over his house and royal
canoe (the Union Jack has been retained in Hawaii's state flag). The upshot of this and subsequent encounters was that the British helped Kamehameha to unify the islands thereby cultivating a Hawaiian dynastic af-
fection for Britain.

PRE-CONTACT TRADITIONS

Historical accounts of socioreligious rituals reveal both the power held by and constraints on Hawaiian women, even exalted ones.

Keakealaniwahine was once the ruler of all Hawaii . . . As there was no other chiefess her equal, she was kept apart . . . Though a woman, Keakealaniwahine was permitted to enter the *heiaus* (temples) to give her offerings and sacrifices. However, she was not allowed to eat any of the offerings and gifts with the priests and the men, who ate by themselves . . . Keakealaniwahine ate in her own house of the food permitted to women.

. . . Kamehameha [the great] and all the chiefs waited until the death of [the high chiefess] Kalola. They wailed and chanted dirges . . . and the chiefs tattooed themselves and knocked out their teeth. Kamehameha was also tattooed and had his eyeteeth knocked out . . .

Source: Jocelyn Linnekin, *Sacred Queens and Women of Consequence: Rank, Gender, and Colonialism in the Hawaiian Islands* (Ann Arbor: University of Michigan Press, 1990), pp. 25, 62. Reprinted by permission of the University of Michigan Press.

The second phase of Western-Hawaiian contact was dominated by starchy New England Protestant missionaries who landed in 1820 as part of an oceanic extension of American evangelical revivalism known as the Second Awakening. The impact of this contact was plainly evident at the 1823 funeral of the highest ranking Hawaiian, the sacred queen Keopuolani. Just before her death, the queen was inconsolable, profoundly agitated over the state of her soul. Though a recent adherent of the teachings of Christ, she had not been formally admitted into the church. Contemplating an eternity in flames, she begged the missionaries to baptize her before she died, proclaiming her love of Jehovah and Jesus, and renouncing the Hawaiian gods. She instructed her son, king Kamehameha II, and the assembled chiefs to protect the missionaries, observe the Sabbath, follow Christ's example, and see that she was interred in a casket and buried in solemn Christian fashion. Within moments of these edicts, Keopuolani slipped into unconscious, received baptism, and died.

As word of the great queen's death spread, deafening moans rose up drowning out the cannons of saluting foreign ships. In accordance with ancient practice, the wailing persisted for days. But new Yankee Protestant ways were also evident in the burial procession with its Christian liturgy, black-draped coffin and cortege, and mourners filing past the coffin in measured columns. After the royal remains were placed in a tomb, commoners built a surrounding wall out of stones brought from a place where the Hawaiian gods had been worshipped. As they did so, a missionary deplored what he saw as their disrespectful gaiety. He was even more shocked by the king's drunkenness from cherry brandy that a merchant had given him. This display of emotion, which the missionary condemned as self-indulgent, was as alarming as the fact that the king had acquired the brandy from the "ungodly" community of American, British, and European traders and sailors. His reaction was a portent of things to come. In different ways, Hawaiians' absorption of Cook's *mana*, Kamehameha's appropriation of British insignia, Keopuolani's deathbed embrace of Christ, the missionary's hostile reaction to Kamehameha II's inebriation by Western liquor, and the odd marriage of Hawaiian and American funeral rites set the stage for decades of cultural intrusion, adjustment, and resistance.

During the 1820s Keopuolani and then Kaahumanu—widow of Kamehameha I and Hawaii's virtual ruler until her death in 1832—backed Protestantism both as a new state religion and as a means of confirming their own power. Chiefly women, and Kaahumanu in particular, were instrumental in the spread of Christianity by supporting the missionaries. But even before the advent of the Yankees, the two queens had persuaded Kamehameha II (Liholiho, ruled 1819–1824) to renounce the traditional religion, its gods, its *kahunas* (priests), and its *kapus*, the collective prescriptions and prohibitions that governed daily life. *Kapus* defined acts, places, times, and persons as sacred or profane, purifying or defiling. They determined how and when to fish, where and how to pray, what foods were to be eaten with whom, and so on. Some *kapus* privileged noble men over noble women. One, for instance, prohibited women from eating purifying foods such as pork, which were reserved for males. These *kapus* were especially irksome to the king's wives, Keopuolani and Kaahumanu, and other female relations who defied them with growing boldness and frequency.

In part, the collapse of the *kapus* was caused by contact with Western sailors and traders. Hawaiians had noted that the failure of Westerners to honor the *kapus* and pay homage to Hawaiian gods failed to provoke divine reprisals. Gradually, the *kapus* lost their hold on the elite. Commoners, taking their cue from their leaders and chafing under the restrictions of the *kapu* system, did not rise up to preserve it. It also seems that while the decline of the old dispensation demoralized some male chiefs whose new status was not what it had been, it emboldened female chiefs whose powers expanded with the passing of the *kapus*. Another factor was political. With Kamehameha I's death in 1819, challenges to his carefully groomed successor would be sanctioned under the old system. Thus, Kamehameha II's repudiation of the *kapus* sent a chilling signal to ambitious high chiefs. It was in this climate that organized Christianity appeared (1820) and it seems that the de facto ruler during the 1820s, the influential Kaahumanu, recognized the value of a new religion as a buttress for a young state.

Still, the old order's demise was far from instantaneous or total. The king and some of his successors maintained several useful and cherished mythico-religious practices. At the same time, chiefs and chiefesses who had embraced Christianity carefully reshaped it to accord better with traditional concepts and institutions. Thus Christian sins supplanted tabus and one missionary was made Kaahumanu's head priest (*kahuna nui*). And though the Kamehameha state and Protestant Christianity reinforced each another into the 1830s, many commoners remained privately faithful to their ancestral and nature gods, *kahunas,* and *kapus* as well as to established pastimes. Many worshipped the old and the new faiths side by side and only occasionally did they overtly protest or defy the Yankee "*kahunas*" and their aristocratic patrons. In any event, it is important to note that the spread of Protestantism was conditional on the actions of Hawaii's rulers, the American missionaries, and on the concomitant decline of the old beliefs.

A CULTURE DISPOSSESSED

The missionaries had their own motivations and objectives, of course. They came to save souls, having become aware of Hawaii after two Hawaiian youths were brought to New England by returning merchant vessels. As religion suffused the lives and thoughts of the true believers, no aspect of Hawaii's culture was immune to reform. The devout beheld Hawaii as a heathenish land ripe for redemption. Although heartened by the recent royal rejection of idols and *kahunas,* much continued to excite their ire. They deplored public nudity and gambling on everything from swimming to surfing and grass sledding contests, and were horrified by *hula* dances which they considered lewd and vulgar.

Initially hesitant, missionaries became more brazen in identifying "immoral, indolent, and wasteful" activities. They argued that Hawaiian culture was all frivolity and devilry. They searched in vain for what they could recognize as thrift, industry, and private property. Occasional praise for Hawaiian ways was couched in patronizing, derisory terms. For example, Hawaiian houses were commended for the skill used in their construction only to be likened to ridiculous birdcages encased in hay stacks. And *poi*—a sticky paste made from taro root and a staple of the Hawaiian diet—was considered useful, not for ingestion, but for the binding of books. Ethnocentric judgments were, of course, at the core of colonial encounters. But in the case of the missionaries, ethnocultural criticism was based on a genuine desire to improve the welfare of Hawaiians.

As in the Congo, critical thoughts and speech informed colonizing deeds. Besides their faith, the missionaries brought tools to restructure the environment to more closely resemble the one they had known in America. They brought clapboard houses and equipped them with ovens, window panes, shutters, engravings, and chandeliers. They fenced in their yards, designed straight roads, planted tidy orchards, and sowed crops in neat rows. In the new subtropical world of the missionaries, Bibles, ploughs, and trousers went hand in hand. (Evangelicals considered civilization and Christianity as the twinned pillars of an advanced society.) Before long, many Hawaiians lived in Western structures, donned Western garb (the unauthentically Hawaiian *muumuu* was invented by the missionaries), cooked dishes in the Western fashion, and filled up Protestant pews and schoolhouse seats. For some it seemed that a primordial paradise had become civilized and that anguished souls had been saved for Christ.

It is important to stress that despite the dominant acculturative role of Westerners, Hawaiians were not mere passive recipients of cultural transfer. Some zestfully embraced the new order and a few—such as Keopuolani and Kaahumanu—were powerful enough to guide the pace and manner of the initial stage of acculturation. The response of commoners was guided by that of their revered chiefs. Hawaiians were also attracted by the intriguing customs and bizarre appearance of these strangers. Historic celebrants of ritual and rhetorical dexterity, Hawaiians were instantly drawn to the delivery of church sermons and to the new curriculums. So great in fact was the response that in little more than a decade the missionaries had provided some basic instruction to some two-fifths of the entire population. Mass conversion followed in the late 1830s and 1840s when a new generation of evangelical missionaries—less reserved and more exuberant but just as tireless as their predecessors— brought some 80 percent of Hawaiians into the fold with their electrifying sermons on an everlasting, loving god and his redemptive son.

Christianity, English, and Western secular knowledge were jointly disseminated through missionary and other private institutions as well as state schools beginning in the 1840s. By the 1850s, the sons of the elite were instructed (in English) in natural science, philosophy, history, and geography (their sisters were tutored in the domestic arts). Even in non-elite schools, Western curricula and methodologies predominated. Such schools played a crucial role in transforming many Hawaiians into Westernized, English-speaking Christians by the last quarter of the nineteenth century. In all this language proved critical. Perhaps surprisingly, most missionaries were staunch defenders of the Hawaiian language, arguing that English was the tongue of depraved traders and shiftless riffraff. Besides, conversion would occur sooner if Hawaiian was the medium of instruction.

In any event, Hawaiians embraced English as the vernacular of commerce and the idiom of the new god. Of course language is far more profoundly influential than that and English conveyed not only a new vocabulary but also new structures of thought that subtly undermined indigenous patterns of thinking about the world. Thus, fluency in English opened up a conceptual vista Hawaiians had not known before, a vista framed by alien norms.

The nonconformity of leading "traditionalists" whom the missionaries called "backsliders" was a troubling exception to the general diffusion of Christian morality. One illustrious example will make the point. King Kamehameha III (Kauikeaouli, ruled 1824–1854) repeatedly offended pious morality by independent, pleasurable behavior, especially at the outset of his reign. Particularly repugnant to missionaries was his intimate, sexual relationship with his sister, Nahienaena. Traditionally, matings between royal siblings were regarded as the noblest of couplings, sanctioned by the *kahunas* but condemned as blasphemous incest by the missionaries. The king's refusal to end this liaison triggered a bitter and painful controversy that led to the devout and pregnant princess' excommunication. Her death at the unripe age of twenty soon followed, just after that of her infant child. The controversy and Nahienaena's death broke the king's spirit, effectively ended his resistance to the missionaries and their chiefly supporters, and led to his partial, demoralized withdrawal from politics.

Despite Kamehameha III's personal rebellion against the evangelical Yankees and their chiefly allies, the king—who, from the mid–1830s, fell under the influence of Christian and Westernizing nobles—authorized several constitutional and legal changes. In 1835 he all but installed the Ten Commandments as Hawaii's national charter by criminalizing murder, theft, adultery, drunkenness, perjury, and other Biblical offenses. Five years later a new constitution completed the process and proclaimed Hawaii a Christian nation and outlawed any regulation "at variance with the word of the Lord Jehovah." In 1852 yet another constitution established a British-style parliamentary monarchy. The result was a diminution

PROTESTANTS IN PARADISE *By the 1830s many Hawaiians had converted to Christianity thanks to the efforts of New England Protestant missionaries who were supported by many Hawaiian leaders, especially women.* (Reprinted by permission: The Hawaiian State Archives)

of the powers of the crown and chiefs, an increased role for all adult Hawaiian males who acquired the vote by secret ballot (something then unavailable in either Britain or the United States), and a considerable increase in the powers of the legislature and the cabinet. The last was most significant because ministers were almost exclusively *haole* (white). Foreign influence was also exerted through an independent judiciary and the missionaries who transmitted the principles of Western government and political economy to Hawaiian chiefs.

Constitutions were the means by which the Polynesian monarchical state articulated its powers and authority vis-à-vis its own subjects and resident foreigners. They also enabled the Hawaiian state to assert its sovereignty in its dealings with increasingly interfering foreign powers (especially the United States, France, and Great Britain) in internationally recognized forms. Occasionally the Hawaiian people also invoked Western forms to resist the encroachments of *haoles* and their national governments. In the 1840s, for instance, thousands prayed to the Christian god for deliverance from the curse of white domination. In 1848 others, noting with approval the revolutionary tumult in Europe, clamored for an anti-white coup at home. Three years earlier, some 1600 Hawaiians petitioned Kamehameha III to halt foreign influence and prevent *haoles* from becoming citizens, buying land (see the discussion of the Great *Mahele* below), and monopolizing high office. They also implored him to safeguard Hawaii's delicate independence. By this time, however, the dispirited king passively supported the coalition of *haoles* and Westernizing chiefs. The petition was shelved.

These early expressions of Hawaiian nationalism were echoed by the resounding reactions to cultural disintegration of two remarkable men. Each was a product of a hybridized culture and was greatly troubled by the decline of native society. One was a scholar, the other a prophet. Both were the glimmering products of Protestant schooling, well educated and with a Christian faith that was fervent and solid. Of modest birth, David Malo was formally educated and converted as an adult, becoming the fourth Hawaiian to be ordained a Protestant minister. Devoted to the missionaries and to his pastoral duties, Malo was recognized for his scholastic talents and appointed the first superintendent of state schools. At the same time, he was a living repository of Hawaiian legends, lore, history, royal genealogy, sacred ceremonies, and the *kapus*. It was Malo, historian and scholar, author of the acclaimed *Hawaiian Antiquities*, and devout Christian, who traced with poignant empiricism the growing envelopment of Hawaii by the West.

In contrast to Malo's sober prognosis were the stark forecasts of Joseph Kaona. His "moment" arrived in the ominous vortex of surging racial strife and geological volatility. Like Malo, Kaona had merged spiritual and temporal careers, having been a district judge, a legislator, and a preacher. In 1869 he had a vision in which the second coming of Christ and the end of the world were foretold, a prediction made frighteningly tangible by severe volcanic eruptions and earth tremors. His inflammatory message of a doomed world (not to mention his slaying a constable) could not be tolerated by the government: he was arrested and his flock was dispersed. Both Malo and Kaona were sirens of a deep cultural crisis, one in the Western "scientific" mode, the other in the guise of a messianic *kahuna*. Their warnings were instantly grasped throughout the kingdom but despite the erudition of one and the charisma of the other, neither could stem the flowing tide of Western influence and control.

HISTORICAL TIDES

David Malo in an 1837 letter to the high chiefess Kinau, offered a gloomy outlook for Hawaii's future.

. . . you must not think that this is anything like olden times, that you are the only chiefs and can leave things as they are . . . This is the reason. If a big wave comes in, large fishes will come from the dark Ocean which you never saw before, and when they see the small fishes they will eat them up; such also is the case with large animals, they will prey on the smaller ones. The ships of the white man have come, and smart people have arrived from the great countries which you have never seen before, they know our people are few in number and living in a small country; they will eat us up, such has always been the case with large countries, the small ones have been gobbled up . . .

Source: Ralph S. Kuykendall, *The Hawaiian Kingdom, 1778–1854* (Honolulu: University of Hawaii Press, 1938), p. 153. Reprinted by permission.

Loyal protests, solemn warnings, an emergent Hawaiian nativism, and the cultural medley that characterized Hawaiian life in the third quarter of the nineteenth century—the *kahunas* were venerated just as Sunday worship was observed and Hawaiian kings patronized *luaus* and *hulas* along with dinner parties and ballroom dances—were reflections of and responses to the islands' fateful demographic metamorphosis. If Westernization was unstoppable, it was because the foreign element was increasing in numbers and had achieved economic and political dominance. At the same time, the native population plunged from a pre-contact (1778) figure variously estimated from 250,000 to 800,000 to a little more than 60,000 by 1870.

Deadly labor regimens or genocide did not play a large role, in contrast to the Congo or the continental United States. The principal culprit of population decline was Western diseases unleashed on some of the most epidemiologically isolated people on earth. The aptly named "fatal impact" consisted of epidemics of measles, typhoid, whooping cough, smallpox, leprosy, and venereal disease, the "great waster" of the kingdom. Some of Cook's men were tubercular and transmitted venereal diseases in 1778–1779 and the first missionaries also carried tuberculosis. In between devastating pathogenic outbreaks, the population was ravaged by more commonplace but equally lethal attacks of dysentery, influenza, and the common cold as well as such psychologically conditioned responses as alcoholism, abortion, and infanticide.

Missionaries were shocked by the precipitous decline. Some blamed it on the wages of sexual sin, others on alcohol, but few *haoles* held themselves in any way responsible. Religiously minded observers tended to view the demographic collapse as a failure to obey the Bible's commandments while amateur Darwinians said it was a natural working out of the laws of evolution in which only the fit survive. Increasingly, Hawaiians recognized that the survival of their culture was dependent on the health and numbers of their people. But their options were tragically few. Western medicine offered precious little defense against the onslaught of Western diseases (especially if Hawaiians refused to vaccinate themselves) and the desperate scheme of replenishing Hawaii with Polynesians from other Pacific islands proved unfeasible.

THE SUGARED ECONOMY

Most foreigners came to Hawaii to push trade. For some years after Cook's visit, a lively traffic developed in sandalwood. Indigenous to the Pacific Islands, it was prized by the Chinese for incense, fans, and ornaments. Since the China trade was so lucrative and the West had so little the Chinese wanted, sandalwood became a staple of transpacific commerce. Moreover, Hawaii was ideally situated on the route linking America to China, which was the reason China-bound Western merchants stopped there in the 1790s and early 1800s to exchange furs for tea and silk. When sandalwood grew scarce, Hawaii's commerce shifted to whaling. Again, its location made it a suitable provisioning base for merchant ships, especially those from America hunting north Pacific whales for their oil and bones. Whaling became so important that it dominated Hawaii's economy from the 1820s through the 1850s. It brought considerable money with which merchantmen purchased Hawaiian beef, fruits and vegetables, fresh water, wood, safe harbors, materials for repairs, and miscellaneous recreations.

Between 1860 and 1880, whaling rapidly declined, both because the whale population had been depleted by excessive harvesting and because petroleum, cheaper and more plentiful, had become available. Yet the legacy of the whaling era was that the *haole* community grew and closer ties were forged between Hawaii and the United States. The industry was dominated by New England, which annually sent hundreds of vessels to Hawaii. The success of American entrepreneurs increased Hawaii's economic dependence on the United States just as it enabled them to exert more influence over local economic and political life. It was from this time that American warships first began to lurk in Honolulu's harbor when some vital interest of a U. S. citizen seemed in jeopardy. As it happened, American gunboat diplomacy played a critical role in the events of 1887 and 1893 (described below).

By the mid–1860s, sugar had overtaken whaling as Hawaii's leading product, helped by the Civil War, which had placed the sugar-producing South beyond the Union's reach. The growth of Hawaii's new industry was rapid and sustained. Throughout the 1870s tens of millions of pounds were exported annually. Twenty years later it mushroomed into half a billion pounds. By 1900 10 percent of all the sugar consumed by Americans came from Hawaii.

To achieve this, planters needed control over land and labor. Access to land was obtained through legislation in the 1840s known as the *Great Mahele* (the great division) which dramatically transformed Hawaiian land ownership and tenures. Before the *Great Mahele* most of the land had been held by the chiefs and their retainers under "feudal" titles conditionally granted by the king. Commoners were obliged to perform customary duties and share their produce with landholding aristocrats though they had the right to leave one landholder's domain for another. Now land was divided into surveyed lots and apportioned to king, chiefs, and commoners in fee simple titles. The owner could do what he or she liked with the lot, even sell it (women controlled land in their own right or on behalf of their families). In addition, aliens—whether naturalized citizens or not—were able to purchase and work the land on the same terms as native Hawaiians. The upshot was that more Hawaiian land came under cultivation, much of it in sugar. Yet capital-wielding whites were quick to buy land from commoners for whom ready cash and employment opportunities in the towns were more attractive than eking out a life on the soil.

The result was a socioeconomic revolution. By 1890 only 15 percent of Hawaii was owned by Hawaiians (and a meager one percent belonged to native commoners). The missionaries had miscalculated when they thought land reform would break the aristocracy's hold on the people and transfer the basic means of production to a large, thriving class of peasant proprietors. Instead of tilling small but productive plots as independent and enterprising farmers, the Hawaiian people lost their customary patrimony altogether.

The consequences of the intrusion of the global economy were enormous. In the first century after Cook's visit, poverty increased as self-sufficient subsistence peasants became landless tillers and unskilled laborers. The required payment of taxes in money increased the exodus from the land to the towns where foreigners paid workers in cash. Relations between commoners and chiefs deteriorated. Coveting foreign products, the nobles had put peasants to work hewing sandalwood and raising crops desired by Western merchants. These the nobles exchanged for such status objects as crystal, silver, brocades, and porcelains. Noble exactions caused cultivators to neglect their own fields, contributing further to spiraling impoverishment. Just as ominous, the trade in provisions exports and luxuriant imports increased the political and economic dependency of the nobles on the *haole* merchant community.

The adoption of Western agricultural methods also changed the demographic complexion of the islands to the disadvantage of native Hawaiians. To offset the decline of the native population (it fell to 30,000 by 1900), Chinese, Japanese, and Portuguese laborers were imported under one-to-five year contracts. But settlement, not repatriation, followed the termination of those contracts. The result was that Hawaii was no longer a Polynesian society but had become a heterogeneous community demographically dominated by East Asians. In 1876 Hawaiians and part-Hawaiians still comprised nearly ninety percent of the population. By 1900 they were a mere twenty-six percent. Over the same years Caucasians rose from six percent to nearly eighteen percent while East Asians shot up from less than five percent to more than fifty-six percent.

Given these numbers, the economic needs of planters had ramifications that went far beyond the concerns of labor procurement. Of great concern was what should be the ethnic complexion of Hawaii and to what extent ought state policy be determined by the sugar interests. These questions divided the various Hawaiian communities and sometimes shaped the parliamentary fortunes of ministries. Anglo-Saxon fears of the "Yellow Peril" as represented by Chinese and Japanese immigrant laborers were matched by native Hawaiians concerned about Polynesian deracination. In the end, both yielded to the short-term requirements of

THE "DE-POLYNESIANIZATION" OF HAWAII   The importation of foreign workers—such as these Japanese plantation hands—to work in Hawaii's burgeoning agricultural industry made Hawaiians a minority in their own country. (Reprinted by permission: Bishop Museum Press)

economic growth and sanctioned the importation of laborers to harvest the sugarcane that kept the economy buoyant.

KALAKAUA AND RECIPROCITY

Having acquired satisfactory access to land and labor resources, planters and their agents concentrated on lowering the prices of their products as they entered the vast U. S. market. This pricing was to be achieved by eliminating import duties that could reduce retail prices by as much as one fifth. This reduction, of course, would benefit more than just the sugar industry. Since the booming days of the California gold rush (late 1840s), the rapid settlement of the West coast of the United States sparked a demand in foodstuffs that Hawaiian farms and ranches rushed to satisfy in the form of meats, vegetables, coffee, and sugar. But it was difficult for Hawaiian goods to compete with tariff-protected American-produced goods, and Hawaiian producers dreamt about future fortunes if and when U. S. import duties were abolished. That was accomplished in 1876 with the signing of the reciprocity treaty by which Hawaii was precluded from ceding any of its territory or granting reciprocity rights to any other power. Upon its renewal in 1887, the Americans won a concession they had long coveted: a lease on Pearl Harbor which, as the best sheltered inlet in the North Pacific, would make an ideal U. S. naval base.

TWO HAWAIIAN VIEWS ON PEARL HARBOR

As one prominent part-Hawaiian politician argued that leasing Pearl Harbor to the United States would actually secure Hawaiian independence, a poem printed in a newspaper argued just the opposite.

I say if Puuloa [Pearl Harbor] is given to America, that would give us independence forever ... America ... will spend millions of dollars there ... hasten the laying of the proposed telegraphic cable. If we give away Puuloa to America, we will fear no longer about annexation, for America does not want another inch of our land ... If we give Puuloa to America, England may want a coaling station here also. Well, give her Koolau [Kaneohe Bay]; that is the only way of maintaining our independence.

I am the comrade of the winds,	Truly desiring annexation,
And the companion of the rain;	Greatly desiring their own good;
I am a shield against the cold	They have no thought of good for you,
And darkness cannot dwell with me.	A presuming set only are they,
I am a messenger forbidding you	A proud and haughty set,
To give away Puuloa.	Ever soliciting, at the same time
Be not deceived by the merchants,	flattering,
They are only enticing you,	Desiring that you should all die,
Making fair their faces,	That the kingdom may become
they are evil within;	theirs.

Sources: Ralph S. Kuykendall, *The Hawaiian Kingdom, Volume III, 1874–1893, the Kalakaua Dynasty* (Honolulu: University of Hawaii Press, 1967), p. 503; and the Honolulu Hawaiian paper, the *Nuhou*, 18 November 1873. Reprinted by permission.

The effects of the treaty on Hawaii were momentous and far-reaching but here it is only necessary to discuss those which influenced the growing American hegemony over Hawaii. Largely as a result of the treaty, Hawaii became irrevocably locked into America's commercial and strategic orbit. The remark of a United States minister to Honolulu in the 1860s that Hawaii under reciprocity would come to resemble a state of the union proved prescient. To the extent that the treaty boosted trade and helped the sugar industry to prosper, the influence of American businessmen (some of them Hawaiian citizens by now) over domestic Hawaiian politics became all but absolute and, in consequence, highly controversial.

Having tethered itself to the dynamo of American consumerism, the Hawaiian state guided by king David Kalakaua (ruled, 1874–1891) became more, not less, determined to preserve its shadowy independence and imperiled way of life. This determination was evident in the style and policies of the king who tried to balance an economic policy that bound the United States and Hawaii closer together with a program of limited revitalization of Hawaiian culture. The king made it a priority to appoint Hawaiians to high office. Prior to 1874, only one Hawaiian had ever held ministerial office. But during his reign, 11 part or full-blooded Hawaiians were appointed to cabinet positions as against 26 *haoles*.

Heading his Hawaiianization agenda was fortifying the monarchy, easily accomplished under the royalist constitution of 1864. His trip around the world, sumptuous coronation, and construction of the grand Iolani palace as well as his (unsuccessful) attempt to build a navy and establish Hawaii as a Pacific power were designed to revive Hawaiian pride and increase the prestige of the dynasty. But the king's gestures were utterly overshadowed by the sharp drop in Hawaii's native population. Moreover, the foreign community considered his lifestyle pretentious and wasteful and his policies absurd and dangerous. Hawaii was repeatedly caricatured in the *haole* press and in official dispatches as a Polynesian toy kingdom. And no matter what Kalakaua did, *haole* influence continued to grow. In fact, his flamboyance only further antagonized and united foreigners who came to distrust his every move.

The reciprocity treaty confirmed sugar's status as king of the economy. Because it was so profitable, cane acquired a dominance that effectively transformed Hawaii—like so many colonies—into a monocultural export country. This was paralleled by increasing planter influence over the Hawaiian government which was most spectacularly illustrated by the Hawaiian career of Claus Spreckels. Spreckels was a cunning businessman with a knack for amassing gigantic profits and for exploiting new markets and technologies. A German immigrant to the United States, Spreckels became a capitalist grocer almost overnight. He bought and sold stores and blithely entered the sugar refining business knowing only that it could make him a very rich man. He worked hard, learning the trade as he transformed it into a thriving enterprise. Fearful of the impact of untaxed Hawaiian imports on his California-based business, Spreckels initially opposed the reciprocity treaty. But when it passed, he boarded the first ship to Hawaii and once there bought over half of that year's crop before the value of sugar shot up. He then gobbled up Hawaiian land, won rights to build irrigation ditches, and created a model sugar plantation at Spreckelsville on the island of Maui. Within a short time he came to control the Hawaiian sugar industry to a degree no one else has matched, before or since.

Spreckels could not have accomplished this without the help of persons in high places, above all Kalakaua himself. He ingratiated himself with the king and either gave or lent him considerable sums of money. In turn, Spreckels exerted an unhealthy political leverage over the king. Between 1878 and 1886 Spreckels made and unmade ministries, earning the tart nickname "His Royal Saccharinity." Despite his massive ego, Spreckels was less interested in political power than commercial profits and in a stable economic climate in which he could best amass them. Unfortunately, his alliance with Kalakaua and the erratic if brilliant prime minister, Walter Murray Gibson, was not conducive to stability. It certainly alarmed much of the *haole* community and considering the numbers of scandals it hatched it is amazing that the triumvirate lasted more than half a decade.

Spreckels was the first to go, in 1886. His downfall was as spectacular as his rise and has entered into Hawaiian lore. As the story goes, he was playing cards one day with Kalakaua and two admirals. When Spreckels remarked that he would have the winning hand if they had been playing poker, one of the admirals called his bluff showing his own three aces. Spreckels, undaunted, displayed his hand of three kings but claimed that he had four. When the perplexed Kalakaua asked where the fourth king was, the sardonic "Sir Claus" shot back: "I am the fourth king!". The offhand remark deeply wounded the king who stalked out as his band played "God Save the King." Spreckels added further insult by standing up and bowing in mock acknowledgment to the royal bandmaster. The incident capped a series of sour dealings between the two. Now Kalakaua was galvanized into action. That evening he negotiated a new loan with London capitalists. With this, Kalakaua paid off the meddlesome grocer and dispensed with his political services. Spreckels' powerbroker days were over.

Unfortunately for Kalakaua, so were his days as a interventionist monarch. The foreign community was incensed at his corrupt cronyism, nativist policies, and extravagance. Kalakaua saw this as freely exercising his rightful prerogatives and so did his people. But for whites accustomed to republican or parliamentary forms of government and used to having their own way, rule by royal fiat had become intolerable. More galling was the racial affront of being subject to the rule of a bronze-skinned

Polynesian. Racism also tinged the contempt many had for the American-born Gibson. A clever and able politician he was also a shameless opportunist, dishonest, and easily tempted. He won a following among Hawaiians with his fluent Hawaiian, his respect for native ways, and his audacious electioneering slogan, "Hawaii for Hawaiians." His white foes, by contrast, were appalled by what they saw as a clear case of race betrayal and campaign demagoguery.

The following year (1887) Gibson was removed on the order of the resident U. S. minister backed by a warship when his support of selling an opium license to a local Chinese merchant burst into print. Fortified by U. S. intervention, a *haole* militia formed and took to the streets, forcing Kalakaua to accept a new constitution. Kalakaua's powers were trimmed and those of the mercantile class expanded. The vote was given to alien white residents but denied to Asians and even to some native Hawaiians. The business and commercial interests had pulled off a bloodless *coup d'etat*. Paradoxically, the king who began his reign allied to American merchants and planters (he had helped to secure the reciprocity treaty) had increasingly identified himself with the Hawaiian cultural-political revival movement as a means of recovering Hawaii's *de facto* independence. This, as much as the blunders of king, minister, and financier, account for the *haole* mutiny. In any event, Kalakaua never accepted the "bayonet constitution" of 1887 but was unable to reverse it. After his death in 1891, his strong-willed sister and successor, Liliuokalani, seemed even more determined to restore royal power. Two years later, royal movements in that direction gave her opponents the justification they needed to move against the monarchy.

THE WRITING ON THE WALL

According to an 1881 letter by Secretary of State James G. Blaine, Hawaii would drift toward America in accordance with immutable laws and irresistible necessities.

The steady diminution of the native population of the islands . . . is doubtless a cause of great alarm to the government of the kingdom . . . The problem, however, is not to be met by a substitution of Mongolian [East Asian] supremacy for native control . . . The Hawaiian Islands cannot be joined to the Asiatic system. If they drift from their independent station it must be toward assimilation and identification with the American system, to which they belong by the operation of natural laws, and must belong by the operation of political necessity.

Source: Ralph S. Kuykendall, *The Hawaiian Kingdom, Volume III, 1874–1893, the Kalakaua Dynasty* (Honolulu: University of Hawaii Press, 1967), p. 141. Reprinted by permission.

SOVEREIGNTY LOST: FROM REVOLUTION TO ANNEXATION, 1893–1898

The revolution of 1893 occurred in the midst of economic hardship resulting from the McKinley tariff of 1890 that reimposed import duties on Hawaiian products. As Liliuokalani's government failed to negotiate a new commercial accord with America (through no lack of trying), support for U. S. annexation grew among the *haole* community. This support, however, did not include the sugar oligarchy which feared a Congressional ban on vital Asiatic labor and tighter regulation of contract labor in tandem with annexation. At the same time, native Hawaiians and part-Hawaiians voiced intense dissatisfaction with a government increasingly beholden to American commercial interests. Between 1887 and 1892 nativist nationalism mounted one unsuccessful coup (1889), nearly spawned three others, and coalesced into a major political party.

Hawaiian politics were plunged into crisis. Racial, economic, and social divisions eroded the popularity of the Reform government which fell from power in 1892 after five years in office. In the next twelve months, there were four separate ministries. The legislature was as fractured as the populace and Reformers, National Reformers, and Liberals jockeyed for power. The Reform party (Reformers), representing *haole* business and propertied classes, stood for the 1887 constitution, cheap and "clean" government, and closer ties to the United States. The National Reform party was the queen's party. It favored a strong monarchy and Hawaiian independence and enjoyed broad native Hawaiian support. The Liberal party wanted a new constitution and represented part-Hawaiians, some full-Hawaiians, and a number of less privileged whites. The Liberals, with their kaleidoscopic agenda and sense of impending national catastrophe, were the volatile variable in Hawaiian politics. Twice they reversed their stance on the two cardinal issues of the day: the monarchy and annexation. The queen became a foil for both sides' mounting apprehensions, labeled an autocrat by much of the foreign community and accused of neglecting her people by some Hawaiian nationalists.

The spark of revolution was ignited by Liliuokalani herself when she proposed a new constitution. She had made little secret of her unhappiness with the 1887 document and had tried unsuccessfully to make changes through the legislature. Her determination to act was bolstered by petitions signed by some two thirds of the registered electorate urging her to set aside the current constitution. Convinced of popular and cabinet support, she unveiled her new constitution before a surprised assembly of ministers, diplomats, legislators, and leading citizens on 14 January 1893. Her ministers refused to sign it, counseling the less authoritarian remedy of amending the existing constitution by legislation. They had hoped to buy time with this proposal knowing that the legislature would not reconvene for many months. The ensuing quarrel between queen and ministers over the next few days led to confused and contradictory initiatives by the Hawaiian government.

By contrast, the announcement of a royalist constitution galvanized the queen's opponents. They responded immediately and with more unity than Liliuokalani's cabinet could muster. The Annexation Club, a secret association formed in 1892, spearheaded the revolt against the queen. Led by the ex-cabinet minister Lorrin A. Thurston, the club was supported by Anglo-Saxon *haoles* of the professional and lower middle classes whose politics were radical by comparison to the conservative capitalists and planters. From 14 to 17 January, Thurston was in constant contact with the resident U.S. minister, John L. Stevens, from whom military support was believed to have been promised. Thurston and his compatriots knew that the American government was not likely to annex Hawaii unless pro-American forces had seized power on their own and made an official request for union. On the 14th, the annexationists openly declared themselves, confident of armed victory and optimistic about U. S. annexation. Two days later, Thurston took the crucial step of negotiating with U. S. officials for the deployment of American marines. On that very afternoon, 154 U. S. sailors and marines, armed with two Gatling guns and two artillery pieces, landed under the joint orders of the warship's commander and minister Stevens. Though posted menacingly close to the seat of the existing government, Stevens claimed that the troops were merely dispatched to protect American lives and property.

Meanwhile, the queen had been persuaded to withdraw her proposal. On the very day that U.S. forces landed in Honolulu, her government distributed a promise that no changes would occur without the consent of the legislature. The cabinet tried to win over the conservative business community and minister Stevens but the latter proved unreceptive. The next day the rebels struck as U.S. troops looked on. The mere presence of American forces and the failure of the cabinet to prevent their landing, secure their removal, or win their support, convinced ministers that Stevens would back the rebels. Fearful of confronting well-armed troops, ministers advised the queen to give up. She did so under protest, yielding, as she put it, to the "superior force of the United States." In so doing, Liliuokalani voiced her view that she had lost her throne not to domestic revolutionaries but to foreign interlopers. The fall of the monarchy occurred without a fight or a single fatality, only a minor gunshot wound sustained by a royal policeman. In America there was little sympathy for what many considered the decadent oceanic monarchy. Typical of the reaction was a "Valentine to Hawaii" from the Yankee heartland that had played such a profound role in the islands' history:

> You half-drowned chick in a waste of waters,
> Poor fatherless, motherless thing,
> Be one of Columbia's fair daughters,

And rest 'neath her ample wing.
Don't fly by yourself any longer,
A stranger outside our gates;
Resolve to be bigger, and better, and stronger,
And join the United States.

Critical to the success of the coup was minister Stevens. Ever since his appointment in 1889, he had railed against the monarchical system and delivered biting indictments of Hawaii's regime. He flouted diplomatic protocol by joining the Annexation Club. Once the uprising began, Stevens actively aided it and effectively immobilized the queen's forces. He had further crushed the queen's will to resist by recognizing the provisional government before it had gained control of Honolulu. He authorized the landing of troops over the government's protest and despite its assurances that it was capable of maintaining control and keeping the peace. And although U. S. troops fired no shots, their presence was sufficient to intimidate the government. It was the first time in Hawaiian history that American forces had landed in defiance of the wishes of the legally constituted government. Had not U. S. forces intervened so decisively and had Liliuokalani ordered it, the royalist contingent—with ten Gatling guns and twelve artillery pieces—might have overawed the *haole* annexationists.

Still, revolution did not automatically turn into annexation. It took five years for Pacific and American developments to spur the United States into annexation. One key factor was the replacement of the anti-annexationist Grover Cleveland by the tepidly pro-annexationist William McKinley as president in 1897. Because McKinley had also proposed new tariffs against all foreign products, Hawaii's sugar barons swung their support behind annexation (because such tariffs would not apply to an annexed territory). The rise of Japan as a Pacific power of the first rank (it had decisively beaten China in 1894–1895) further tilted the scales in favor of annexation. The rapid influx of Japanese laborers into Hawaii— over 20,000 between 1884 and 1893—and a range of disputes between Japan and Hawaii over labor, immigration, and import duties on Japanese products, had led to the deployment of a Japanese warship to Hawaiian waters in 1897. Tensions rose even higher when Japan protested Congress' discussion of annexation

In 1898, two crucial events made annexation a certainty. The first concerned China where several powers—notably Britain, Germany, Russia, Japan, and France—had wrung economic and political concessions that threatened to close what many believed was a teeming Asian market for surplus American goods and capital. America would need to act swiftly and decisively before the Chinese bonanza was hoarded by others. Hawaii possessed a perfect base for launching and defending future American interests in the Far East. The second event was the outbreak of war between the United States and Spain in April. The pretext was Cuba, an object of American economic interest, which had been in rebellion against Spain since 1895. But the war quickly spread to other Spanish possessions which were seized in a turn-of-the-century naval blitzkrieg. By July American forces had attacked the Philippines, occupied Guam and Wake Island, and invaded Cuba and Puerto Rico.

In the same month, Congress approved a joint resolution favoring Hawaiian annexation that McKinley swiftly endorsed. Sovereignty was formally transferred to America on 12 August 1898 in a ramshackle ceremony in Honolulu that Hawaiians conspicuously boycotted. Those few compelled to participate as musicians and escorts refused to lower the flag or play "Hawaii Ponoi," the national anthem, one final time. Embarrassingly, the ceremony had to be conducted almost entirely by Americans. A few days later the war with Spain was all but over and America emerged with an instant empire. Its possessions straddled the Caribbean and Central America and forged an insular chain across the north Pacific to the Far East. By 1914 Hawaii, Guam, Wake Island, the Philippines, Puerto Rico, and the protectorates of Cuba, Panama and the Dominican Republic were added to the older noncontiguous possessions of Alaska, the Aleutians, Johnston Island, and Midway Island (all acquired in the 1850s and 1860s).

THE WHITE MAN'S BURDEN

In 1899 the British "poet laureate of empire," Rudyard Kipling, urged America to "Take up the White Man's Burden."

The first stanzas are from Kipling's poetic civilizing ethic of imperialism. The next are from a lampoon penned by the anti-imperialist American poet Ernest Crosby.

Take up the White Man's burden—
Send forth the best ye breed—
Go bind your sons to exile
To serve your captives' need;
To wait in heavy harness,
On fluttered folk and wild—
Your new-caught, sullen peoples,
Half-devil and half-child.

Take up the White Man's burden;
Send forth your sturdy sons,
And load they down with whiskey
And Testaments and guns.
Throw in a few diseases
To spread in tropic climes
For there the healthy niggers
Are quite behind the times.

Take up the White Man's burden
The savage wars of peace—
Fill full the mouth of Famine,
And bid the sickness cease;
And when your goal is nearest
the end for others sought,
Watch Sloth and heathen Folly
Bring all your hope to nought.

Take up the White Man's burden,
And if you write in verse,
Flatter your Nation's vices
And strive to make them worse.
 Then learn that if with pious words
You ornament each phrase,
In a world of canting hypocrites
This kind of business pays.

Sources: Rudyard Kipling, *McClure's Magazine*, Vol. XII, 4 February 1899, pp. 290–291.4; and Ernest Crosby, *The New York Times*, 15 February 1899.

AMERICA'S IMPERIAL QUEST: MOTIVATIONS AND RESERVATIONS

The specific and proximate triggers that accounted for the timing and form of the United States' annexation of Hawaii—war with Spain, the rapidly deteriorating situation in China, and the rising Japanese presence—overlaid broader international and domestic factors that produced the conditions that made annexation practically inevitable. The bloodless conquest conducted by Yankee missionaries and *haole* merchants between 1819 and 1887 was simply confirmed by United States officials and politicians between 1893 and 1898 with the connivance of American navalists and capitalist merchants. In 1893 Americans in Hawaii held the initiative. By 1898 the impetus had shifted to the United States where domestic factors—economic and psychological—played important roles in the debate that surrounded Hawaii's annexation.

By the mid–1890s America had experienced unprecedented economic growth despite the intermittent downturns of the 1880s and 1890s, some of them having serious economic and psychological ramifications. Periodically, industrial strife erupted into violent clashes between workers and police. Businesses went bankrupt and much of the misery was attributed to a saturated market caused by industrial overproduction. Failure to unload swollen inventories meant business slowdowns, closures, and widespread layoffs. Overseas outlets were seen as a partial solution and in fact U.S. industry and agriculture boosted overseas exports by some 240 percent between 1895 and 1914, from $800 million to $2.3 billion. Capital investments abroad quadrupled over the same period. Most of this went to Europe not to the colonies, underscoring the divergent aims of colonial and economic expansionists. The state participated with higher tariffs for vulnerable home industries and a twin consular offensive in Latin America and China—the so-called "Open Door" policy. These offensives were supported by a host of government bureaus and agencies and, most vitally, by a large modern fleet. Navalism, whose ideological godparent was the influential naval strategist Alfred Thayer Mahan, meant a powerful global presence as much as a commitment to an ambitious naval building program.

Thus, *fin de siècle* American buoyancy was riddled with doubt and anxiety. Fears that opportunities for breaking into the world's markets were rapidly evaporating partially explain the haste with which some private companies and the government embraced colonialism. This mood was fueled by frantic international competition but it also grew out of a gnawing sense that America urgently required a fresh outlet for its dynamic energies. For years these energies had been engaged with pioneer settlements and economic enterprise along America's elastic frontiers (expressed as Manifest Destiny). But by the 1890s continental expansion had reached its limit, dramatized by the occupation of the immense area bordered by Canada, Mexico, and the Pacific Ocean and cemented by the final elimination of Amerindian resistance at Wounded Knee (1890). In 1893 the historian Frederick Jackson Turner pronounced the American frontier closed. It had, he claimed, defined the American experience but it would no longer do so. With British Canada and independent Mexico unobtainable without a costly war and international censure, some Americans turned an anxious and hopeful gaze on overseas territories as the next beneficiaries of America's great democratic and capitalist experiment.

In part, the outward orientation of some Americans was a reflection of pressing domestic ills of the 1890s. Along its bustling Eastern seaboard, urban populations expanded rapidly and municipalities grappled with tenement squalor and overcrowding. The problem was aggravated by a re-energized Anglo-Saxon nativism. Most of the urban dwellers were recent immigrants from culturally "inferior" Southern and Eastern Europe who were relegated to the bottom rungs of the economic ladder. In the West, Native Americans were corralled into barren reservations and Chinese laborers were barred from entering the country. Those already in place were subjected to extraordinary legal restrictions. For black Americans, the limited gains of Reconstruction were rolled back by a new era of socioeconomic segregation enshrined in the Supreme Court's *Plessy v. Ferguson* (1896) and by disenfranchising Jim Crow laws in the South made chillingly real by a host of lynchings.

This formed the background to what was probably the most incisive debate on imperialism anywhere during the era of high imperialism. The debate emerged belatedly (by comparison with Europe) and climaxed suddenly in 1898–1899. It concerned not only Hawaii, of course, but the Philippines, Cuba, and America's other colonial war prizes. Since the issues, arguments, and participants in the Hawaiian annexation debate (1893–1898) and the Spanish-American war debate (1898–1899) were often the same, the two can be collapsed together for the purposes of analysis. Although unsuccessful, the anti-imperialists mounted a vigorous opposition that will be briefly sketched here to better reveal what was at stake in America's impulsive leap into overseas colonialism.

American imperialists offered a range of rationales, of which economic reasons figured repeatedly. Adventurous capitalists contended that Hawaii would be good for business. The "Crossroads of the Pacific" was fated to become the "American Hong Kong," a mid-oceanic emporium where Chinese and American commerce would meet. A few labor union leaders joined prominent manufacturers and visualized an industrialized Hawaii capable of supporting a population and workforce ten times its present size. Indeed, America's various dependencies were capable of economic development that partisans claimed would benefit colonizer and colonized alike. Champions of popularized Social Darwinism predicted that economies, like nations, either expanded or withered. Accordingly, a pressing concern of pro-imperialists was that the United States secure for itself a fair share of finite and fleeting global investment and merchandising opportunities.

Closely tied to economic arguments were strategic concerns. Few imperialists failed to emphasize that Hawaii was perfectly situated to harbor a large fleet. This fleet would afford protection to a bustling transpacific trade and help the United States defend its West coast and the Nicaraguan isthmus where canal construction was underway to link the Caribbean and the Pacific. Mahan saw Hawaii as the "Key of the Pacific," a crucial satellite for a modern global power. Numerous others used a preemptive argument: it was necessary to seize Hawaii to keep it from falling into the grasping hands of others. The Japanese danger was new and palpable, paralleled by the long-standing threat to America supposedly posed by an encircling chain of British naval bases at Halifax (Nova Scotia), Bermuda, Saint Lucia (West Indies), and Esquimalt (British Columbia).

Racism and the civilizing mission were popular refrains throughout the debate. Many argued that Hawaiians were incapable of defending themselves or of keeping the peace on their own streets—an odd point in view of growing violence in American cities. This and other "failings" were attributed to racial and moral inferiority, a belief that inspired press depictions of the Hawaiians as drunken and diseased and Liliuokalani as a "debauched" and "battered harpy" spellbound by her *kahuna* "sorcerers." Further evidence of Hawaiian incapacity for self-rule was cited in the recent history of the islands where the rapid rise to dominance by New England traders and preachers was interpreted as proof of Hawaiians' need of uplifting Western rule. America, it was said, not only had the technological wherewithal to improve the lives of other peoples but the moral obligation to do so. Some put it in terms of a heavenly mandate. A few annexationists distinguished between Hawaiian annexation and European imperialism. America, they averred, was not a land thief and therefore not comparable to aggrandizing European nations. Unlike a European dependency, Hawaii was bound to become a territory and, afterwards, a state. Of course, such naively spurious distinctions would be shattered in the aftermath of vigorous resistance to American occupation of the Philippines when Americans finally understood what it meant to be in the empire business.

It is significant that the anti-imperialists also combined high morality with unsavory racism. In the first category were arguments that assailed the subjugation of other peoples as inimical to U. S. traditions of liberty and progress and a betrayal of the virtuous republican principles of representative self-government. It was also dangerous. Even well-intentioned colonial rule was fundamentally arbitrary and irresponsible. Imperialism would therefore seduce Americans into despotism abroad and tempt them with authoritarianism at home. Once one island chain was gobbled up, the appetite for plunder and confiscation would grow and the United States would embark on a colonizing spree in the European mode. It would also increase the power of the state, a deeply troubling prospect to many Americans. Some opposed overseas acquisitions on constitutional and historical grounds. Imperialism was portrayed as an immoral departure from the past and a violation of an implicit

THE ANNEXATION DEBATE:
TWO VIEWS

*The first excerpt is from Representative Charles F. Cochran and the
second excerpt from Representative Champ Clark, both of Missouri.
The first is triumphantly self-congratulatory, the second wildly sarcastic
of racially inspired expansionism.*

The rescue of these islands from the absurd, grotesque, tottering native dynasty was only another step in the onward march of liberty and civilization; another forward movement in the conquest of the world by the Aryan race . . . Sir, the fittest will survive. Under the providence of God, Anglo-Celtic civilization is accomplishing the regeneration of the planet.

. . . If we annex Hawaii and you, Mr. Speaker, should preside here twenty years hence, it may be that you will have a polyglot House and it will be your painful duty to recognize "the gentleman from Patagonia," "the gentleman from Cuba," "the gentleman from Santo Domingo," "the gentleman from Corea" . . . or, with fear and trembling, "the gentleman from the Cannibal islands," who will gaze upon you with watering mouth and gleaming teeth!

Source: William Adam Russ, Jr., *The Hawaiian Republic (1894–1898)* (Selinsgrove, Penn.: Susquehana University Press, 1961), pp. 311, 318. Reprinted by permission.

constitutional prohibition against adding noncontiguous lands, especially those peopled with non-European stock.

Opponents also pointed out that trade and investment were more likely to thrive without the offsetting costs of imperial defense and administration. Labor unions feared directly competing with low-waged workers in colonial offshoots. Many others objected to the Hawaiian republic, which was seen as "of the sugar interests, by the sugar interests and for the sugar interests." Conversely, American sugar magnates and fruit farmers, including Claus Spreckels, dreaded the influx of cheap produce and inferior grades of sugar that had been excluded under reciprocity. More generally, many believed that Polynesians, Asians, and Latin Americans were incapable of assimilating into Anglo-Saxon society. Democracy, liberty, and the tropics were thought to be incompatible. Close association with "barbarous archipelagoes" would debase Americans of "civilized" habits and "superior" bloodlines. Contact with new races overseas would somehow add to racial burdens at home. As the *New York World* crudely put it in June 1898: the country already had a "black elephant" in the South; why would it want a "leper elephant in Hawaii, a brown elephant in Porto Rico and perhaps a yellow elephant in Cuba"?

Pro-annexationists and expansionists prevailed, in the short term at any rate. Their arguments seemed more persuasive. They outnumbered the anti-imperialists in Congress and the press. They were not as divided as their opponents nor as inconsistent in their arguments. And, in any event, it was easier to argue to keep something already won than to propose giving it up. The anti-imperialists seemed to be small-minded nay-sayers moaning about the loss of innocence at a time when America was being summoned to greatness. In fact, the actual debates were not always clear-cut and it is likely that most Americans felt ambivalence, perhaps of the kind expressed by President Jordan of Stanford University when he said of overseas expansion: "It is un-American; it is contrary to our traditions; it is delicious; it is intoxicating."

CONCLUSION

From the moment of Cook's landing, Hawaii was forced to take account of the outside world on terms over which it had very little control. Quite remarkably, under the circumstances, its indigenous rulers managed to transform a chiefly dominated hierarchical society into a centralized state system that retained its formal independence until 1893. Kamehameha I's military ambitions and skills, assisted by British arms and Western seamanship, brought about interisland unification. But such achievements and devices could not prevent the corrosive impact of internal and external forces that gradually undermined its culture and sovereignty. Internally, the new order often helped to diminish the power of the chiefs as the new state monopolized administrative authority and as the new commerce in foreign goods delivered them into debt and made them dependent on Western merchants. But, in actuality, the erosion of chiefly power foreshadowed and contributed to the collapse of the monarchy.

The primary instruments of native decline were Western businessmen and missionaries though the two rarely worked in concert and often detested one another. With ample capital, imported labor, state-sanctioned privileges, and access to Hawaiian land and water, *haole* traders and planters acquired an effective control over the local economy and polity. Spreckels was a prime example of *haole* prowess and it was highly significant that his downfall did not in any way disturb the power of the planter-merchant class that he so spectacularly epitomized. The missionaries also increased Hawaii's dependence on the West though their intentions were more complex. Through religion and education, but also as royal advisors on such matters as constitution-forging and land reform, and as the transmitters of idealized Western customs, habits, and norms, they helped to create conditions that were more favorable to outside economic influence and eventually to foreign political manipulation. No less important, Westerners were the agents of pathogenic calamity. By the 1890s, Hawaii's demographic and economic plight had grown so desperate and the monarchy's powers so circumscribed that when Liliuokalani ventured to loosen the shackles of Western domination, her efforts were easily crushed and her throne disposed of in a coordinated *haole*–United States coup d'etat.

The revolution of 1893 and the annexation of 1898 confirmed America's rise to dominance in both the Pacific and the global economy.

The latter was apparent by 1900 when the United States had already surpassed Britain as the leading industrial power—whether measured in terms of steel, pig-iron, or coal production. America's formal entry into the imperial sweepstakes in 1898 was not only a departure from prior U.S. policy, it symbolized a new mood shared by the Great Powers that unilateral annexation was not only an acceptable but even a legitimate, almost "natural," recourse for powerful states confronted by energetic rivals, vulnerable "natives," and a finite supply of *free* space. Accordingly, in the Pacific of the 1880s and 1890s, cultural (typically missionary), economic, and diplomatic tension—especially between the United States, Germany, and Great Britain—resolved itself in favor of the expanding empires and against the maintenance of Pacific Islander independence. In such an atmosphere, it scarcely mattered whether the islanders were cooperative or not, but the imperial conscience was eased and annexation became even more compelling where Western missionaries, traders, and planters had helped to render the indigenous regimes of Micronesia, Polynesia, and Melanesia unstable. Whether annexation resulted from the request of resident foreigners or indigenous rulers or was initiated solely by the metropolitan state, the Pacific succumbed to partition just as Africa had. Thus, Hawaii's fate was shared by the Pacific islands generally as Europe and America engaged in a rush to seize the last of the world's available markets, resources, and strategic linchpins however small their area or decimated their populations.

The annexation of Hawaii, President McKinley observed, was "a consummation" of America's long-standing involvement with the Polynesian kingdom. By that he meant that American interests in Hawaii had been paramount for decades and that American culture there was entrenched. He also acknowledged that the pressures to intervene had been building during the previous decades. Few resident Americans favored annexation in the 1850s, 1860s, or even the 1870s, and their agitation for United States involvement was half-hearted and short-lived. But as the perception that other powers might intercede in Hawaii's affairs grew in the minds of resident Americans, more and more of them clamored for the establishment of permanent bonds with the United States. Ironically, these demands increased as Britain and France exhibited ever greater reluctance to embroil themselves in Hawaiian politics.

What seems to have pricked Yankee sensibilities most was Britain's respected reputation among Hawaii's dynasts who displayed their Anglophilia in a variety of ways: borrowed Hanoverian names (Albert, Victoria, Edward, and William), the national flag with the Union Jack in its upper hoist quadrant, royal patronage of the Church of England from the 1860s, and the persistent usage of the name "Sandwich Islands" in deference to Cook's nomenclature in honor of his patron, the earl of Sandwich, first lord of the admiralty and "inventor" of the humble sandwich. More alarmingly, Hawaiian rulers had tried (unsuccessfully) to use Britain as a counterweight to America (in the South Pacific, Fiji's rulers had succeeded in winning British annexation partly to prevent a repeat performance of American gunboat diplomacy).

British interests and inclinations were, as it happened, insufficient to thwart American initiatives that became bolder as the century wore on. Growing American involvement in Hawaii's internal affairs resulted mostly from the close ties that arose between U. S. ministers to Hawaii and the local American community. It was rarely orchestrated from Washington, D. C., which frequently overruled high-handed consular interference. Instead, U. S. ministers acted on their own and strove to shape local politics. In 1880 and 1887 they forced Kalakaua to dismiss his prime minister against his will. On several occasions they threatened or actually used force and clandestinely worked with groups opposed to Hawaii's dynasts. From the 1860s ministers became open advocates of U. S. intervention and annexation. Such contemptuous views were reinforced by the presence of U. S. warships intermittently deployed to influence Hawaiian political developments. Hawaiian independence was thus compromised long before 1893 and every ruler from Kamehameha III on wrestled with the distinct possibility of some power annexing Hawaii.

When annexation finally occurred in 1898, the act was prompted by strategic and economic considerations. Hawaii's location was perfectly suited to the naval designs of the new imperial American state. Moreover, the archipelago was to become a part of a more stable and enlightened world order that American expansionists predicted would arise from a vigorous global presence. And although hardly critical to the American economy, Hawaiian produce sweetened and added variety to America's stock of edibles and offered limited outlets for capital investment. More importantly, Hawaii was midway along the oceanic highway to the supposedly gigantic markets of East Asia. At the same time, formal takeover was made easier and politically more acceptable in America because Hawaii was already substantially Westernized, indeed Americanized.

Hawaii can, and should, be seen in the broader context of American history in which expansion and conquest were hardly novel components. In fact, America's territorial growth began before the American Revolution and accelerated afterwards. By the end of the 1780s, the America of the thirteen colonies had more than doubled with the passage of the Northwest Ordinance. In 1803, Thomas Jefferson negotiated the Louisiana Purchase with France at the expense of a sizable indigenous population. In so doing, he set a precedent followed by successive presidents with the result that the country finally consumed the entire middle swath of the continent from "sea to shining sea." The settlement of the newly won areas by white Americans was achieved, of course, by killing and displacing millions of Amerindians.

While the Louisiana Purchase consisted of *neighboring* territory, America's covetous eye soon wandered beyond its shorelines. President James Monroe enunciated in his famous doctrine of 1823 that he intended to reserve the hemisphere for prospective American activities by warning

LILIUOKALANI'S PLEA

In 1898, Hawaii's last monarch sent a spirited, desperate plea to the Americans.

Oh, honest Americans, as Christians hear me for my down-trodden people! Their form of government is as dear to them as yours is precious to you. Quite as warmly as you love your country, so they love theirs. With all your goodly possessions, covering a territory so immense that there yet remain parts unexplored, possessing island's that, although near at hand, had to be neutral ground in time of war, do not covet the little vineyard of Naboth's, so far from your shores, lest the punishment of Ahab fall upon you, if not in your day, in that of your children . . .

Source: Liliuokalani, *Hawaii's Story by Hawaii's Queen* (Boston: Lothrop, Lee & Shepard Co., 1898), p. 373.

off potential European rivals. Consistent with this outlook, Monroe described Cuba as a part of the greater Mississippi river delta while his successor, John Quincy Adams, christened the Caribbean islands the "natural appendages" of the United States. (Though largely rhetorical, such pronouncements reflected an expansionist mind-set that in this century led to a number of military occupations in the Caribbean and Central America). When Whitelaw Reid, imperialist editor of the influential *New York Tribune* advised McKinley in 1896 that if he took Hawaii and Cuba his administration would rank with Thomas Jefferson's, he hit upon a central expansionist thread that ran right through the history of the United States.

U. S. expansion was as much cultural and economic as it was political. In Hawaii, American influence both preceded and prepared the way for formal annexation, although this does not mean that the intricate and protracted process of acculturation of which merchants and Protestant evangelists were the main architects was consciously intended to deprive Hawaii of its political sovereignty. Yet American—and Western—cultural influence in Hawaii was a form of cultural imperialism even if it was not premeditated or core-directed. Early on, Americans refashioned society at the expense of the indigenous culture, using religious conversion, educational institutions, and economic practices to extend their cultural dominance. In the process, Hawaii was nearly turned into an "ethnographic museum" whose breathing exhibits were the "primitives" themselves. Before the close of the nineteenth century, Americans were venturing to Hawaii as tourists. There, where the indigenous population had been decimated, rendered harmless, and picturesque, Westerners "went native" without fear of compromising their own cultural identities. Thus denationalized, *luaus* and *leis* soon became the festive and exotic adornments of the civilized on holiday.

But it is important to stress that the introduction of Western symbols, rituals, ideologies, and social conventions was not a simple unilinear, involuntary process. As we have seen, cultural imperialism included varying degrees of initiative by indigenous rulers and active participation by indigenous peoples. Kaahumanu, Kamehameha III, and Kaona engaged in "cultural appropriation," that is, the limited or conditional absorption of Western practices, technologies, and beliefs. Frequently such appropriations were adapted to better suit the norms and conventions of the local cultural system.

Retaining considerably more autonomy than conceded by Western observers, Hawaiians offered both resistance to, and voluntary acceptance of, selective foreign practices and beliefs. Yet attempts to control the velocity and scope of the transfer so as to minimize social disruption proved largely illusory. The limited degree of control exerted by Hawaiians with respect to cultural transfers was even apparent early on, during Captain Cook's visit, Keopuolani's funeral, and the missionary-led assault on Hawaii's material and moral environment. As time went on, the forces of Westernization became beyond anyone's power to control. The irony here is that Hawaiian cultural resistance only became genuinely organized in the 1870s when it was too late to stem the acculturative tide.

As we now well know, the circumstances that once supported imperialism in the Pacific were superseded in this century by others that did not. By the 1970s colonies became independent nations. Hawaii, however, is an anomaly, for its remains fastened to the old colonizing power, more or less accepting its statehood status though the embers of nativism continue to smolder today as Hawaiians and part-Hawaiians rally to rescue themselves and their heritage from oblivion.

FURTHER READING

Ralph S. Kuykendall's three-volume *The Hawaiian Kingdom, 1778–1893* (Honolulu: University of Hawaii Press, 1937–1968) is the monumental narrative history of the postcontact period. But more readable and current is Gavan Daws' revisionist *Shoal of Time* (Honolulu: The University Press of Hawaii, 1968). Hawaii's experience of Westernization and colonialism is successfully placed in a Pacific Islands context by K. R. Howe, *Where the Waves Fall* (Honolulu: University of Hawaii Press, 1984) which ends with the nineteenth century; K. R. Howe, Robert C. Kiste, and Brij V. Lal, eds., *Tides of History* (Honolulu: University of Hawaii Press, 1994) which covers the present century; and I. C. Campbell, *A History of the Pacific Islands* (Berkeley: University of California Press, 1989). Over a decade ago, Hawaiian studies were stuck by a wave of structuralist histories, especially those of Marshall Sahlins, with their productive coupling of anthropology and history: Sahlins, *Historical Metaphors and Mythical Realities* (Ann Arbor: University of Michigan

Press, 1981) and *Islands of History* (Chicago: University of Chicago Press, 1987). For an anthropological challenge to Sahlins and to the West's mythologizing of Cook and his fatal encounter, see Gananath Obeyesekere, *The Apotheosis of Captain Cook* (Princeton, N.J.: Princeton University Press, 1992). Sahlin's response is *How Natives Think: About Captain Cook, For Example* (Chicago: University of Chicago Press, 1995). A feminist complement to a gender-blind structuralism is the quantitative ethnohistory by Jocelyn Linnekin, *Sacred Queens and Women of Consequence* (Ann Arbor: University of Michigan Press, 1990). Another example of recent scholarly trends is Elizabeth Buck's assessment of cultural dynamics under American domination, *Paradise Remade: The Politics of Culture and History in Hawai'i* (Philadelphia: Temple University Press, 1993).

From the American side of the colonial ledger, the standard work on U.S.-Hawaiian relations is Merze Tate, *The United States and the Hawaiian Kingdom: A Political History* (New Haven, Conn.: Yale University Press, 1965). The imperialist spurt of 1898–1900 during which Hawaii was annexed is covered in: David Healy, *U.S. Expansionism: The Imperialist Urge in the 1890s* (Madison: University of Wisconsin Press, 1970) and Richard H. Miller, ed., *American Imperialism in 1898* (New York: John Wiley & Sons, 1970) which presents pertinent primary source excerpts in a debate format. For the U.S. "imperial" prologue to 1898, see Frederick Merk, *Manifest Destiny and Mission in American History* (New York: Vintage Books, 1966). For an engaging look at America's imperial prologue and epilogue by a leading revisionist historian, see William Appleman Williams, *Empire as a Way of Life* (Oxford: Oxford University Press, 1980).

5

PATTERNS AND CONTEXTS

Imperial Diasporas

The spread of Europe's capitalist economy and its overseas empires resulted in a demographic dispersal that permanently altered the racial and ethnic complexion of the world. This change began in the sixteenth century and continued into the twentieth. But our concern is only with the brisk traffic in humanity that occurred in the age of high imperialism. The transatlantic African slave trade—estimated to have transported some 10 million Africans to the New World between 1500 and 1880—had collapsed with the abolition of slavery between the second and fourth quarters of the nineteenth century. The only significant African slave trade that survived into this period was carried on by Arabs and Swahili-Arabs out of East Africa. By 1914 even that had ended. Thus international migration between 1870 and 1914 was dominated by emigrating Europeans. Most of it was voluntary, private, and undertaken by individuals or by small family units. This migration contrasted sharply with the great diasporas of the past that tended to be enforced, massed, and often "state"-coordinated, usually in response to severe military, ecological, or demographic crises. Yet the voluntarist characterization can be misleading. Millions of non-white migrants were bonded or served as indentured labor (as distinct from chattel slavery) until well after 1870; much of this labor filled the vacuum created by the abolition of slavery.

In other words, the global migrations that occurred during the era of high imperialism were gigantic transfers of labor. In this respect they were a continuation of former migrations dating back to the early 1500s when the transatlantic commerce in enslaved Africans and indentured

Europeans commenced. But where prior labor migrations had been dominated by blacks and browns, a majority of the new migrants were white. Most of this migration went outside the European empires to such independent states as the United States, Argentina, and other South American republics. Yet since there are several important parallels between the United States and white settlement colonies within the empires—which together may be termed the New Europes—and because America eventually became an overseas imperial power, it will not be excluded here. This section concentrates on the aggregate patterns, experiences, and impacts of imperial migrations. Five separate movements will be traced with more attention being given to those involving the greatest numbers. These are: Europeans who settled in the New Europes; Europeans who journeyed to the tropical colonies; Asians and Pacific Islanders (mostly Melanesians) who toiled in the New Europes; Asians, Africans and Pacific Islanders who were sent to the tropical colonies; and indigenous peoples who migrated within the New Europes.

The historical peak of European emigration coincided with and profoundly shaped the development of empires between 1870 and 1920. Some 35 million people settled in the Americas, the Antipodes (Australia and New Zealand), and the temperate zones of Africa as additional millions ventured eastward into Russian Siberia. Wherever they had settled in large numbers they created New Europes. As the new dominant racial group, they retained much of the social customs, structures, and relationships as well as the culture, religion, and language of their homelands. France was much in evidence in its premier settlement colony of Algeria and not only Canada, Australia, New Zealand, and South Africa but also the United States necessitated minimal social adjustments for the nineteenth century waves of immigrating Britishers. Parts of South America such as Argentina, though not part of any European empire, also absorbed considerable waves of European immigrants at this time and may also be classified as New Europes. The result of this unprecedented, gargantuan transfer of Europeans was a cultural-spatial extension of Europe. All told, that portion of the globe's landmass stocked with European majorities is estimated to have risen from nearly 30 percent to just under 40 percent between 1850 and 1920. This by itself was a remarkable historical development.

The European exodus to the New Europes reflected both the "push" of unprecedented population increases and dislocating economic changes at home and the "pull" of widely advertised economic and social opportunities abroad. Most migrants were poor and sought betterment where it was most likely to be found. Carried in steamships, they experienced safer, faster, and cheaper crossings than any their predecessors had known. They left on their own, rarely with state sponsorship but sometimes with charitable or private assistance. Often relatives already settled overseas helped pay their way or sponsored them on arrival. They landed in the centers of established settlements and many stayed put, massively contributing to the industrial and commercial growth of their new homes. Yet some ventured into the hinterlands and plied the agricultural and artisanal skills they had learned at home. A few, especially in sparsely populated Canada and Australia, rushed towards the frontiers herding livestock or prospecting for gold or diamonds.

For the vast majority who had more hope than resources, none of this was easy and their ordeal should not be romanticized. Many struggled against unemployment and ethnic prejudice. Some did not survive and a considerable minority returned to Europe. All of this is well recorded in the accounts of immigrant histories but their contributions also went the other way. In Europe, the incomes of many peasant families were supplemented by earnings posted back by New World relatives. Beyond this, emigration contributed to the easing of labor competition and the lessening of social and political pressures in Europe. Still, so great was Europe's population rise that the flood of emigrants barely accounted for two-fifths of the increase.

To the extent that Europeans settled in an independent country or the dependency of another power, no direct advantage accrued to the country of origin. And despite the acknowledged benefits of siphoning off surplus populations from densely inhabited, urbanized, and industrialized Europe, concerns were expressed about the loss of national strength and well-being caused by the departure of fellow citizen-workers. Those who welcomed the removal of the unemployed, criminal (the transporting of British convicts to Australia ended in 1868), and potentially "seditious" classes were alarmed at the much greater volume of emigrating labor power. Especially after 1880 when international economic and military competition became acute, the idea of emigrationist colonialism came to be seen as an ideal way of channeling excess populations overseas while keeping their productivity tied to the national economy. There need be no further loss of skills, earning power or production-generating consumption nor any fears of an army marching off to war desperately short of manpower. In Germany some claimed that it was no longer necessary for emigrants to forego their national customs and identity. In Italy imperialists argued that settler colonies could turn "lost sons" into faithful ones who would continue to participate in the ennoblement of the Italian state and culture. Even in demographically stagnant France, such pressure groups as the *Union coloniale française* hoped to boost imperial emigration. They did so primarily by publishing lists of names, occupations, and areas of origin of each French resident of particular overseas colonies in the hopes of drawing emigrants from those of similar backgrounds at home.

Colonial emigrationist ideologies and schemes had a marginal impact. Despite the promise of cheap land and philanthropic assistance, opportunities were limited. France lacked not so much the "pull" of suitable outlets—Algeria, Tunisia, Morocco—as the "push" of severe population pressures. Germany had no colonies before 1884 and apart perhaps from Southwest Africa it acquired none capable of supporting a sizable settlement.

Anyway, marked economic growth from the 1890s reduced German emigration to a trickle. Imperial enthusiasts in prewar Italy cited Libya (acquired, 1911–1912) as a "safety valve" for social unrest but Italian emigrants preferred the United States, Brazil, Argentina, and French Tunisia.

It was otherwise with Britain, which was best situated to shepherd its sons and daughters to its temperate zone colonies. Not only did its multiplying population yield the largest number of European emigrants, it possessed in Canada, Australia, New Zealand, and South Africa a "Greater Britain" of attractive territories. Between 1870 and 1920 hundreds of thousands from the British Isles—between one third and one half of the total number of British emigrants—were absorbed into the settler populations of those colonies, no doubt pleasing imperialists like Cecil Rhodes who predicted that overpopulation at home, if unchecked, would lead to mass pauperization and political upheaval. Thus two aims were met: Britain's stability and security were enhanced and the settlers gained from exchanging a diseased and corrupting urban environment for a morally cleansing and physically invigorating rural colonial life.

There is no doubt that the colonial New Europes benefited the metropolitan states. White settlers engaged in agriculture and commercialized pastoralism geared to the metropolitan market as they absorbed manufactured goods and utilized capital from Europe. Commerce prospered and investments burgeoned between Britain and its white colonies in the prewar years though strategic gains from the vibrant Greater Britains were less visible. Authoritarian rule imposed on Asian, African, and Pacific Island colonies could not be extended to white colonials whose customs, numbers, economic viability, and institutions seemed to merit self-rule. Gradual autonomy was extended to Canada, Australia, South Africa, and New Zealand partly in the hopes that they would shoulder more of the burden of imperial defense. To some extent they did and the Dominions—as they came to be called—made tremendous sacrifices on Britain's behalf in the Anglo-Boer and First World wars.

By contrast, in the more densely populated tropical colonies hundreds of thousands of Europeans maintained a relatively thin presence. A large subgroup consisted of the military with smaller numbers engaged in business activities, civil administration, the professions, and missionary work. One of the largest concentrations of Europeans was in British India where, in 1901, some 60,000 out of 170,000 were soldiers. Such populations were transitory and most Europeans who made their careers in the tropical colonies returned home, handsomely compensated for their efforts. They were predominantly male though the numbers of women increased throughout this period. They were also preponderantly young, not only to better survive the arduous tropical life but also to better sustain the image of Western vigor and vitality. It was not unusual, for example, to return home before progressing on into deep middle age. Most, apart from the soldiers, were middle class though persons from lower social strata, including a few soldiers, permanently settled in the colonies where they were able to enjoy a lifestyle far superior to ones they had left behind. Buttressed by numbers and a sense of cultural-cum-racial superiority, Europeans in the tropics maintained a conspicuous social and physical distance from the colonized. They were shielded by a circle of servants and lived in "white towns" that, if possible, occupied higher elevations than the adjacent "black (native) towns."

As we have already seen, imperial economic development occurred mostly through the labor of the third stream of humanity to be considered here, the millions of non-white workers transported to the New Europes where indigenes were few or unresponsive to workforce discipline. There, roads and railroads were constructed, crops were cultivated, and minerals were dug by armies of Asians, Pacific Islanders, and Africans. These people toiled under contracts as bonded or indentured laborers. Chinese peasants were conscripted or hired to work in mines and construction projects from South Africa to Australia and from Hawaii to the United States. Indians worked from Canada to Natal (South Africa) mostly as agricultural laborers. Pacific Islanders were recruited to toil on Australian plantations. And Africans from Nyasaland and Mozambique were signed up to dig in the gold and diamond mines of South Africa.

By the 1880s, however, the New Europes were beginning to grow uneasy at the presence of such "foreigners," however invaluable they might have been. The tight surveillance and regimentation afforded by barrack-like compounds in which bonded labor was typically housed no longer provided sufficient reassurance against social disharmony, "criminal" behavior, or racial mixing. Growing European populations and heightened race prejudice induced the regimes of the New Europes to stem the influx of black, brown, and yellow workers. America banned further Chinese immigration in 1882 and Indian immigration into Natal ended in 1911. The majority of those in place opted to remain and Indians outnumber whites in Natal today. Where the political situation permitted, where outrage erupted over the "new slavery," or where the use of such labor was no longer seen as a necessity, repatriation followed. Humanitarianism and race prejudice combined to send Chinese coolies back home from South Africa by 1910. In Australia, racism and trade union opposition to the use of competing, virtually wageless Melanesian labor resulted in their removal between 1900 and 1906.

The fourth group was indentured non-white labor in the tropical colonies where the demand for their toil was even greater, especially in the plantation areas where, in the aftermath of emancipation (1830s–1880s), former slaves deserted the fields for other opportunities. Tropical migration of this sort was dominated by Indian peasants. It was supplemented by Chinese, Japanese, Javanese, and Pacific Islanders who, in terms of their small population base, were the most extensively exploited. Mostly these workers harvested sugar, cotton, and other foodstuffs and industrial crops. On the expiration of their contracts many stayed put, especially Indians who today comprise around half of the

population of Fiji, Trinidad, and Guyana. There are numerous other examples, however, including the Japanese of Hawaii and Peru, the Indians
of Sri Lanka and Malaysia, the Indian-Indonesian-East African creoles of
French Réunion, and the Chinese of Cuba, and Southeast Asia (though
much Chinese settlement there occurred before 1870 or after 1914).

Indentured communities integrated with others or remained isolated to varying degrees. The mixed ethnic groups of Hawaii and Réunion are countered by the homogeneous Indian communities of the
Caribbean and Oceania. For the most part, integration depended on sex
ratios. Where women comprised almost one third of Caribbean-domi-
ciled Indians, the Chinese were almost exclusively male, which accounts
for their relative assimilation into Cuban society, for example. Race and
cultural distinctions also played a role and there was far less mixing, especially socially sanctioned mixing, than in previous periods when inter-
marriages were commonplace. In any event, much of the value of such
labor to planters and mine owners was that it was hardy and young (typically 15 to 30 years old). The simple motivation for a peasant to inden-
ture himself (where he was not coerced) and for remaining on afterwards
was money. This motivation was a constant and the supply of willing
labor never evaporated. Rather, the cessation of the intercontinental migration of bonded labor—ending within the British empire by 1920—
owed more to an increasingly critical public climate both among liberals
in the metropole and nationalists in India and China.

This is not to say that indentured contracts offered a rosy existence.
Many had been impressed into work with vague promises or fraudulent
claims. Work was grueling and living conditions squalid. Once placed,
the barriers to social improvement were absolute. Even though most survived the sea voyage easily enough, mortality rates were high upon arrival and as many as one fourth of the Melanesians laboring in Queens-
land died, mostly due to disease. Often wages were not payable until the
expiration of the contract, resulting in massive indebtedness that had to
be paid off after the bonded worker had reverted to free labor. Many expressed frustration by malingering, engaging in petty sabotage, alcoholism, or drug addiction or, less commonly, by resorting to murder, suicide, desertion, or strikes.

Still, many overcame the hardships and fashioned a satisfactory life
for themselves, very probably a better one than awaited them back home.
This was even sometimes true of those who did not have far to go and it
should be pointed out that in addition to the legions of workers shipped
overseas, throngs of others were shifted across much shorter distances
overland to the advantage of European administrators, merchants, and
industrialists. Thus hundreds of thousands of Indians were recruited
from various Indian provinces to work in Bengali textile factories, As-
samese tea gardens, Punjabi public works projects, or to serve in the army
of the British *raj*. Of the perhaps 20 million Indian laborers who were

domestically or internationally indentured between 1834 and 1920, approximately 25 percent returned home after their contracts had expired.

Besides menial laborers, another imperial transfer consisted of Asiatic middlemen. Merchants, clerks, and moneylenders served as vital socioeconomic links between European overlords and indigenous subjects. The middlemen were frequently preferred by the colonial rulers to local businessmen partly because of their dependency on the colonizers and the social insulation they provided and partly because of the extensive financial networks and considerable entrepreneurial resources they commanded. Such persons included higher caste Gujarati traders and Chettiar creditors who operated in East Africa, Burma, and Malaya; Armenian, Jewish, and Eurasian labor subagents who were found throughout colonial Asia; Chinese clerks, planters, merchants, and lenders who stoked the economies of Southeast Asia; and Levantines who ran small businesses and shops in West Africa.

Though small in numbers, such middlemen exerted a distinct and important influence in colonial economic development that in some instances continued after decolonization. They also became easy targets for the pent-up frustrations of the subjugated indigenes. Occasionally they suffered from militant local nationalism whether during decolonization or in its wake as was the case with the Asians of Idi Amin's Uganda. As with other migrants, their contributions were also often felt in their original homelands, not only in financial but sometimes in political terms as well. For instance, two famous nationalist leaders, Mahatma Gandhi and Sun Yat-Sen, had returned home with crucial political skills and outlooks acquired in other colonial settings. Gandhi had developed his peculiarly Indian form of nonviolent protest (*satyagraha*) while a lawyer in South Africa between 1893 and 1915. And Sun Yat-Sen's political ideas were partly shaped by the contradictory examples he had been exposed to as an impressionable adolescent residing with his Chinese relatives in Hawaii between 1879 and 1883: the liberty-affirming republicanism of resident Americans and liberty-crushing American colonialism.

Last to be considered here are the original inhabitants who encountered the Europeans in the areas here called the New Europes. Sometimes, where space allowed, they migrated to avoid cataclysmic collisions with white communities. But after 1890, relatively little internal migration occurred as conquest and settlement pushed imperial frontiers to their geographical and climatological limits. The process of corralling indigenes into reserved areas—reservations in the United States and Canada, black areas in South Africa—culminated or was well underway in this period. In other places, such as French North Africa, expanding *colon* settlements shifted Arabs and Berbers away from the coast. In America, Canada, and Australia, resettlement policies were finally making real the old expansionary myth that Europeans had primarily settled in empty spaces.

By 1900 Europeans greatly exceeded North American Amerindians, Australian aborigines, and New Zealand Maoris in their homelands.

Native Americans in the United States, for example, whose pre-Columbian numbers may have ranged from over 5 to 10 million, sank to 300,000 in 1865 and 220,000 by 1910. Hawaiians declined to the brink of extinction and Tasmanians were simply wiped out. Westerners dispassionately referred to the "Dying Savage" and the "Vanishing Primitive" as the natural victims of their own cultural and biological deficiencies. It seemed to be the destiny of such peoples to disappear whether this fate was foreordained by the Bible or scientifically "proven" by Social Darwinists. For it appeared to the Victorians that the "natives" had been degenerating for centuries. Western intrusion was regarded as simply the final act in a long, inexorable process of extinction.

At the same time, the era of high imperialism paradoxically witnessed a recovery in the numbers of many indigenous peoples in the New Europes. This resulted partly from policies designed to preserve endangered populations, partly from wholly internal factors including spiritual and cultural revival, and partly from enforced isolation from Western contagions that ravaged Pacific Islanders and others. Today, for example, Amerindians in the United States number some 2 million and in 1989 there were 300,000 Maoris in New Zealand, up from some 42,000 in 1896.

The causes of such demographic calamities were many but the most important—and which continued to exact a terrible toll throughout this period—were the biological-ecological assaults unleashed by invading Europeans. The supreme biological culprit was new diseases against which the epidemiologically inexperienced local populations had no protective immunity. In absolute numbers, the apocalyptic decimation of Carribeans and Central Americans in the sixteenth century was repeated on a smaller scale in the Pacific in the nineteenth century as the Hawaiian case illustrated. Smallpox was a great scourge but other Old World germs combined to destroy New World societies, especially venereal diseases that made people sterile and therefore incapable of replenishing their own stock.

Frequently compounding these disasters were innumerable armed contests with settlers, militias, and imperial regulars. Settlerdom also damaged or destroyed the ecological basis of indigenous life by such means as cutting and burning down forests, exterminating game, polluting and rerouting rivers, confiscating land, and decimating livestock with animal pathogens unconsciously brought from Europe. Thus, the purposeful elimination of the Great Plains buffalo by American hunters and the devastation of South African cattle by the chance arrival of the virulent rinderpest virus had similar impacts: they killed the animals that socially and symbolically defined the societies they had physically supported.

Not surprisingly, such experiences frequently triggered a psychological crisis among the indigenes characterized by widespread confusion and depression. Narcotic addictions, sexual abandon, and infanticide were both the symptoms and culprits of cultural despair. As we have seen, Hawaiians exhibited each during the nineteenth century even though the Western invasion was a peaceful one. With their numbers and their arms, their ploughs and their illnesses, their alcohol and drugs, their fears and prejudices, Europeans presented an ominous challenge to those societies whose long isolation and scant numbers made them far less capable of effective resistance.

Others, as in Africa, fared better. Even in settler South and North Africa, indigenous populations were larger, had more experience of outsiders, and were better equipped to save themselves. In the late nineteenth century the Xhosa of South Africa responded with regenerative social and religious movements, reforming traditional institutions and systems of wielding power that enabled them to better endure the engulfing whites. In North Africa, as French control spread, Arabs and Berbers retreated further into the desert. These responses replicated the pattern of avoidance or protest migrations as practiced in nonsettler colonies. And conspicuous among the aboriginals of the New Europes, the Maoris were able to adapt with remarkable speed, preserving much of their culture as they assimilated into the capitalist economy of settler New Zealand.

Throughout the world, migratory patterns in the age of high imperialism combined with earlier and later population redistributions to produce the mixed populations and ethnic heterogeneity of many of today's societies. Most of this migration was in response to labor demands occasioned by the expansion of a capitalist economy to which the major empires were closely tied. But some of it was politically, strategically, or culturally motivated. The final incarnation of modern imperial diasporas did not evolve until much later though there were early signs of it during World War I. That was when some North Africans voluntarily went to France to take over the jobs vacated by Frenchmen fighting in the trenches. After the Second World War that metropolitan-destined rivulet broadened into a stream resulting today in minority communities of Afro-Caribbeans and South Asians in Britain and North Africans and Indochinese in France. In a limited way, the empires had managed to strike back.

FURTHER READINGS

The history of the various strands of human traffic associated with late nineteenth century imperialism has yet to be written. Most information is anchored in disparate studies devoted to global migratory flows and circuits, intercontinental slave trades and bonded labor transfers, national and area studies, and economic and/or ecological colonialism. Those that explicitly link empire with massive demographic shifts are not confined to the era of high imperialism. Composites of varied and selectively useful articles appear in two recent overviews edited by P. C. Emmer: *Colonialism and Migration: Indentured Labor Before and After Slavery* (Dordrecht, Netherlands: Martinus Nijhoff, 1986) and (with M. Mörner as co-editor) *European Expansion and Migration* (New York: Berg, 1992).

On the impact of settler populations and their plants and animals on indigenous peoples see Alfred Crosby, *Ecological Imperialism: The Biological Expansion of Europe, 900–1900* (Cambridge: Cambridge University Press, 1986). A useful introduction to a burgeoning literature on the natural environment of the tropical colonies under imperialism is Madhav Gadgil and Ramachandra Guha, *This Fissured Land: An Ecological History of India* (Berkeley: University of California Press, 1992). Global demographics are addressed in several works by William H. McNeill. See his recent *The Global Condition: Conquerors, Catastrophes, and Community* (Princeton, N.J.: Princeton University Press, 1992), penned with his usual suggestive erudition. On post-slave trade bonded labor within the British Empire, see: Hugh Tinker, *A New System of Slavery: The Export of Indian Labour Overseas, 1830–1920* (London: Oxford University Press, 1974) and Kay Saunders, ed., *Indentured Labour in the British Empire, 1834–1920* (London: Croom Helm, 1984). Finally, for overviews of the experiences and consequences of colonial immigrants on Britain, see: Rozina Visram, *Ayahs, Lascars, and Princes: The Story of Indians in Britain, 1700–1947* (London: Pluto Press, 1986) and Paul Gilroy, *"There Ain't No Black in the Union Jack": The Cultural Politics of Race and Nation* (Chicago: University of Chicago Press, 1987).

6

Conflicting Ideologies in British India, 1875–1900

In contrast to the Congo and Hawaii, which came under Western rule during the era of high imperialism, large portions of India had been governed by Britain since the turn of the nineteenth century. From the early 1600s, officers and merchants of the English East India Company had trafficked between Europe, India, and China. From 1765 onward commercial ventures gave way to political dominion and by 1850 the British had extended their power throughout India. The suppression of revolt in 1857, which was part army mutiny, part regional uprising, and part sporadic protest against British policies, confirmed Britain's dominance just as it encouraged new patterns of governance. The late Victorian Indian Government firmly asserted its right to rule but was more modest in its aims than its predecessor had been and was far from certain of its purpose. It practiced a quiet, conservative paternalism, interfering sparingly in Indian society. It was mostly content to preserve order and reap the handsome harvest of agricultural-based revenues. At the same time, the introduction of metropolitan-based socioeconomic forces induced changes that tended to upset the deferential order devised by the British.

This chapter explores certain aspects of the imperialist ideology that buttressed the British raj (rule), especially in its civilizing mission guise. That idea was predicated on the cultural and racial superiority

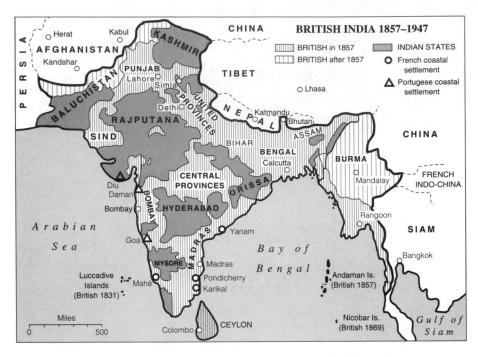

THE DOMINION OF THE BRITISH RAJ   Britain's chief dependency was an unmatched source of military power, prestige, and earnings. (Reprinted by permission: G. P. Putnam's Sons, New York)

of Westerners and on the ability of the colonized to Westernize. At their best, Europeans saw themselves as tutors, healers, guides, and builders. The question that bedeviled ruler and ruled alike was how far and how fast Westernization could proceed. Debates over this issue flared up with growing frequency and controversy in the late 1800s. One such instance occurred in 1883 when the British raj proposed giving high-ranking native civil servants powers and responsibilities commensurate with their qualifications. This proposal was virtually shelved in the face of fierce opposition from the resident British community. This opposition in turn prompted India's disappointed middle classes to increase pressure on the raj. They became more impatient with the spirit and performance of British rule and slowly began to chart a path that eventually led, by many twists and turns, to independence in 1947. In consequence, an entrenched ideology of dominance, evident in state policies as well as in an imperial lifestyle supported by privilege and prejudice, was by 1900 confronted by conditional cooperation and Indian self-assertiveness.

BRITISH PRIDE AND INDIAN ASSETS

More than any other colony, India instilled pride among the imperialists. It was a land of topographical superlatives and climatological extremes. The sheer presence of India—the striking variations in landscape and the intensity of its heat and monsoons—made an instant and lasting impression. The hardiest of Victorians—whether driven by profit, adventure, hubris, or humanity—contended with punishing climate and tough terrain. They also gazed delightfully upon sublime Rajasthani deserts and snow-capped Himalayan peaks. Everything was on a grand scale. Indeed, India was no mere territory but an entire subcontinent. And, at more than 1.5 million square miles (about half the size of the continental United States), it was easily the world's largest tropical dependency.

It was also the most populous. Containing over 300 million persons by 1914, India was home to more than half of the world's colonized population. That is, nearly six out of every ten persons ruled by Westerners were Indians. The subcontinent boasted a dozen different languages and hundreds of dialects. Approximately 70 percent of Indians were Hindus and 25 percent were Muslims, with lesser numbers of Sikhs, Parsis, Christians, Jains, and Jews. Caste, locality, and ethnicity formed important distinctions that, along with religion and language, forged identities that separated Indian from Indian. For the British overlords, India seemed on the brink of disintegration, collapsing under the weight of cultural diversity and religious enmities. For reasons both plausible and self-serving, the colonizers credited Indian unity to their own vigorous government and claimed that they had fashioned order out of fragmentation. They also pointed to Indian productivity as the result of the steady, nurturing hand of empire. As a result, late Victorian India became a showcase of civilizing colonialism. It was England's most prized possession and the one most envied by its imperial rivals.

British pride was partly based on India's fabled former glory. The British were aware of the attainments of past civilizations and had marveled at the immense inventory of texts, buildings, and other artifacts bequeathed by such monumental states as the Mauryan (fourth to second centuries B.C.) and Gupta empires (fourth to sixth centuries A.D.). Many also appreciated India as the cradle of Hindu and Buddhist philosophy as well as the birthplace of Sanskrit literature. The British also critically admired the great Muslim Mughal dynasty (1526–1858) and its record of conquest, plunder, administrative talent, revenue extraction, cultural production, and architectural adornment. Britons congratulated themselves on the impressive legacy they had inherited: tombs, temples, mosques, forts, palaces, artwork, cities, and canals. Perhaps the clearest testament of this was the proclamation of Queen Victoria as "Empress of India" in 1877 (making her the first British sovereign to assume an imperial title).

They were equally astonished that such a civilization had declined so severely by the time of their own rise as a subcontinental power.

Imperial pride was also grounded in a pragmatic assessment of India's strategic and economic value. The enormous importance of the "jewel in the imperial crown" was reflected in the size, efficiency, and mobility of its army. Numbering approximately 140,000 in 1880 (supplemented by 60,000 British troops stationed in India) the European-officered Indian army confirmed Britain as a formidable land power at a time when its own all-volunteer forces fluctuated between 175,000 and 250,000. From 1850 to 1900 the Indian army fought in countless colonial campaigns and defended British interests in Persia, China, Ethiopia, Hong Kong, Singapore, Afghanistan, Burma, Egypt, Nyasaland, Uganda, and the Sudan. During World War I (1914–1918), England's "barracks in the Oriental seas" furnished over a million soldiers to help defend England against the Kaiser. While war raged elsewhere, India was held by a force that contained a trifling 15,000 British troops.

India's strategic significance was, in turn, related to Britain's economic stake in the subcontinent. A steady increase in British-Indian trade occurred throughout the second half of the nineteenth century. In addition, British economic involvement expanded with new agricultural, shipping, financial, and industrial firms as well as with the construction of a modern transportation system. By 1900 the Indian railway network was one of the world's largest with more mileage than the rest of Asia combined. India also absorbed more British products—mostly cotton goods—than any other part of the empire. In turn, Britain imported more than half of India's exports, mainly jute (for rope), raw cotton, indigo (a dye), tea, and coffee. A lucrative trade was accompanied by a boost in British investments in India. By the 1880s, India's share of Britain's *total* overseas capital investments equaled one fifth, much of it going to finance the railroads. The important point is that the profits on trade and returns on investment were so favorable to Britain because the British controlled the levers of exchange at both ends. While the trade surplus with India offset nearly half of Britain's trade deficit with Europe and North America, Indian industries in direct competition with British enterprise often languished.

Nor did the colonizers themselves bear the massive expense of occupation and administration. Escalating expenditures and salaries (Indian Civil Servants were the highest paid bureaucrats in the world) were charged to the Indian people and consumed some 80 percent of the Indian Empire's budget. The pensions of British officers and administrators retired from India, payments for English-made military and civil merchandise consigned to India, and the cost of the Indian-manned, British-officered Indian army were all borne by Indian taxpayers. Thus, Indians financed their own subjugation. It is hard to exaggerate India's economic importance to Britain at this time. All considered, India kept Britain economically competitive in the international economy at a time when its own productive capacities were in relative decline.

The British countered the image of a predatory power devouring Indian resources with statistics pointing to gains marked by Western technology, entrepreneurship, and humanitarianism. These the *raj* published in annual "Moral and Material Progress Reports." Most frequently cited were construction projects: canals, railroads, telegraphs, tunnels, bridges, and sanitation works. Equally important were social, legal, and policing reforms that had been put into effect by the early 1860s. Heading the list were the outlawing of *sati* (widow immolation), infanticide, human sacrifice, and slavery. Moreover, Hindu widows were legally permitted to remarry for the first time in centuries and women could own their own property (a legal entitlement married women in England were denied until 1882). The *raj* presided over a rise in domestic order and interpersonal safety. Internal warfare ceased though frontier flashes persisted unabated. The *Pax Britannica* (parodied by Britain's critics as the *Pox Britannica*) eliminated or domesticated hereditary and professional criminal groups (including the notorious strangling cult, the "thugs"). Legal practices were simplified and codified, the death penalty greatly restricted, and several forms of corporal punishment abolished. Other sources of official pride were the introduction of Western medicine, famine relief schemes, and English education.

Results, however, did not always match intentions. Infanticide and the taboo against widow remarriage persisted. In addition, government and science accomplished rather less than their most optimistic sponsors had forecasted. For instance, infectious diseases persisted in the face of interventions by Western physicians (plague took more than ten million lives between 1897–1917). Famine killed additional millions in the 1890s. And English literacy was confined to less than one percent of the population. India was changed by British rule and international capitalism in important ways, but fundamental transformation was another matter. India in the 1920s was virtually as agricultural, rural, illiterate, capital impoverished, and deindustrialized as it had been a century before.

During the early nineteenth century, the colonial state promoted the English language and a Western curriculum as the principal agents of Anglicizing select groups of Indians. Evangelical Protestantism and secular Utilitarianism influenced proposals that were meant, in the words of Thomas Babington Macaulay, member of the Governor-General's Supreme Council, to make Indians "Indian in blood and color, but English in taste, in opinions, in morals, and in intellect." Britain's rule was seen as a preparatory trusteeship under which Indians would be transformed into "brown Englishmen" capable of self-rule.

By the late 1800s, however, this experiment in cultural reform became stalled, a casualty of several factors: a hardening racism in Europe that stressed biological immutability over environmental transformation as the chief determinant of each race's developmental potential; a more populous, self-supporting, and exclusive British community in India; and the discouraging lessons British officials drew from the uprising of 1857. British interventions in Indian socioreligious life had always been limited, hesitant, and prompted by local agitation, but they were even fewer and more tentative after 1857. The 1857 revolt had resulted in an appalling loss of lives, money, and trust and the victorious British emerged wary of further antagonizing Indian sensibilities (the revolt was commonly seen as a reaction against British attempts to Westernize India).

British reluctance to interfere in Indian society was fueled by a rejection of "Macaulay's" vision of "brown Englishmen" running an independent India. Instead of disseminating the "new learning" to other Indians as the British had expected, India's Anglicized elite used it for their own purposes, mostly, it seemed, to challenge Britain's administrative monopoly in India. Not coincidentally, the British concluded that Anglicized Indians lacked the moral and intellectual fiber to govern themselves. Inasmuch as Anglicization was now considered pointless (because of racial limitations none could overcome), Britons all but persuaded themselves that their imperial tenure was inevitable, necessary, and permanent. Western-educated Indians, unable and unwilling to unlearn what they had acquired, began to indict British rule. In doing so, they employed Western reasoning and modern methods of organizational protest and judged the realities of British rule according to the rulers' own ideals of beneficent progress.

THE PROMISE OF IMPERIAL RULE

Conflicting attitudes about the purpose of their rule as well as Indian expectations of a greater role for themselves in administrative and political life collided dramatically in 1883 in a fevered debate over an unlikely bill. Though trivial in itself the bill was of great symbolic importance. The bill in question was the Criminal Procedure Amendment Act, which first appeared in the Viceroy's council in early 1883. Popularly known as the Ilbert Bill because it was introduced by the council's legal member, C. P. Ilbert, it modestly proposed to invest the highest ranking "native" members of the colonial service with the specific authority to try European British subjects in criminal cases in the countryside ("natives" were already invested with such powers in civil cases in rural areas and in all

A SOLEMN PLEDGE

In the aftermath of the 1857 revolt, Queen Victoria issued a proclamation on 1 November 1858, outlining some cardinal principles about imperial governance, two of which are excerpted here.

We hold ourselves bound to the natives of our Indian territories by the same obligations of duty which bind us to all our other subjects, and those obligations, by the blessing of Almighty God, we shall faithfully and conscientiously fulfil. Firmly relying ourselves on the truth of Christianity, and acknowledging with gratitude the solace of religion, we disclaim alike the right and the desire to impose our convictions on any of our subjects . . . And it is our further will that, so far as may be, our subjects, of whatever race or creed, be freely and impartially admitted to offices in our service, the duties of which they may be qualified, by their education, ability, and integrity, duly to discharge

Source: C. H. Philips and B. N. Pandey, eds., *The Evolution of India and Pakistan 1858 to 1947, Select Documents* (London: Oxford University Press, 1962), p. 11. Reprinted by permission of Oxford University Press.

cases in the principal cities). At the time, only civil servants who were British by blood or birth were allowed to judge such cases which could carry a sentence of two years' imprisonment or a 1,000-rupee fine (£75 or $375 at 1883 values) and a flogging.

The bill was not aimed at Indian society at large but only at a segment of the colonial state itself and at a minuscule portion of the Indian population that was directly affected by it. Ilbert's wish was simply to bring criminal and civil law and town and country judicial practice into alignment by equalizing the powers of senior native and British civil servants. The issue had been raised in 1882 through a critical memorandum written by Behari Lal Gupta, one of a handful of Indian members of the elite thousand-man Indian Civil Service (ICS). The bill was faithful to the spirit of Queen Victoria's pledge of 1858 that admission into and promotion within India's administration would be determined by merit, not by race or creed. Given the small number of Indians affected by the measure (fewer than a dozen Indians would have been empowered by the bill), the bill was regarded by its sponsors as a trivial matter.

They were wrong. Right away Anglo-Indians (European merchants, planters, and professional people) erupted in opposition. The controversy ignited by Ilbert was fueled by the tense political climate which began in 1880 when the first Marquis of Ripon was appointed India's Viceroy (1880–1884). Ripon, the most progressive proconsul of the era, raised Indian hopes along with British anxieties by his zealous reforms. He was a self-contradiction: a Radical nobleman who favored democracy and an imperial ruler who disliked colonialism. He favored the older ideal of offering efficient, impartial government as a preparation for Indian self-rule. He rejected the attitude that the authority of empires rested on brute force and existed solely to benefit the conquerors. Ripon was a cultural chauvinist who believed Indians possessed the aptitude to rise to the level of Western civilization. Moreover, he despised the racism some Britons hurled at the "damned niggers."

AN IMPERIAL DILEMMA

In a letter written to a member of Parliament in March 1883, Lord Ripon presented two choices available to the imperial masters.

The question at issue is not the passing of this particular Bill, but the principles upon which India is to be governed . . . Is it England's duty to try to elevate the Indian people, to raise them socially, to train them politically, to promote their progress in material prosperity, in education, and in morality; or is it to be the be all and the end all of her rule to maintain a precarious power over . . . 'a subject race with a profound hatred of their subjugators?' . . . I feel pretty sure . . . that our future policy in India will be established on just and liberal lines; but if you fail us now, all my . . . work will be wholly wrecked, and the effect upon the minds of the natives will . . . be disastrous in the extreme . . .

Source: Edwin Hirschmann, *'White Mutiny': The Ilbert Bill Crisis in India and the Genesis of the Indian National Congress* (Columbia, Mo.: South Asia Books, 1980), pp. 70–71. Reprinted by permission.

Given the constraints placed on him, Ripon succeeded in putting his ideas into practice to a surprising degree. In his first two years he ended the censorship of the Indian press imposed by his predecessor; protected child labor with India's first factory act; set up a commission to look into expanding public primary education; sponsored a tenancy bill designed to bolster Bengal's rich peasantry; and increased the numbers and powers of Indians serving on local government boards. He had tried, without success, to grant to Indians the same right to carry arms as Europeans. All of this won Ripon the respect of many Indians.

But it had also annoyed many British officials in India who felt that Ripon's acts were flagrantly reckless. By the close of 1882, the Anglo-Indian community was virtually alienated from the Viceroy. Some 80,000 strong, Anglo-Indians exerted an influence over the colonial state far in excess of their numbers. Concentrated in Bengal province, Anglo-Indians tended to view India as their long-term home. This, along with their membership in the ruling race, tended to pit them against the rising and competing aspirations of Western-educated Indians. Anglo-Indians loathed Ripon for supporting the reviled "baboo" (or *babu*, members of Bengali's scribal class; in this context a derisive term for Westernized Indians).

The excitement created by Ilbert proved more disruptive than any since 1857 and was swiftly dubbed the "White Mutiny" (evoking the "Sepoy Mutiny" of 1857). Within weeks, monster rallies were held, incendiary speeches were delivered, and scurrilous letters saturated the Anglo-Indian press. One anonymous contributor who styled himself "Britannicus" fanned racial animosity with no fewer than 90 letters to the editor. Ridiculing any such notion as a unified Indian identity, "Britannicus" discounted the "mawkishly sentimental cry" of "India for the Indians" as a ruse to rob the "British of a land which their fathers had purchased with their blood" and had maintained "by their bravery." Petitions bearing thousands of signatures begged queen and parliament to abort the bill. A play called *A Glance in Advance; or What's in Store for '84* packed a Calcutta theater with its acid parody of the bill and its gloomy forecast of what would ensue if Indians dared to judge Britons.

More serious was the formation of EADA—the European and Anglo-Indian Defence Association—which, with over 1100 members, rapidly became an effective lobby for Anglo-Indian interests. So solid was Anglo-India's opposition that only four Europeans in all of Calcutta were said to have openly supported the bill. Race affinity prompted resident Americans, continental Europeans, and even many of the 62,000 mixed-race Eurasians to oppose the bill even though they could already be tried by Indians (the bill applied only to European British subjects—those of British birth or background).

The Ilbert bill exposed the fears and prejudices of the British in India. One socially prominent speaker stated that Indians could not be trained to become impartial and competent judges just as Ethiopians could not vary their pigmentation or leopards change their spots. Another delivered a racial slur along with a challenge to the *"greasy baboo's"* masculinity: Bengali civil servants were likened to snakes who slithered on the ground and got into places where men who, because they walk upright, could not enter. These remarks conveyed base appeals to fear. British males who lived in isolated settings upcountry feared a rash of charges by their native subordinates if Indian judges and magistrates presided. Given the widespread mistreatment of Indian workers and servants by European planters and estate managers, such concerns were not entirely unfounded. But neither were they realistic considering the minute number of Indians empowered by Ilbert as well as the exceptional courage required of a worker to bring a suit against an employer.

Another fear was gender-based. It was claimed that English sisters, wives, and daughters would be left defenseless if men were jailed or if they themselves were tried by Indians. In fact, the rallying cry "women-in-danger" raised Anglo-Indian outrage to hysterical levels. Women who feared for their families and their dignity thronged to the opposition. They held separate meetings, sent their own petitions, and boycotted glittering viceregal social events, which, by their own account, was the toughest sacrifice of all. One of the staunchest defenders of white feminine privilege was Annette Akroyd Beveridge. Though the wife of one of the few pro-Ilbert members of the ICS, Beveridge split with her husband

and openly discoursed on the degraded condition of Indian society. Speaking for the memsahibs (Englishwomen), she argued that the "ignorant and enslaved" status of Indian women particularly rendered Indian men unfit to judge Western women who were accustomed to more "civilized" standards of conduct. For Beveridge, the prospect of trial by "savages" was unnerving. Others elaborated on Beveridge's theme with lurid insinuations that vulnerable Englishwomen would be molested by sex-crazed Indians.

INDIAN HATE AND ENGLISH REASONING

A leading member of the Anglo-Indian opposition to the Ilbert Bill was the lawyer James Branson. In this speech he refuted Ripon's assessment of Indian capabilities and sentiment.

You cannot suddenly educate a Hindu into a full appreciation of his freedom . . . Look at the history of India. Here you have a country that has been for all historical times, I say, the victim of one conquering nation or another. The conquered have hated the conquerors . . . with an intense hate, which unmistakeably characterizes the races in India . . . If . . . [however] the Hindu has no patriotism . . . if he does *not* hate us, then it follows that he has not a single quality which we can understand or appreciate.

Source: Edwin Hirschmann, *'White Mutiny': The Ilbert Bill Crisis in India and the Genesis of the Indian National Congress* (Columbia, Mo.: South Asia Books, 1980), p. 299. Reprinted by permission.

The impact of Beveridge's remarks was all the greater because she did not fit the stereotype of the memsahib. Indeed, she had shown little patience with many Anglo-Indians whom she considered boorish and provincial. Her own life in India had been unusual from the start when, at the age of thirty, she responded to the plea of a Bengali reformer visiting England to travel to India to teach middle class Indian women how to become modern wives. Akroyd (her maiden name) was what became known in the *fin-de-siècle* as a New Woman: highly educated (a graduate of Bedford College), unmarried, independent, and career-minded. She learned Bengali and translated from Persian the memoirs of the sixteenth century founder of the Mughal dynasty. This she did while working in a school for Hindu girls run by a Bengali reform society. In 1873 she founded her own school. Throughout, she acquired a reputation as a friend of the Indian people. Two years later she quit her vocation and married Henry Beveridge. Her first daughter was given a Sanskrit name and she and her husband continued to socialize with members of the Bengali respectable classes (the *bhadralok*).

But her remarks regarding the Ilbert bill severely damaged her image in the opinion of leading Indian supporters of the bill. The *bhadralok* newspaper, *The Bengalee*, denounced her as a hollow liberal. This accusation finds surprising substantiation in her own diaries, which reveal a secret dislike of India and Indians. The Beveridge that emerges from those private entries was condescending and prudish, preoccupied with replacing the "obscene" sari with the more chaste petticoat. She despaired of expecting anything more than shiftlessness and delirium from a people who worshipped stone idols and sanctioned juvenile marriages. Despite her extraordinary background and unconventional experiences, her opinions and those of Anglo-India on Ilbert were remarkably congruent.

Meanwhile, the Anglo-Indian outburst caught the ICS unawares. By the close of 1883 many high officials who had supported the bill reversed themselves and privately urged postponement or withdrawal. In part, members of the ICS feared the prospects of growing numbers of Indians entering their ranks. For officials and the Indian middle classes alike, Ilbert and the larger question of increased Indian participation at the highest administrative echelons became confused. The significance of this was that the weight of officialdom counted more with Ripon than did nonofficial opinion. Lacking solid support from London, Ripon compromised. In the end, Britons were guaranteed the right to be judged by a jury of their own countrymen if an Indian presided.

Ripon's compromise was widely seen as a capitulation and Anglo-India's victory as a setback for the educated Indians. Indeed, disillusionment over the Viceroy's defeat played a pivotal role in subsequent Indian politics. Indian leaders applied organizational and methodological lessons of the anti-Ilbert agitation effort to an all-India nationalist movement that evolved from the founding of the Indian National Congress two years later (1885).

The Ilbert controversy illustrates two important features of British imperialism in late nineteenth century India. The first concerns the mechanics of administration. At the time the Ilbert bill was proposed the *raj* was becoming increasingly bureaucratized. It was hardening into a routinized regime that privileged the status quo over progressive initiatives. It also contained numerous specialized departments (police, public works, forestry, medicine) and levels (India, province, district, and sub-district) that functioned as an informal system of legislative brakes. Lengthy consultations and deliberations were standard. Proposals similar to Ilbert had appeared before the *raj* since the 1860s. And even when the Viceroy, provincial governors, and bureaucrats were in agreement, final approval from London was necessary. London's role actually increased as submarine cables brought it nearer to Calcutta and permitted it to be a close participant in the shaping of policy. The result was that the Secretary of State for India in London became the Viceroy's senior policy partner. In this instance, bureaucratic schisms and the Secretary of State's tepid support had eroded Ripon's resolve.

The second point relates to ideology. The Ilbert bill highlights the tension between the civilizing and noninterventionist tendencies of the colonial state. Indeed, it demonstrates that the colonial state housed diverse opinions. The dominant, prevailing element was especially strong among the Anglo-Indian community and was more obviously influenced by racist attitudes. The authority for this position rested on the supposed absolute rights of conquerors. To its most vehement proponents, India should be governed exclusively for the benefit of Britain. Concessions to the colonized beyond those necessary to maintain peace, subsistence level incomes, and production for the international market should be resisted. Against this, a minority element, almost entirely confined to official circles, was more paternalistic. Espousing a vaguely supremacist ideology based more on cultural than racial criteria, it urged a more benevolent approach to imperial rule. At its most advanced, it pushed for substantial material and legal progress.

THE *RAJ*, SEX, RACE, AND VIOLENCE

As the Hawaiian case illustrated, the transfer of Western culture overseas was a distinguishing feature of European economic and political expansion. To a considerable degree, European social orders and customs were replicated in various colonized niches throughout the world. This pattern was particularly prominent in the age of high imperialism when borrowings from indigenous peoples were rare. Far fewer Victorians wore Indian garb, took Indian wives, or engaged in Indian pastimes than did their Georgian forbearers. It is important to recognize that the social experiences of the colonizers were determined by such ideological influences as racial attitudes, gendered distinctions, Christianity, and sexual taboos.

"Going native" was a paramount fear and signaled a precipitate fall from civilized grace. Such a fate had befallen Kurtz in *The Heart of Darkness*. Beyond personal calamity, it was believed that fraternization with the colonized imperiled others. In E. M. Forster's restrained critique of empire, *A Passage to India*, Adela Quested, a young woman fresh from England, wanted to see the "real India" and "real Indians," a craving her Anglo-Indian hosts found distasteful and puzzling. Bored with staged soirees and stale conversations with hand-picked "natives," Adela accepted Dr. Aziz's invitation to visit a set of mysterious caves. Thrilled to be guided by an Indian, she shrugged off protests that such outings must be British supervised. The adventure started badly as the sole invited English male failed to join the group, leaving Adela and her companion Mrs. Moore "unprotected." It ended in tragedy when Adela accused Aziz of sexually assaulting her in the recesses of a stifling, black cave. Inevitably, the Indian and Anglo-Indian communities polarized, each rallying around its victim. But Adela's Anglo-Indian compatriots could not conceal their satisfaction at having been proved right. And Adela herself grew disillusioned, apparently having grasped Forster's awful truth that real friendship between Indian and Briton was impossible under imperialism.

In real life, misadventures of this kind were rare. Perhaps this was because Europeans in tropical dependencies took such great pains to erect effective barriers between themselves and surrounding populations. Desirable spots were selected for their healthy climate, altitude, or military-commercial value. They were then seized, declared "European," and occupied. By the early twentieth century separate and exclusive enclaves of European neighborhoods and towns dotted the empires. Within those areas, the presence and activities of Africans, Asians, and Oceanians were limited and strictly regulated.

This segregation was mirrored in India where the British strained to preserve their racial purity and cultural homogeneity by keeping the ruling and ruled communities apart. An apartheid-like colonial social system allotted to each race its own sphere and roles. British civilians were clustered into "little Englands" and British soldiers were barracked in strategically sited compounds called cantonments. Removed from the tumults of the great indigenous urban centers, they offered protection to nearby Anglo-Indian communities and ensured the loyalty of Indian soldiers housed beside them. English society, whether in the cities, large towns, or remote district headquarters known as civil stations, revolved around the clubhouse, church, private bungalow and, for the men, the office. Life was regimented, routinized, and parochial.

It was also contentedly derivative. Colonial society mimicked society back home as faithfully as local conditions permitted. English plants perennially struggled in the inhospitable Indian soils and climate. The interiors of bungalows were often transformed into homey shrines to English decor as furnishings and mementos from home claimed every available space. The most exact replicas of "Home" were the hill stations, prized mountainous retreats to which the British fled from both heat and Indians. Bathed in fresh alpine air and surrounded by neo-Gothic churches and timbered Victorian hotels, Anglo-Indians could fantasize they were in England. Lady Betty Balfour's rapture is unmistakable in the following notation: "The afternoon was rainy and the roads muddy, but such beautiful English rain, such delicious English mud."

Anglo-Indian life was at once dynamic and rigidly stratified. Anglo-Indians seem to have been driven by a hard-boiled pursuit of wealth and a desire to leave a tangible mark on the world. They managed plantations, directed business firms, ran shipping and transport lines, operated large commercial companies, practiced law, edited newspapers, and controlled financial houses. Each occupation carried a particular social status. At the summit were members of the "heaven born" ICS, followed by lesser officials and army officers, the professions, "box wallahs" (merchants and businessmen), and skilled workers. Social distinctions were so meticulously observed that the Anglo-Indian social hierarchy was known as the British caste system.

Encounters between Britons and Indians were highly formalized, distanced, and unequal. At the same time, the requirements of social

distance had to yield before the necessity of daily contacts with the colonized. Colonial regimes were always dependent on widespread indigenous cooperation and collaboration. Without this, the *raj* would have
been unsustainable. Never exceeding 170,000, the British in India were
too few to manage on their own a subcontinent whose population increased from about a quarter to nearly a third of a billion people between
1850 and 1920. They succeeded only with the aid of tens of thousands of
Indian soldiers, policemen, and junior officials as well as the support of
innumerable servants, laborers, and economic go-betweens. But collaboration was not a one-sided affair and Indians were often able to influence
the direction and impact of the *raj*. Indian collaborators and servants
were neither mindless imperialist tools nor blind to their own interests.
They sometimes could direct policies by wielding their own literary and
administrative expertise, capital resources, local command structures,
military systems and traditions, and networks of production and distribution. In these ways, they exercised an informal influence on British rule
in India and, by extension, on British imperialism overseas wherever Indian soldiers, officials, merchants, and creditors ventured.

QUIET AND BENEFICENT IMPERIALISM

*The image of the conscientious, hard-working, selfless, and caring ICS
district officer shines through in the recollection of John Beames, whose
official career spanned the 1850s and 1880s.*

. . . we were in the saddle by five in the morning and worked on horseback for
two or three hours, riding about inspecting police-stations, roads, and bridges
and public buildings under construction, tree-planting, ferry-boats, settling
disputes about land and property between villagers, and such-like business.
Or we would walk, with our horses led behind us, through the narrow lanes
of the ancient town accompanied by a crowd of police officers, overseers and
others, giving orders for sanitary improvements, repairing roadways and
drains, opening out new streets, deciding disputes . . . [Beames would then
preside as a court magistrate from 10 am until 6 pm].

Source: Philip Woodruff, *The Men Who Ruled India, Volume Two: The
Guardians* (New York: Schocken Books, 1964), p. 48.

Cooperation was elicited in part with demonstrations of overwhelming force, whether these took the form of blasting rebels from the
mouths of cannons or displays of stupendous military pomp. Loyalty
was also purchased through an elaborate system of inducements that
bound colonized and colonizer together: employment, education, titles,
medals, participation in grand ceremonies, and service on official boards,
councils, and commissions.

A constant hazard of colonial encounters was the violence—mostly
beatings, maimings, and rapes—perpetrated on the colonized. Between
1880 and 1900, for instance, Indian officials recorded 81 unauthorized

shootings of Indians by Britons. Lord Curzon, the Viceroy (1898–1905) was alarmed by these statistics, which he knew were a small fraction of the real number. He also knew that those few cases that went to trial usually ended in acquittals. Late Victorian India witnessed a number of cases where European planters who had clubbed their coolies and British soldiers who had smashed property and roughed up bazaar merchants were found "not guilty." In one notorious case a British soldier admitted killing an Indian tailor in a fit of pique but the European jury still refused to name him as the guilty party. Curzon decided to take action.

His impulses were paternalistic. He was an arch-imperialist whose reign coincided with the climax of British rule in India. He could not imagine a relaxation of imperial authority much less a transfer of power. Nor did he share Ripon's estimation of the *babus'* aptitude for self rule. Yet for Curzon, ruffian racism blighted Britain's imperial reputation. He conceded that racism was rampant but not that it was inherent in imperialism. Indeed, his view of racism as a conscious reflex undergirded his belief that it could be uprooted by a diligent government. Accordingly, he made an example of the military, reopening files on incidents that high-ranking officers had previously quashed. He dismissed officers whose soldiers had gone on rampages and transferred others who had failed to discipline their men. He also punished entire regiments, canceling their leaves for an entire year or assigning them to "hellish" outposts like Aden. For all this he had to endure the public humiliation of standing silent as one such regiment passed by in review to the deafening cheers of a crowd of Anglo-Indian spectators.

With respect to prosecuting racially motivated violence Curzon was an exception. More representative were his attempts to police another form of interaction between the races: sexual intimacy. Some such contacts were, of course, unavoidable. Adequate outlets had to be found for what (middle class) officials presumed were the uncontrollable lusts of (working class) enlisted men. These men were not allowed to bring their wives with them, nor were they encouraged to turn casual affairs with Indian women into steady relationships. Taking a native wife was forbidden and more than one soldier who tried to do so was sent back to England. The solution was to supply the men with low caste prostitutes. These were housed on military bases where they were periodically examined by army physicians and where the diseased could be quarantined in special hospitals.

Still, even state-regulated sex had its attendant hazards and sexually transmitted diseases disabled thousands of British soldiers during the nineteenth century. Moreover, by officially sanctioning prostitution, singling women out as vectors of disease, and subjecting prostitutes to invasive surveillance, the *raj* became the target of an organized moral protest. In particular, feminist moral purity campaigns were launched against the British and Indian Contagious Diseases Acts that victimized females suspected of prostitution but allowed male clients to escape unprosecuted.

In Britain the Acts were repealed in 1886. In India, the colonial state out-maneuvered its critics with limited reforms and continued to provision its soldiers with sex more or less on demand.

Class, race, and sex under colonialism interacted in complex ways. In 1893 the Maharaja of Patiala, a leading supporter of the *raj*, announced his intention to marry Miss Florry Bryan. The viceroy signaled his instant disapproval: the proposed union would violate both race and class taboos. As a European, Miss Bryan occupied a privileged position. But she was an Irishwoman of obscure social origins and as such was the maharaja's social inferior. As such she would not win the respect that was normally accorded to the wife of a prince by Europeans. The viceroy vigorously argued that the prince's polygamous propensities would offend the moral sensibilities of any memsahib, however lowly her background. Despite all these warnings and the official ostracism he courted, the maharaja married the music hall entertainer anyway.

Central to the viceroy's apprehensions and evident in his reference to the maharaja's polygamous habits were white fears of the "native" libido. Accordingly, patriarchal authorities felt bound to protect European women from the wanton lusts of Indians and other subject races. At bottom, this was deemed necessary to preserve the purity of the master race. Curzon went to considerable lengths to keep the races from mingling sexually, even preventing maharajas who seemed too fond of white women from traveling to Europe. He also hoped to suppress the "special Oriental vice" (sodomy) among the maharajas by an incredible scheme to identify young homosexual princes and enroll them into the all-male Imperial Cadet Corps where their sexual "irregularities" would miraculously cease in such hypermasculine surroundings.

In each of these cases, the British *raj* intervened in the personal lives of its subjects, confirming that in the colonial world private conduct carried public implications. Other steps taken by the *raj* can only be cited here as fascinating indicators of the kind of image the British liked to project of themselves. They kept the white vagrant population small, removed impoverished whites from public view, sequestered the infirm and mentally ill in remote asylums, and mandated an early retirement for officials. With such precautions, the rulers could be beheld by the "natives" at their most youthful, vigorous, intelligent, and gainfully employed.

More often, Anglo-Indians policed themselves. The Victorian cult of self-control that supposedly made members of the ICS impartial, incorruptible, and untiring, also governed domestic life where gentlemen were expected to stifle their carnal urges or keep their affairs hushed. Good breeding was thought to impart the virtue of self-regulation. When it didn't, scandal exploded. One apt example concerns a European missionary. Missionaries were a particular worry, occupying as they did the social margins of Anglo-India. Not only did many live among Indians, some spurned established codes of conduct and wore Indian garb or adopted other Indian customs. Some even went further. When a Protestant minister first converted an outcaste woman, then married her, and began having children by her (eventually numbering 21), the English religious community was stunned.

By accusing persons of having interracial sexual relations, the transgression was publicized and social conformity was presumably achieved. This is precisely what happened to Mary Pigot and K. C. Bannerjee though it remains doubtful that any sex had occurred between them. Still, the Presbyterian lady missionary and her Bengali friend, a theologian, were charged with fornication. The accuser was Pigot's supervisor, the Reverend William Hastie, who alleged that the two had shared a lounge chair and that Bannerjee had draped his arms over Pigot's bare feet. Pigot took the unusual step of suing Hastie. The case went to trial at the height of the Ilbert turmoil. Anglo-Indians, including the presiding judge, intuitively sided with Hastie. But as the trial unfolded and the accuser failed to produce any evidence, other issues surfaced. Pigot, it seems, had resisted Hastie's authority and Bannerjee had criticized Hastie's doctrinal views in print. Reluctantly, the judge decided for Pigot, but awarded her the derisory damages of one anna (roughly one English penny). However, she won 3,000 rupees (about £225) on appeal. Pigot's suit was significant because it was brought by a European woman (it would have been far more difficult for an Indian to sue a European). In effect, Pigot was obliged to erase even a hint of indiscretion but her rebuttal still left Anglo-Indian norms intact.

THE CLOISTERED WORLD OF ANGLO-INDIA

Yet other Victorian notions governed the clothing and nourishment of the Anglo-Indian body (though solar topees and mosquito nets were unavoidable concessions to India's clime). Memsahibs were layered in confining starched underwear, petticoats, and full cotton dresses, as sahibs worked in suits and close-fitting collars. The unadventurous English palate dictated cuisine throughout the empire. This was especially true after the opening of the Suez Canal in 1869 through which refrigerated steamships eventually conveyed customary English fare. Morning eggs, toast, and coffee were followed by mid-day creamed soups and cheeses, mid-afternoon teas and cakes, and evening dinners of meat pies, roasts, salads, and puddings. With Indian cooks it was inevitable that local staples and flavors infiltrated the Anglo-Indian diet and the British acquired a taste for such delectables as saffron rice and curried fowl.

The vernacular of Anglo-India was known as Anglo-Indian or Brindian, an English enriched by borrowings from Hindi and Hindustani along with invented words and phrases that made it unique within a galaxy of British imperial dialects. The Anglo-Indian vocabulary teemed with practical, everyday terms necessary for communicating with servants: *burra-beebee* (important lady), *chota peg* (small whisky), *juldi* (hurry up), and *pukka* sahib (a real gentleman). Such expressions remained peculiar to British India (though some, like memsahib, traveled throughout the empire) but other Indian words (more than 1,000 of them by one count) have become part of British and American English, such as chutney, guru, juggernaut, pajama, verandah, bandanna, thug, and calico. Some Anglo-Indians bothered to learn Urdu, Hindi, Bengali, or another language. A few acquired sufficient linguistic skills to translate, like the Indian Civil Servant John Beames who authored a *Comparative Grammar of the Modern Aryan Languages of India.*

But for the English *baba-log* ("baby people") the first requirement was to learn proper English. Parents feared that their young, possibly having had an Indian wet nurse and reared by an *ayah* (nursery maid), would become Indianized before a British identity could take hold. Thus by the age of five or six, Anglo-Indian sons and daughters were routinely packed off to England for several years while their parents remained in India. As one sahib who happened to be the father of the Bloomsbury author Lytton Strachey observed, when a child "jabbers away in Hindustani" it was time to send him home. Such separations were invariably painful and sometimes devastating for both parent and child. Kipling himself bore the psychological scars of unhappy years in England following a captivating and lordly "Indian" childhood.

Anglo-Indian pastimes were as vigorous as their working lives. Some, like cricket, were imported while others, like polo, were wholly indigenous. Pig sticking often substituted for fox hunting as bagging tigers did for shooting grouse. Horse racing, cards, and billiards amused the less active. Sundays—begun with robust Protestant sermons and climaxed by splendid military parades—offered both spiritual and secular visions of masculine vitality. Sports in particular cultivated a moral athleticism that Victorians regarded as invaluable to the maintenance of empire. The "games ethic," a development of the English public school, was an instrument of character formation in which team sports imparted the virtues of group loyalty and self-reliance, of stamina and resourcefulness, of knowing when to command and when to obey. A peculiarly English blend of team spirit and individual initiative was immortalized in these lines from *Vitae Lampada* by Sir Henry Newbolt:

> The sand of the desert is sodden red—
> Red with the wreck of the square that's broke;
> The gatling's jammed and the colonel dead,
> And the regiment blind with dust and smoke,
> The river of death has brimmed its banks
> And England's far and Honour a name,
> But the voice of a schoolboy rallies the ranks:
> Play up! Play up! And play the game!

Colonizers felt a constant need to impress the colonized. They were always on view, always having to set an example to affirm their "superior" identity. What but the preservation of race prestige can explain the odd habit of solitary planters in the thick of a tropical forest formally dressing for dinner in case any "native" should happen by? As an official's widow once explained why she dressed up for dinner on a steel canoe in the middle of a Nigerian river: "When you are alone, among thousands of unknown, unpredictable people, dazed by unaccustomed sights and sounds, bemused by strange ways of life and thought, you need to remember who you are, where you come from, what your standards are." A French African official put it more baldly: "When a superior race ceases to believe itself a chosen race, it actually ceases to be a chosen race."

What accounted for the Anglo-Indian bastions of pride, privilege, and prejudice? First, Anglo-Indians were acutely race conscious, fearful of racial degeneration and cultural contagion. Second, the British were convinced that a governing group could retain its *izzat* (prestige) only by maintaining a certain distance from the colonized. Third, the British had the practical fear of Indian riots and revolts. Distance and concentrated numbers supplied a degree of safety that, Britons reckoned, might prevent a repetition of the butchering of unarmed English women and children that occurred in 1857. Fourth, Europeans often saw Indians as diseased and feared epidemiological transmissions. This was one reason for choosing higher ground where cool breezes were believed to disperse deadly germs. In their cantonments and civil stations, Anglo-Indians assembled behind a line that was, in reality, much more a psychological than a physical *cordon sanitaire*.

HOME AWAY FROM HOME   *The Late Victorians in India made few concessions to local habitat and climate as this foxhunt at Lucknow in 1893 strikingly attests.* (Reprinted by permission: The Mansell Collection)

There was another, more positive rationale for creating habitats in the image of home: simple comfort and familiarity. India, for all its opportunities and delights, was a hostile place. Dangers abounded and Victorians were assaulted by broiling sun, choking dust, poisonous snakes, wild animals, restive villagers, cholera, dysentery, and fevers. That life in late nineteenth century India was harsher than in contemporary Britain was evident in the tombstones of infants and women that crowded Anglo-Indian cemeteries. (The child mortality rate of late Victorian Anglo-India was double that of Britain.) Families were often split up. Children were shipped off to England. Wives and husbands passed long separations from each other as memsahibs migrated to the cool hill stations each summer leaving the men behind to work on the hot plains. Periodic transfers uprooted households and shifted them hundreds of miles away. Moreover, Anglo-Indians lacked the customary support of family and old friends as well as many conveniences commonly available in Britain. Under such circumstances, the gritty Englishness of Anglo-Indian domestic life offered some compensation.

Two views of the Anglo-Indians stand out. The first is one they and their admirers preferred to advertise. This view might be summarized as an image of perseverance overcoming adversity. Such a spirit is evident in the titles of books and poems by and about the British in India: *India Called Them*, *The Necessary Hell*, *Bound to Exile*, and *The Land of Regrets*. The heaven-born Sir Walter Lawrence called his time in India a "divine drudgery," a "splendid happy slavery." Indian obstacles and English tenacity animated Anglo-Indian diaries and letters. They believed in themselves and in the good they did. Part of this was English vanity, but a sincere belief in their own worthiness undoubtedly helps us to understand the attitudes and deeds of those who lived under strenuous and sometimes perilous conditions.

The alternate view is one of racial insularity, arrogance, and greed. Anglo-Indians lived among Indians but not with them. Unlike other foreigners who had invaded India only to become absorbed by it, the Anglo-Indian resisted comprehensive cultural exchange much less integration. India was an unrivaled opportunity to make money, build things, command others, and improve conditions. Self-interest drove the colonizer just as it does all of us. But owing to advantages reserved for them as conquerors and rulers, Anglo-Indians amassed larger incomes and acquired a higher status than would have been possible under less privileged circumstances. They themselves believed that colonialism afforded better prospects than those available in England and they were probably right.

INDIAN MIDDLE CLASS RESPONSES TO THE *RAJ*

Colonizing attitudes and lifestyles inevitably disrupted preexisting patterns of indigenous thought and social life. This was especially true of the Westernized middle classes for whom British rule first provided a welcome expansion of conceptual horizons but which later induced a psychological-intellectual crisis. Early expectations of benefits that India could derive from British military, administrative, and economic hegemony had, by 1900, depreciated into anxieties about the harmful consequences of armed occupation, political domination, and economic manipulation. At the height of imperial expansion (1870–1914), an anti-colonialist consciousness formed that began to challenge the manner—even the legitimacy—of British rule.

What British colonialism sparked in the last half of the nineteenth century was a wide-ranging intellectual inquiry by India's middle class intelligentsia that produced unprecedented changes in outlook. Indian social reformers, religious revivalists, nationalists of varying stripes, and cultural patriots investigated and meditated on the meaning of colonial rule and the state of their own society. As they reassessed the West, they also began to form a new vision of India. As was the case with Europe at the time of its Renaissance, India of the late 1800s generated a cultural flowering and a new world view.

Without discounting the impressive volume, creativity, or intellectual impact of nonpolitical literature, poetry, music, and sectarian tracts, our focus will be the sociopolitical ideas of middle class leaders who fashioned a nationalist ideology that was used to combat the *raj*. As the first group of its size and influence to develop a national consciousness among the colonized Africans and Asians, India's Westernized middle classes established a prototype for bourgeois nationalisms in other European possessions. This first assumed form in Bengal, from where the following examples are mostly drawn. As a prominent politician from Western India said over a century ago, "What Bengal thinks today, all India thinks tomorrow." In part this was due to Bengal's unequaled size and wealth, but it was also because Anglo-Indians and Westernized Indians were most numerous there. More than any other Indian province, Bengal was subjected to a prolonged and penetrating Western presence.

Many early political thinkers began by praising British rule. They believed that on the eve of British conquest India had been anarchic, impoverished, exhausted, and morally adrift. If India had had a golden age, it was situated far in the distant past. It followed that if India's decline preceded the rise of British subcontinental power, Indian social critics could not argue that British rule was a reign of darkness that had descended on a bright, buoyant India. British paramountcy was a symptom, not a cause, of India's recent historical predicament.

In contrast to retrograde India, Britain was hailed as a beacon of progress: enterprisingly prosperous, militarily powerful, politically united and purposeful, scientifically and technologically advanced, and morally guided by Evangelical Protestantism and reformist Utilitarianism. These attributes imbued Britain with the power and the will to govern India as well as the responsibility to improve it. K. C. Sen, a leading contemporary socioreligious reformer, extravagantly claimed that British rule was part of a divine plan. Mid-century Indians sharply critical of their own culture largely accepted the Western diagnosis, put forward by imperialist and Marxist alike, that British rule was engaged in a regenerative enterprise. In speeches and writings, they acknowledged British social, moral, and material leadership.

MODERATE CRITICISM

Moderates could be both admonishing and supportive of British rule as the "Grand Old Man" of Indian nationalism, the Bombay politician Dadabhai Naoroji, was in this memorandum of 1880. Note how he relates a specific group's plight to India's fortunes.

The Europeans are not the natural leaders of the people. They do not belong to the people. They cannot enter into their thoughts and feelings; they cannot join or sympathize with their joys or griefs. On the contrary, every day the estrangement is increasing. Europeans deliberately and openly widen it more and more. [A glaring example of this was barring well-educated Indians from government employment] . . . the thousands that are being sent out by the universities every year find . . . there is no place for them in their motherland . . . The educated find themselves simply so many dummies, ornamented with the tinsel of school education, and then their whole end and aim of life is ended. What must be the inevitable consequence? . . . the power that the rulers are, so far to their credit, raising, will, as a nemesis recoil against themselves . . . He who runs may see, that if the present material and moral destruction of India continues, a great convulsion must inevitably arise, by which India will be more and more crushed under the iron heel of despotism and destruction, or may succeed in shattering the destroying hand and power. Far, far is it from my earnest prayer and hope that such should be the result of the British rule.

Source: Wm. Theodore de Bary, ed., *Sources of Indian Tradition, Vol. II* (New York: Columbia University Press, 1958), pp. 120–121.

To a large extent these positive assessments derived from the social positions that their authors occupied. Known as the *bhadralok* in Bengal, the new middle classes evolved from those who, a century before, had served as commercial middlemen to the British. They were largely composed of Hindu scribal (*kayasthas*) and merchant (*banias*) castes. As agents, interpreters, and brokers they responded swiftly to a new order created by commercial colonialism. As the British acquired greater economic and political control over Bengal, the compradors evolved into a collaborative service-professional-landholding-administrative class. By the mid-nineteenth century, they achieved considerable social mobility as lawyers, doctors, teachers, journalists, clerks, and lower level bureaucrats. Moreover, many had adopted specific cultural traits of the new rulers. Most had acquired a Western education. Some absorbed Christian teaching and forged a religious synthesis of Western and Eastern spiritual learning known as the *Brahmo Samaj*. Others remained more firmly moored to their Hindu origins and attempted to reform society in light of religious and rationalist Western notions. Many were proficient in English. The best known *bhadralok* family was the Tagores, large landowners with considerable banking and commercial interests, who were social reformers and cultural leaders (Rabindranath Tagore (1861–1941) was modern Bengal's most famous poet and novelist).

The middle classes became financially and psychologically tethered to the British. New jobs brought higher incomes and prestige. Social advances inevitably resulted in a measure of ideological affiliation with the colonizers. The Bengali middle classes had been singularly loyal during the 1857 revolt and continued to cooperate with the British well into the twentieth century. Many became moderate nationalists who assessed the worth of British rule more by its performance than with regard to its alien origins.

THREE BENGALI HINDU NATIONALISTS: MODERATE, PROTO-EXTREMIST, AND CULTURAL

The middle class enchantment with Western ways was epitomized by the Bengali moderate nationalist Surendranath Banerjea (1848–1926). The precocious product of a Eurasian school, Banerjea was pushed by his Anglicized physician father to compete for entry into the ICS. Well educated in a Western curriculum, Banerjea easily passed the exam. As a result, he became one of a handful of Indians who entered the ICS prior to World War I. Three years later he was dismissed on a technicality. The underlying reason appears to have been race discrimination. Banerjea took his grievance to England but failed to win reinstatement. He then tried to become a lawyer but despite his mental agility, he failed at that as well. Undaunted, he returned home and launched successful journalistic and political careers. In 1876 he founded a middle class interest group, the Indian Association, and nine years later (in 1885) he joined the Indian National Congress, the organization that subsequently spearheaded the nationalist movement against the *raj*. Banerjea served as president of the Congress and remained an influence within it into the early 1900s.

Banerjea's politics were typically restrained and plaintive. His horizons were set by principles acquired through Western learning and laid down by India's British rulers. He favored legal and orderly protests in defense of threatened Indian rights. He repeatedly reminded the British of their ideals. In 1883 he found himself thrust into the political fray when, in his capacity as newspaper editor, he publicly accused a British judge of religious insensitivity when he allegedly ordered a Hindu stone idol brought into court as case evidence (a blasphemy in Hindu eyes). In an atmosphere made tense by the Ilbert agitation, Indian criticisms of the British became less tolerated and despite an apology, Banerjea was jailed for contempt of court. "Surrender Not" Banerjea became an overnight hero, the darling of Calcutta's Westernized students, a victim of heavy footed imperialism.

Twenty years later, at a pivotal moment in modern Indian history, Banerjea was conspicuously out of touch with more militant nationalist currents. The crisis began in 1905 when Lord Curzon, the viceroy, administratively divided the province of Bengal. Justified by Curzon that the province was too large and unwieldy, partition was interpreted by Bengalis as a divide and rule ploy intended to defuse nationalism by breaking up the Bengali political community and placing it under divided jurisdictions. Partition sparked instant and widespread protests. Bengal exploded with strikes, street demonstrations, and a boycott of British goods (called *swadeshi* meaning a reliance on domestically produced goods). Sympathetic demonstrations were held in other provinces. Within a couple of years a revolutionary terrorism emerged among Bengal's bourgeois youth that resulted in a number of shootings, bombings, and assassinations.

In this climate, Banerjea's call for peaceful, legitimate protest appeared flaccid. He was vilified by the extremist nationalist press as a brown sahib, more at ease in British than Indian circles. Some evidence of this has been supplied by Banerjea himself in his autobiography, *A Nation in The Making*. In many ways, the work is a classic artifact of the Anglicized mind-set. It is replete with British historical and literary allusions and is written in a style highlighted by English idioms. Capable of fiery indignation and stumping oratory, Banerjea more often engaged in quiet work on behalf of *bhadralok* and broader Indian interests. He preferred reform from within. Between the 1890s and 1920s he held various nominated and elected posts on Calcutta's municipal corporation (city council) and the provincial and Imperial legislative councils. Later he served as a minister exercising executive authority on behalf of the *raj*. Rewarded with a knighthood toward the end of his life, the gadfly "Surrender Not" Banerjea had become the pliable Sir Surendranath.

Along with other moderates, Banerjea carved out a position that was both loyalist and patriotic. In the late 1800s it was possible to see imperialism and nationalism as compatible ideologies. Not only was (Indian) national development conceived of as consistent with (British) imperial management, it was argued that imperialism was actually necessary to the nation-building process. Like others who saw no contradiction in being pro-British and patriotic, Banerjea regarded British rule as vital to Indian moral and material recovery. Though increasingly impatient with alternating policies of coercion and conciliation, moderates remained fairly well disposed to their masters.

For Bankimchandra Chatterjee (1838–1894), the foremost Bengali literary figure of his day, Western knowledge led to a detailed re-examination of Indian culture and history that spawned a renewed pride in India and a less worshipful view of Britain. From there others proceeded to a systematic criticism of British rule. Although Bankim—as he is known—never articulated such a blanket critique, his patriotic novels, songs, and poems contributed mightily to a more favorable reassessment of Indian capabilities.

Bankim came from the same Westernized high caste Hindu background as Banerjea. A graduate of Calcutta University, he served the imperial administration for more than thirty years as a deputy magistrate. Steeped in the Western aesthetic tradition, he considered Shakespeare superior to Kalidasa (the Indian classical poet) and preferred Greek sculpture to Indian statuary. But his politics remained more resistant to Western biases. Although his literary works utilized a Western form of critical analysis, he relied on familiar Bengali images. He used both on behalf of Bengali patriotism. The British comprehended the seditious potential of his works and perhaps his most famous patriotic novel, *Anandamath* ("The Abbey of Bliss," 1882), was the cause of Bankim's demotion. This turned out to be a prophetic if backhanded tribute to the work's popularity. After his death it was adopted as the unofficial bible of Bengal's first generation of revolutionaries. That Bankim had intended a greater impact for his works was indicated by his decision to write in the vernacular Bengali. Indeed, he became a master of Bengali prose and elevated his native language into a respected and spirited form of literary expression.

In his historical novels, Bankim contributed to a revival of indigenous cultural forms without indiscriminately denouncing the British. Bankim's examples of national vitality blended Indian elements with Western ones. At times, he contrasted the vigor, initiative, and persistence of the English with the fatalistic languor of his own people. Much of the latter he attributed to the crushing impact of earlier Muslim rule. But he also reached back into Indian history and lore, where he found instructive examples of Hindu strength and purpose. He celebrated lord Krishna of the ancient Indian epic the *Mahabharata* as an inspirational example of courage, determination, and personal sacrifice on behalf of the larger community.

Bankim's thought is a good illustration of the middle class' dual reliance on colonial and Indian sources of inspiration. Acculturated Indians of his time often found themselves estranged from their own culture. But Macaulay's prophecy of equality with the colonizer still eluded these "brown Englishmen." Frustrated personal ambition, along with less self-interested concerns, led to the formation of the Indian National Congress and a politics of discontent. What is important to stress here is that their concerns were increasingly referenced to indigenous thought and practice. Sometimes this took a symbolic form as when Banerjea, who acknowledged the orthodox Hindu influence of his grandfather, donned the sacred thread—a religious initiation emblem worn only by the higher castes—at an anti-partition rally in 1905.

BANDE MATARAM

Bankim is well known for his Bengali anthem, Bande Mataram *(Hail to Thee, Mother), the "Star-Spangled Banner" of the early twentieth century nationalist movement. In these two stanzas from a longer poem, note the primordial love of place, the invocation of unity based on a shared cultural and geographical identity, and the not-so-implicit revolutionary threat.*

Mother, I bow to thee!
Rich with thy hurrying streams,
Bright with thy orchard gleams,
Cool with thy winds of delight,
Dark fields waving, Mother of might,
Mother Free.

Who hath said thou art weak in thy lands,
When the swords flash out in twice seventy million hands
And seventy million voices roar
Thy dreadful name from shore to shore?
With many strengths who are mighty and stored,
To thee I call, Mother and Lord!

Source: Wm. Theodore de Bary, ed., *Sources of Indian Tradition, Vol. II* (New York: Columbia University Press, 1958), p. 159.

The selective adulation of India's past and equally selective adoption of Western modes and ideas was also characteristic of Swami Vivekananda (born Narendranath Datta, 1863–1902). As a young man, his plans to study law in England had to be scrapped when his father's sudden death ruined the family's finances. A philosophical adept—the same Reverend Hastie who charged Miss Pigot with fornication declared him the brightest pupil he had encountered at any university, Indian, British, or German—Vivekananda's inquisitive intellect was redirected by a chance encounter with the holy man Ramakrishna. Impressed by Ramakrishna's egoless spirituality, he embarked on a disciplehood that commenced with a decade of worldly renunciation. After his guru's death Vivekananda became the global emissary for Hinduism, "representing" it at the First World Parliament of Religions held in Chicago in 1893. There the relentless intelligence and open sincerity of the man whom the American press dubbed the "Cyclonic Hindu" made a lasting impression on delegates and raised India's global stature. Indeed, prior to Gandhi, he was arguably the best known and regarded Indian on the world scene. His extended visit to Europe and the United States (1893–1897) resulted in a wide following of Western admirers. When he returned home, it was to a growing public acclaim. The Western stamp of approval had transformed Vivekananda into a Hindu hero in India, which was, ironically, yet another sign of India's cultural dependency on the West.

Vivekananda's gospel was one of social uplift. He dwelt among illiterate, struggling peasants, something very few middle class reformers would ever have considered. Through his actions, he demonstrated his conviction that the village community was the seat of Indian civilization and the peasantry India's most vital resource. He invoked generative tendencies within Hinduism to revive village industries and restore self-respect. The West could help by sharing some of its affluence but it could supply no effective model for Indian regeneration. Machines, Vivekananda argued, did not produce bliss and the technological feats of the West, however impressive, were puny compared with the titanic powers of nature. Science, medicine, and gadgetry had their uses but knowledge of the divine soul would ultimately lead to a more sustainable physical and spiritual growth. By such means, India would save itself and instruct the world.

As a nonpolitical exponent of cultural nationalism, Vivekananda focused on Hinduism. He advocated discarding modern corruptions that sanctioned caste prejudice and widow oppression. Like other Hindu revivalists who favored social reform and were sharp critics of unthinking defenders of the status quo, he counseled a return to the fundamentals of Hinduism. He contended that shorn of its impurities, Hinduism's vital forces would surge forth, inaugurating a new golden age for India. To British critics and their Indian allies, he rejected the proposition that morally dubious Hindu practices reflected a deeper cultural malaise. Vivekananda loudly railed against blind obedience to venal brahmins (priests) and instead urged the cultivation of self-reliance. An athlete, gymnast, and dancer he continuously cited the ancient Indian epic, the *Bhagavad Gita*, with its examples of bodily and spiritual strength. He justified beef-eating not only as necessary for combating the British but on the grounds that it was an authentic Aryan practice still observed by certain warrior groups and castes. In all this he sometimes flashed his sense of humor, as when he summed up his own recipe for national revival as the "three Bs": beef, biceps, and *Bhagavad Gita*.

Despite his strong sectarian identification, Vivekananda was more ecumenical than many Hindu revivalists. He borrowed from Jain and Buddhist traditions. And, though put off by the crusading vanity and colonizing propensity of Christianity, he prized Christ's ethical message. More important was his appreciation of Islam's spiritual clarity and his personal friendships with Muslims. This set him apart from Bankim and more orthodox Hindu political figures such as B. G. Tilak whose communal chauvinism helped to drive a wedge between Hindus and Muslims. He also managed to weld an ideological partnership between Hindu spiritualism and Western science.

Each of these figures and the "schools" they represented—moderate, extremist, cultural—helped to mold Indian nationalist thought. Moderates like Banerjea fashioned an Indian nationality based on the borrowed

European experience of nation-building and on Western notions of what constituted a nation. India would be rebuilt along Western lines simply because Europe offered the most compelling model of progress. Their enthusiasm for the West was both genuine and defective because, although they assessed Europe's current condition accurately enough, they failed to appreciate its historical antecedents. They presumed that institutions and practices that had first evolved in the West were universal and transportable anywhere, intact, without serious regard for the particularities of India's past and present.

VIVEKANANDA'S EMPIRE OF THE SOUL

In this speech after his triumphant tour of the West, Vivekananda mapped an Indian course for global domination which might be seen as a form of reverse cultural imperialism. What might have been its real purpose?

This is the great ideal before us, and every one must be ready for it—the conquest of the whole world by India—nothing less than that, and we must all get ready for it, strain every nerve for it. Let foreigners come and flood the land with their armies, never mind. Up, India, and conquer the world with your spirituality! . . . The whole of the Western world is a volcano which may burst tomorrow, go to pieces tomorrow. They have searched every corner of the world and have found no respite . . . Now is the time to work so that India's spiritual ideas may penetrate deep into the West . . . The only condition of national life, of awakened and vigorous national life, is the conquest of the world by Indian thought.

Source: Wm. Theodore de Bary, ed., *Sources of Indian Tradition, Vol. II* (New York: Columbia University Press, 1958), p. 100.

Moderates conceived of an India that corresponded not to the geographical boundaries of the ancient Mauryas or the accomplishments of the early modern Mughals but to British India's borders and achievements. Consistent with their cosmopolitan temperament, the moderates constructed an inclusive definition of "Indian": all the peoples of the British-ruled subcontinent irrespective of caste, religion, or language. Furthermore, they were optimistic that an Indian nation would emerge whose people would share a common identity and a common urge to control their own united destiny. The moderate aim, therefore, was to press the British to progress steadily toward that point.

Moderates conceded that Britain had supplied some of the necessary components for the emergence of an Indian national consciousness. First, the British had imposed a political-administrative unity. Second, the use of the English language enabled interregional discussions among Indians on terms of linguistic equality. Third, the middle classes themselves were the historical product of conditions shaped by colonialism. Fourth, exchanges and diffusions of ideas among nationalists across India were made possible by a British-built infrastructure of a transport-print capitalism: roads, trains, postal systems, newspapers, and telegraphs. Lastly, Westernized Indians were familiar with concrete examples of nation-building. The rise of Britain was revealed in self-congratulatory history lessons and the literary patriotism of the likes of Shakespeare and Defoe. Italian unification (1850s–1860s) provided a more contemporary blue-print and Mazzini's nationalist formulations as well as Garibaldi's popular exploits were greatly admired.

A younger generation of "extremists" who transformed the exuberant literary patriotism of Bankim into an insistent political agenda, offered a vision that was at once narrower and more expansive than that of the moderates. The extremists privileged certain traditions (such as Hinduism) to the exclusion of others. But by venturing into local popular cultures, relying on familiar and cherished religious symbols, and wielding vernacular tongues, they managed to forge tenuous links with urban and rural classes. At the same time, extremists studied past French and Irish insurrections and cultivated an inflammatory anti-British politics that culminated in challenging Britain's right to rule. The goal became *swaraj* (self-rule) and power-sharing with the colonizers was simply a means to that end. Extremists never rejected Western knowledge, norms, or institutions but they utilized indigenous concepts and practices more frequently than did their moderate counterparts.

The extremist critique began with an acknowledgment that Indians were responsible for their own plight at the onset of British colonialism. But from there they rapidly proceeded to indict the British for deepening India's poverty and moral malaise. Extremists questioned the nature, even the fact, of some of the progress that had occurred under British rule. They gradually edged towards a position that many nationalists openly assumed in the post-war period: that alien rule was an incapable and destructive rule because it could not comprehend indigenous patterns of life or understand the people. Physically and psychologically garrisoned, intolerant, and fastened to their metropolitan home base, the British were especially vulnerable to this charge. The extremists grasped with a piercing incisiveness that the British were the first of India's many conquerors to resist assimilation ("Indianization").

Conversant with both indigenous and foreign experiences, cultural nationalists mounted a large scale unearthing of India's past. They promoted the use of local vernaculars in lieu of alien English and sponsored the cultivation of the ancient scriptural language, Sanskrit. They advocated new research into Indian antiquities, sought to reinvigorate Indian medicine, and began to rehabilitate ancient and medieval Indian knowledge. At one end of the cultural nationalist spectrum were the antire-formist orthodox who met the cultural threat of the West with an uncompromising defense of native tradition. At the other end were critics of Indian habits and attitudes who sought reform in harmony with India's precolonial traditions. These proposed a revitalized Indian (usually Hindu) culture as the defining core of a modern Indian identity. As many were highly Westernized themselves, few argued that the West had nothing to offer India. But most maintained that India's greatest asset was its own spiritual tradition.

In the process, India's middle classes had equipped themselves with a formidable nationalist ideology. And although numerous post–1914 international and Indian events intervened between the dawn of nationalism and the attainment of political independence in 1947, the first generation of nationally conscious political, literary, and religious reformers managed to construct a programmatic critique of the legitimacy and impact of British imperialism.

CONCLUSION

This chapter has examined three colonial ideologies: civilizing mission, cultural-racial exclusivity, and Western-inspired indigenous nationalism. British assumptions of superiority whether keyed to culture, race, or material achievement, buttressed and determined their dominion no less than did warships, guns, capital, and asymmetrical economic relations. The inevitable complement to the superior Westerner, was, of course, the inferior Oriental/African. The "debased" habitats and social systems of the colonized became the touchstone of the civilizing ideal. Long before they departed from Europe, prospective colonizers were well accustomed to images of colonial "barbarism" and "decadence." Non-Europeans were exoticized in the portraits of the Orientalist painters Jean-Leon Gerome and Rudolf von Ottenfeld and were caricaturized in the imperial novels of Rudyard Kipling, Pierre Loti, and Ernest Psichari. Overseas, references to "primitives" saturated bureaucratic memoranda, colonial gazettes, censuses, biblical sermons, missionary tracts, popular travelogues, and memoirs.

Superficially crude dichotomies centered on the colonizer-colonized axis also contained more subtle categories of difference defined by traits the British had ascribed to various ethnic components of the colonial population. Subsets of the colonized population (stereotyped as slothful, enterprising, agrarian, pastoral, pristine, cosmopolitan, martial, or mercantile) were ranked in accordance with a hierarchy of European notions of virtue and ability. In India, the Bengali *bhadralok* was singled out for special ridicule by the British for its "opportunistic" Anglicization, cultural "blemishes," and "insolent" politics. A hyper-masculine *raj* scorned the *babu* as effeminate, imitative, and indolent. At the same time, it praised the so-called "martial races" of Northwestern (Aryan) India: Sikhs, Jats, Pathans, and Rajputs, along with the Gurkhas of the Northeast. In the perceived robust demeanor and virile deportment of these peoples, the British fancied that they saw an approximate, if lesser, mirror image of themselves.

Imperialism governed through a denigrating image of Indians who, it was asserted, had been reduced to docile submissiveness after enduring centuries of primeval despotisms, caste oppression, and priestly superstition. According to the imperialist account, the cycle of deterioration was apt to continue because a long period of cultural decline had stunted the Indian personality. This attitude expressed itself neatly in pervasive depictions of the colonized as child. Imperialism was, in fact, aggressively paternalistic and Europeans imbued with the civilizing ethos consciously ruled in ways deemed best for the colonial "child" who, unlike real children, was unlikely ever to grow up. Characteristically, individual British military officers and bureaucrats established a tradition of styling themselves the peoples' "*ma-bap*" (mother and father).

With indigenous confidence undermined, psychological dependence was manifest in the middle class's intoxication with Western ideas and habits. But this dependence can be exaggerated and indigenous culture was resilient, quite capable of withstanding successive waves of Westernizing influences. Furthermore, European criticisms incited hearty resistance. The late-nineteenth century intellectual awakening and cultural renaissance sketched above offered a range of responses to British assertions of dominance and superiority. Of these, nationalism proved enduring and formidable. Nationalists chose selectively from the Western model of modernization as they looked to their own society for developmental guidance. In fact, the recovery of Indian self-esteem was registered in a belief in the worth and viability of native customs, systems, and institutions. Most importantly, it raised the self-image of Indians. After it acquired a mass following in the 1920s, nationalism posed a serious challenge to British rule. However, though nationalist politics had mapped a viable escape route from colonial subjugation, other developments and events—international, domestic, and British—were needed to dislodge the *raj* from the subcontinent.

Nationalism reproduced many features of modern imperialism: purposefulness, a strong group identity, disciplined self-control, and a rationalized world view. Bankimchandra Chatterjee instructed with historical examples of British patriotism. Banerjea unequivocally admired British resolve and self-confidence. Vivekananda countered imperial allegations of Indian effeminacy by building his body up with calisthenics and weights. True, extremists and cultural nationalists had boasted of a great and ancient Indian civilization that flourished when tribal Britons were painting their naked bodies blue. But that civilization had been appraised by self-consciously Western criteria: empirical evidence, inductive reasoning, rigorous logic, and verifiable methods. Themselves the products of a colonial milieu shaped by strong Western influences, Indian nationalists battled the British on terms set by the colonizers. And long after the formal collapse of empire, the psychological-intellectual legacy of imperialism abides in the Westernized outlooks and postcolonial practices of their political heirs, the governing elite of the former colonies.

FURTHER READING

Good introductions to the history of modern India are Stanley Wolpert's *A New History of India* (New York: Oxford University Press, 1993) and Judith Brown's *Modern India* (New York: Oxford University Press, 1994). A more demanding work is the incisive *Modern India: 1885–1947* (New York: St. Martin's Press, 1989) by one of India's leading historians, Sumit Sarkar. There are no comprehensive single volume treatments of British India, but an excellent study of the ethos of British imperialism in India is provided by Francis Hutchins, *The Illusion of Permanence* (Princeton, N.J.: Princeton University Press, 1967). The definitive work on the Ilbert Bill is Edwin Hirschmann, *"White Mutiny" The Ilbert Bill Crisis in India and Genesis of the Indian National Congress* (Columbia, Mo.: South Asia Books, 1980). But also see Mrinalini Sinha, "Chathams, Pitts, and Gladstone in Petticoats": The Politics of Gender and Race in the Ilbert Bill Controversy, 1883–1884," in Nupur Chaudhuri and Margaret Strobel, eds., *Western Women and Imperialism* (Bloomington: Indiana University Press, 1992). Annette Akroyd Beveridge is assessed in a chapter on British feminists and imperialism, "Britannia's Other Daughters," in Vron Ware, *Beyond the Pale: White Women, Racism, and History* (London: Verso, 1992).

British Indian social life is recalled with a heady whiff of nostalgia in: Geoffrey Moorehouse, *India Britannica* (New York: Harper & Row, 1983) and Charles Allen, ed., *Plain Tales From the Raj* (London: Futura Publications Ltd., 1977). The pioneering book on the socio-sexual milieu of the *raj* is Kenneth Ballhatchet's *Race, Sex and Class Under the Raj* (London: Weidenfeld and Nicolson, 1980). For a tantalizing exploration of sexuality in the imperial context, see Ronald Hyam, *Empire and Sexuality* (Manchester: Manchester University Press, 1991). The best overview of the late nineteenth century cultural, political, and intellectual awakening in India remains R. C. Majumdar, ed., *British Paramountcy and Indian Renaissance Part II, Volume X of The History and Culture of the Indian People* (Bombay: Bharatiya Vidya Bhavan, 1981).

An invaluable sourcebook of primary documents dealing with Indian thought under colonialism is William Theodore de Bary, ed., *Sources of Indian Tradition Volume II* (New York: Columbia University Press, 1958). A fascinating sketch of the elite Indian experience of colonialism that combines ebullient and poignant anecdotes that nicely complement those found in Allen and Moorehouse is Zareer Masani's, *Indian Tales of the Raj* (Berkeley: University of California Press, 1987). The authoritative historical sociology of India's middle classes is B. B. Misra, *The Indian Middle Classes* (London: Oxford University Press, 1961). On early Indian nationalist politics see: R. C. Majumdar, *History of the Freedom Movement in India Vol. 2* (Calcutta: Firma K. L. Mukhopadhyay, 1963); Anil Seal, *The Emergence of Indian Nationalism* (Cambridge: Cambridge University Press, 1968); and Charles Heimsath, *Indian Nationalism and Hindu Social Reform* (Princeton: Princeton University Press, 1964). On Banerjea, see Daniel Argov, *Moderates and Extremists in the Indian Nationalist Movement, 1883–1920* (London: Asia Publishing House, 1967). Four recent trends in Indian scholarship are exemplified by: Ashis Nandy, *The Intimate Enemy: Loss and Recovery of Self Under Colonialism* (Delhi: Oxford University Press, 1989), a psycho-analytic essay on the impact of imperialism on the Westernized Indian consciousness; Partha Chatterjee, *Nationalist Thought and the Colonial World* (Minneapolis: University of Minnesota Press, 1993), a theoretical investigation of colonial nationalism informed by French post-structural theory and Antonio Gramsci; Tapan Raychaudhuri, *Europe Reconsidered: Perceptions of the West in Nineteenth Century Bengal* (Delhi: Oxford University Press, 1988), which dissects the didactic cultural nationalism of Bankimchandra Chatterjee and Vivekananda; and Ranajit Guha, *Subaltern Studies* (Delhi: Oxford University Press, 1982) and the group of South Asian "subaltern" scholars who present history from below, detailing the perspectives, acts, and interests of India's vast peasantry and the less privileged inhabitants of town and country.

7

PATTERNS AND CONTEXTS

Women as Colonizers and Colonized

When Lady Nivens arrived in West Africa an official brusquely told her "this is no place for a white woman." It was a truism that empire was a male sphere, too wild and dangerous for the "delicate" sex. A contrary truism was that women posed a special threat to the empire. In 1985 the noted filmmaker Sir David Lean—director of such colonial epics as "Lawrence of Arabia," "A Passage to India," and "Ryan's Daughter"— stated that the memsahib had lost the British their empire. His comment echoed the orthodox view that white women distracted their husbands from their administrative duties, drove a wedge between ruler and ruled, interfered with the widespread practice of concubinage, and poisoned relations with their straitlaced racism. A French historian dismissed white women as parasites while a sociologist of colonialism singled out French-women in Madagascar as perniciously racist. In official and fictional literature, European women in the colonies were stereotyped as petty, bigoted, ignorant, and frivolous. Though trivialized as mere ornamental appendages, they were contradictorily saddled with the heavy responsibility of changing colonial culture for the worse.

Against this, recent scholarship has produced a more complex, subtle, and less damning interpretation. The notion that European women were the prime vectors of racism has been discredited. Outnumbered by European men by ratios ranging from two to one (Dutch East Indies) to more than twenty-five to one (French Ivory Coast), white women arrived at a time when colonial communities had achieved a size that made them more self-sufficient and required fewer informal contacts with the colonized. They also appeared just as trenchant racism was on the rise. Men no less than women exhibited racist behavior and attitudes. Nor were women a homogeneous group. They were spouses, daughters, doctors, nurses, prostitutes, missionaries, travelers, and explorers. Some were feminists who fled the constricting sexism of home in quest of adventure and independence. A greater number sought a higher standard of living in the colonies. Most were the relatives of officials, traders, professional men, and soldiers. All, however, were subject to the legal and customary codes of conduct of a colonial milieu largely set by the male colonizers.

Official attitudes frequently centered on women's sexuality and were based on the European patriarchal conceptualization of women as reproductive and nurturing mistresses of the household. They were the "bearers of their race," the vessels of their culture, and the "angels of the household." It was in this vein that French manuals exhorted colonial wives to "conserve the fitness and sometimes the life of all around them" by keeping the household "happy and gay." Contradictory views of white women as sexualized objects abounded. If unappealing, they were supposedly incapable of keeping their own mates virile and heterosexual. But as coveted members of the ruling race, even the plainest allegedly aroused the colonized male to heights of uncontrollable lust (the "Black Peril" with its overtones of insurgency). In the pages of the popular metropolitan press, the tropics became a zone of threatened sexuality and

FEMALE COLONIZERS AND COLONIZED   *In this photo, Annette Akroyd, the English feminist and wife of an ICS official, is surrounded by her pupils who were from Bengali Hindu bhadralok families. Note the attire.* (Reprinted by permission of the British Library, Oriental and India Office Collections)

deviance. White women became sterile, native women were diseased, native men were oversexed, and white men were apt to degenerate. Europeans projected onto the colonial world a pornographic image of extravagant promiscuity and perversion, dangerous yet alluring. Africa and the Orient became a feminized terrain to be entered, controlled, and possessed.

In accordance with such assumptions, the colonial state avidly policed carnal transgressions. Bowing to white male pressures, authorities in Papua New Guinea passed a "White Women's Protective Ordinance" (1926) that imposed the death penalty on alleged or real Papuan rapists of European females. Turn-of-the-century South Africa banned intercourse between African men and European women. White women were also subjected to tight surveillance. In British Rhodesia and Uganda immorality laws criminalized any lewd suggestion made by a European woman to an African man.

One way of reducing forbidden behavior was to curb the numbers of European women. The Dutch East Indies restricted female emigration by prohibiting soldiers under the rank of sergeant major from taking European wives (1872). Prior to 1920 the British colonies of Africa, Southeast Asia, and the Caribbean discouraged their officers from marrying. (French and German colonies in Africa, however, paid the passages of their officials' spouses.) When French feminists urged skilled women to settle in Indochina, colonial authorities cited a surfeit of French penniless widows and underemployed seamstresses and florists competing against cheap, skilled Chinese labor as countervailing arguments. Rejecting the *petit-blanc* (poor white) model of Algeria, French Indochina actually shipped widows backed to France. South Africa, by contrast, welcomed female domestic servants recruited by the British Women's Emigration Association who promised genteel work, enhanced marriage prospects, and a chance to civilize the world and preserve British culture.

The imperial lifestyle offered middle-class women certain advantages: legions of servants, the support of the state, and certified social privileges. Yet innumerable discomforts and dangers preoccupied women and life in the colonies was in reality more restrictive than in the metropole. Health was a constant worry and confinement and delivery were particularly perilous situations. Miscarriages and infant mortality rates were significantly higher in the tropical dependencies. Moreover, women lacked the support of kith and kin, the comfort of a familiar cultural environment, and the amenities of modern life that they had enjoyed in Europe. Family routine and stability were frequently disrupted. Social life was frequently numbing and middle-class women were compelled to mark time with banal conversations and endless rounds of visitations.

A few women, however, led more independent lives. Throughout French West and North Africa, for instance, many women earned incomes as farmers, boarding house proprietors, and shopkeepers. And then there were the conspicuous exceptions: the African traveler-explorer Mary Kingsley, the anti-imperialist-feminist South African writer Olive

Schreiner, and the theosophist-nationalist in India, Annie Besant, each of whom led famous and somewhat controversial lives. A few delved into indigenous culture. The adventurer Isabelle Eberhardt, for instance, gained notoriety in the French Mahgreb by following a female sufi saint, converting to Islam, and "passing" as an elite Arab male. Some women were "maternal imperialists" who took up "The White Woman's Burden" as nurses, missionaries, and social reformers. Many of these combined feminism and imperialism in the name of the civilizing mission, educating the wives of Westernized indigenes, working for female uplift, and decrying such practices as infibulation, clitoridectomy, and *sati*. At times, French, Dutch, Belgian, and British authorities encouraged such interventionist efforts and many women who worked for women's causes did so within the unquestioned framework of imperialism. Several were leading imperialists in their own right. Arguably the most famous was Flora Shaw who served as the Colonial Editor of *The Times* of London. Shaw became the staunch supporter of archimperialists Cecil Rhodes and Sir George Goldie, and later the influential wife of Frederick Lugard, one of Britain's most influential proconsuls. It was she who coined "Nigeria," the name of Africa's most populous state.

Though clearly subordinate, women had a limited impact on empire. On the one hand, their presence did alter interpersonal relations between ruler and ruled. They opposed concubinage. Their arrival was accompanied by houses partitioned into racially segregated quarters, enclosed household compounds, formalized servant relations, and set prescriptions governing interracial socializing. But almost always these conditions and innovations were initiated by European men. At the same time, women acted as the conscious agents of imperial culture as exemplified by Annette Beveridge. Although capable of serving as interpreters of indigenous societies to the West, colonial women were seldom able to transcend their own racist-imperialist bias or perceive affinities with native women.

It has been argued that the condition of colonized women—their seclusion, domesticity, and overriding function as sex providers—reinforced European women's sense of their own superiority and blunted the impact of the gender discrimination they experienced in their own cultures. European men and women equally rejected indigenous institutions and customs. At the same time, women's prescribed roles as homemaker, nurturer, and the guardian of Western culture were even more imperative in the alien colonial setting than at home. In sum, white women were either disinclined or precluded from exerting much of an impact on the course of colonial interpersonal relations or legislation whether positively or negatively.

With indigenous women the picture is considerably cloudier. Arriving at an interpretive consensus has been impeded by the formative state of scholarship and by the host of variables that conditioned women's lives in the colonial period. To cite only a few, the conditions and experiences of women under colonialism were determined by differing time periods, colonial rulers and policies, local traditions, and the class-social-marital status of colonized women. Another problem arises from the minute number of works currently available. The overwhelming preponderance of textual evidence was written by and for men, yielding a distortive view of women as passive, shadowy, or irrelevant. With these limitations, what follows must be selective. The patterns tentatively proposed here are based on examples drawn entirely from British sub-Saharan Africa and India. Most concern indigenous women and the colonial state and economy, echoing the emphasis of most studies of women in the colonial era, with less attention given to sociocultural agents of empire such as missionaries, doctors, and teachers who also exerted powerful influences over women's lives.

Commercial and industrial capitalism that frequently accompanied colonialism played a crucial, if varied, role. It often increased labor gender differentiation and assigned women to the margins of the export economy, most often as subsistence farmers. In late-nineteenth century Bengal, for example, the participation of women in short-distance trade and local manufacturing declined as European domination of the economy increased. Most new industrial jobs in Calcutta were seized by men, as women were constrained by old prohibitions against physical and occupational mobility. As these prohibitions were usually enforced by male relatives, the majority of women employed in Calcutta mills in the 1890s were either widows or deserted wives without children. But overall, industrializing Calcutta became a male preserve (the female percentage of the urban population of Bengal proper fell from 45 percent in 1881 to 38 percent in 1911) with more women engaged in subsistence agriculture.

The disruptive dynamics of capitalism were frequently supported by the colonial state. In parts of Southern Africa a gender-differentiated dual economy formed with mostly young African men housed in distant same-sex compounds and contracted to work for European-owned mines and plantations while women were consigned to rural reserves where they fed families and subsidized the wages of migrant males through subsistence cultivation. When sexual liaisons in rural reserves suggested to colonial officials the presence of males who had escaped from the work compounds, Southern Rhodesia (Zimbabwe) passed a Natives Adultery Punishment Ordinance (1916). This ordinance was designed to press able-bodied males back into the migrant labor force by imposing severe fines on sexually active men and women. In Nigeria, colonial authorities tried to regulate the location and operation of markets managed by Yoruba women, a good example of efforts to limit the independence of female producers and retailers. Several African colonies passed laws restricting female mobility.

The colonial state and economy also reinforced indigenous patriarchies. In the peasant agrarian economy of the Gold Coast (Ghana), women had traditionally performed much of the farming within the framework of an exploitative indigenous system of female labor governed by male elders. In colonial Gold Coast women found themselves performing a similar role in cocoa production, the colony's chief export crop. As such, they sustained both the indigenous patriarchy and the colonial economy as field laborers, porters, and sometimes as pawns—that is, their labor was literally mortgaged to other relatives so that husbands, fathers, and uncles could buy land for export crop cultivation. While some women became traders and a few owned cocoa farms many more were reduced to debt servitude. In numerous instances, unpaid female labor subsidized the low wages paid to males. This enabled employers to maximize profits and produce exceptionally cheap products for the European market. In addition, women's social status declined as household survival became more dependent on men's wages and less on women's food production.

Many changes legislated by the colonial state resulted from the gendered attitudes of Europeans. A key target of civilizing mission propaganda was the debased condition of indigenous women. Colonialist writers and officials like James Mill argued that the condition of women was a barometer of a society's level of civilization. They cited *sati* and foot-binding, bridewealth and widow oppression, childhood marriages and enslaved labor, and enforced seclusion and genital mutilation as examples of Asian oppression and African depravity as well as justifications for colonialist interventions. Accordingly, a number of reforms ensued. In India, *sati* was abolished (1828), Hindu widows were permitted to remarry (1856), and the age at which an Indian female could give consent to having intercourse was raised from 10 to 12 (1893). Yet recent scholarship has stressed the important role of small groups of indigenous reformers in inducing a reluctant *raj* to act as well as the mixed motives that prompted the British—as much to condemn Indian society (and Indian men) as to alleviate the plight of Indian women, all somehow without unduly antagonizing deeply held native sensibilities. It is also clear that many reforms were unenforceable or effectively resisted by the local populations (*sati* was an exception).

As stated earlier, Europeans brought with them set notions of women as nonproductive; they were relegated to the domestic sphere of the household, excluded from the world of politics and market place, and designated the primary reproductive agent within the boundaries of a monogamous marriage. These ideas shaped colonial practices and policies in various ways. For one, formal systems of female education were introduced that, in India, produced for indigenous elite males wives instructed in the efficient arts of household management, virtuous motherhood, and wifely companionship. These roles harmonized well with the emergent Indian nationalist image of the respectable, self-sacrificing, monogamous, and subservient "new woman." The Hindu reformer Vivekananda advocated female education so that women could better fulfill their natural destinies within the family. With such notions of a fixed female nature, elite indigenous and colonial patriarchies merged. On the other hand, the nationalist movement did accommodate limited female input in areas as diverse as politics and gynecological and infant hygiene even as women's subordinate status remained intact.

The Victorian domestic ideology of separate gendered spheres sometimes produced bizarre results along the colonial periphery. In colonial Africa, it influenced the redesign of homes from a round to a square format supposedly to inculcate civilized habits. Tswana women were banned from plough agriculture by Europeans who judged such activities as unduly onerous. African men were trained as carpenters and women who formerly constructed houses were urged to turn to sewing and cooking. Matrilineal social networks that afforded women some authority and autonomy within a kinship system of male patronage and shared rights and responsibilities were assailed under colonialism. The result was a diminution of security and support afforded to women by customary family arrangements. Among the Bemba of Northern Rhodesia (Zambia), for example, the ritual of temporarily incorporating the groom into the wife's family was subverted by a British law that permitted a husband to remove his bride from her family with the payment of a bride price. With commercialization of the economy under colonialism, bride price was increasingly paid in cash instead of cloth or cattle. This converted a complex exchange that forged interfamilial alliances into a straightforward transaction that was consistent with the mistaken colonial notion that wives were the properties of their husbands in some African societies.

Polygamy was frequently outlawed with results that were not always favorable to women. Monogamous unions often intensified male control and, as the wife no longer shared household duties with other wives, there was often less time and freedom to engage in crafts production and trade. Colonial laws that consistently awarded custody of children to fathers were a setback for the Shona and Ndebele women of Southern Rhodesia, who under customary law, could have cited extenuating circumstances to gain custody. Generally speaking, flexible indigenous custom was rendered rigid by codified colonial law that seems on balance to have worked against women. For example, when the British generalized Indian custom that had traditionally governed only an upper caste minority, they extended to the entire Hindu population bans on female ownership of property, divorce, and polygamy. (Property ownership was irrelevant, of course, to the masses of impoverished peasants.)

Other innovations, such as the institution of conjugal rights (which allowed a husband to force his absent wife to return to him), often had no basis in precolonial law. Another was a wider surveillance of women's bodies. Fears of a depopulated (and therefore unproductive) Uganda prompted officials to apply stringent medical and moral hygiene regimens to women to halt the spread of sexually transmitted diseases. By examining female genitalia and instructing women to mend their "immoral"

ways, colonial doctors placed women at the heart of a physical-moral reproductive order increasingly influenced by European ideas.

One trend in colonial policy apparent by the late 1800s was the active support of traditional institutions and practices, including those of a
patriarchal nature. By that time the reformist zeal of European officials
and missionaries was waning and the colonizers were becoming concerned about threats to the indigenous social order posed by capitalistic
forces. As a result, requests by village elders and chiefs for help in con-
trolling independent women met with sympathetic official responses.
When Akan women of the Gold Coast formally challenged customary
practices that tied them to their husbands and fathers, colonial courts
strongly allied themselves with the customary courts and helped to con-
strain the discontented women.

In Bengal, the British held aloof from local patriarchal efforts to re-
construct a female popular culture. Among the women of the *bhadralok*,
a refined feminine culture was displacing an earthy, less submissive culture expressed by women's poems, songs, dances, and dramatic perfor-
mances. Actresses, female poets, dancers, and players were denounced as
vulgar and driven to the margins of Bengali society. Though an initiative
of the *bhadralok*, this campaign was in part a cultural nationalist response
to biting British criticism of Indian culture and the depressed status of
women. As such it was a part of the self-conscious sanctification of the
private household, symbolized by an idealized (Hindu) mother figure,
and declared off-limits to British interference.

Of course, initiative was no monopoly of colonial authorities and
indigenous men; women's actions and responses shaped their own lives as
well. Some women were able to take advantage of new attitudes and
changing conditions. For instance, the educated wives of the *bhadralok*
absorbed the ideas of their male relatives and put them to their own use.
This was apparent in a turn-of-the-century literary output by women
that expressed a "new woman" household ideology often linked to wider
social, political, and cultural concerns. In addition, Indian female literacy
inched up from 0.4 percent in 1891 to 2.1 percent in 1921. Between 1901
and 1921 the percentage of women who were literate in English more
than doubled (albeit from an infintesimal 0.07 percent to a miniscule 0.18
percent). By 1901 some 250 women were enrolled in Indian colleges. In
the 1880s university-educated Indian women became doctors and Cor-
nelia Sorabji became the first to graduate from Oxford with a law degree
(though women could not practice law in India until 1923). Perhaps the
foremost feminist of the time was Pandita Ramabai (1858–1922).
Schooled in Sanskrit, Indian history, and religion, Ramabai founded
women's organizations, wrote emancipation tracts, toured the United
States, Canada, and Britain, and attended sessions of the Indian National
Congress. A contemporary, Amina Tyabji, was a pioneer of Indian Muslim girls schools.

Other women rejected the models and resisted the intrusions of the colonial state and economy. In Africa, many spurned the companionate helpmate archetype preached by missionaries and resisted state efforts to increase their economic dependence on their male guardians. Older religious and secular traditions empowered women to oppose colonial policies. In late-nineteenth century Southern Rhodesia, Nehanda, a woman spirit medium, led a vigorous anti-colonial movement. In 1857 a Xhosa prophetess, Nonqawuse, had Afro-Christian apocalyptic visions of mass destruction followed by a redemptive resurrection that won her a substantial following in South Africa and sparked a major protest against a culturally and spiritually abrasive colonialism. In eastern Nigeria in 1929, Igbo and Ibibio speaking women rose up in opposition to new colonial taxes. They attacked colonial offices, freed prisoners, and raided European trade depots. But a salient feature of the Women's War of 1929 was the use of humiliating taunts—protesting women openly dared colonial troops to impregnate them—that underscored the unique powers of women based on their fertility and reproductive capabilities, attributes customarily devalued under patriarchal regimes.

Colonial capitalism also created limited opportunities for enterprising women. South African women who were abused or deserted by their husbands or accused of witchcraft were able at times to escape to colonial cities, European-owned mineral or agricultural work compounds, or rural Christian missions. There they became petty brewers and beer sellers, prostitutes, servants, and missionary pupils. That they were willing to endure a life of precarious prosperity, indigenous stigma, or overbearing white supervision suggests that these new circumstances were preferable to those they had abandoned. With or without male patronage, some of the female migrants to these colonial enclaves managed to evade laws that forbad them access to land, housing, or waged employment.

From these examples, the record of imperialism seems a mixed one. Neither the imperialist self-portrait of dogged efforts to emancipate women nor the nationalist vision of precolonial gender egalitarianism quashed by misogynist colonizers has withstood scholarly interrogation. A number of studies by feminist historians and anthropologists have revealed a colonial patriarchy that complexly colluded with an entrenched indigenous patriarchy. Traditionally subordinate, non-elite women became engaged in subsistence agriculture that was increasingly marginalized in an export market-oriented colonial economy.

At the same time, European humanitarianism created a reformist legislative agenda that had a finite impact on women's lives. The most to benefit were elite women. Those in India gained from formal education, new professional occupations, the eradication of *sati*, and diminished enforced seclusion. But improved prospects and new escape routes were also available for women of a lower status who fled and resisted customary forms of gender subjugation in Southern Africa. West African women demonstrated that it was also possible to seize opportunities in a peasant-based cash crop economy. In terms of political objectives, neither imperialism nor prewar nationalism proposed real gender equality. In some ways nationalism fused colonial and traditional practice to maintain women in subservient roles. Thus, while some women's lives improved between 1870 and 1914, these examples suggest that most probably experienced a decline—or at best no improvement—in their status and condition relative to those of men.

FURTHER READING

For white women and modern imperialism a number of important works have appeared over the last decade. Most of these concentrate on the British Empire. Two welcome introductory anthologies are: Mona Etienne and Eleanor Leacock, eds., *Women and Colonization* (New York: Praeger, 1980) and Hilary Callan and Shirley Ardenes, eds., *The Incorporated Wife* (London: Croom Helm, 1984). Nupur Chaudhuri and Margaret Strobel, eds., *Western Women and Imperialism: Complicity and Resistance* (Bloomington: Indiana University Press, 1992) explores the complex intermediate and intermediary role of European women in India, Africa, and the Middle East. Margaret Strobel's model analyses of intention, impact, myths, and realities of women in the colonial empires can be found in *European Women and the Second British Empire* (Bloomington: Indiana University Press, 1991) and in "Gender, Sex and Empire" in Michael Adas, ed., *Islamic and European Expansion* (Philadelphia: Temple University Press, 1993). Ann Laura Stoler has authored a number of pathbreaking articles that weave empire, gender, sexuality, and race together in the setting of Dutch and French Southeast Asia. For example, see: "Carnal Knowledge and Imperial Power: Gender, Race, and Morality in Colonial Asia" in Micaela di Leonardo, ed., *Gender at the Crossroads of Knowledge: Feminist Anthropology in the Postmodern Era* (Berkeley: University of California Press, 1991). Also see Helen Callaway's influential *Gender, Culture and Empire: European Women in Colonial Nigeria* (Urbana, Ill.: University of Illinois Press, 1987). Finally, for a comparative set of biographies of "lady" explorers, travelers, and missionaries in Africa see Caroline Oliver, *Western Women in Colonial Africa* (Westport, Conn.: Greenwood Press, 1982).

With a dearth of macroimperial synthetic surveys or comparativist collections, the experiences, voices, and significations of colonized women viewed as active agents and not as passive victims (as traditional historiography has tended to view them) is still best found in a number of specific, more narrowly focused studies. This is especially true of sub-Saharan Africa. These works have typically appeared in women's studies and feminist journals (e.g., *Journal of Women's History, Signs, Women's Studies International Forum, and Feminist Review*) or are embedded within other transgendered topics (e.g., legal, labor, social, sexual, development, and anthropological histories and studies). A worthy exception to this is Cheryl Johnson-Odim and Margaret Strobel, eds., *Restoring Women to History* (New York: Organization of American Historians, 1988) which sketches a cross-cultural historical overview that encompasses the colonial period.

The impacts of colonialism on sub-Saharan African women are treated in some of the contributions to Claire C. Robertson and Iris Berger, eds., *Women and Class in Africa* (New York: Africana Publishing Co., 1986) and in Margaret Jean Hay and Marcia Wright, *African Women and the Law: Historical Perspectives* (Boston: Boston University Press, 1982). Focused explorations of ruptures and continuities in the lives of South African women as they experienced capitalism, acculturation, and new forms of patriarchy are presented in Cheryl Walker, ed., *Women and Gender in South Africa to 1945* (Cape Town: David Philip, 1990).

India has been better served. Kumkum Sangari and Sudesh Vaid, eds., *Recasting Women: Essays in Indian Colonial History* (New Brunswick, N.J.: Rutgers University Press, 1990) offer a variety of selections that are indebted to the nonelite school of subaltern studies and examine gender in connection with the paradigms of modernity versus tradition, class and caste, capitalist modes of production, and colonial nationalism. Also for India see: M. Kaur, *Women in India's Freedom Struggle* (Delhi: Sterling Publishers, 1985) and Bisheswar Nanda, *Indian Women: From Purdah to Modernity* (Delhi: Vikas Publications, 1976). For articulate, upper caste Bengali women (*bhadramahila*) see Meredith Borthwick, *The Changing Role of Women in Bengal, 1849–1905* (Princeton, N.J.: Princeton University Press, 1984) and Ghulam Murshid, *Reluctant Debutante: Response of Bengali Women to Modernization, 1849–1905* (Rajshahi: Rajshahi University Press, 1983).

CONCLUSION

Whatever the multiplicity of forces and complexity of circumstances that promoted the formal extension of the Western empires, the actual colonial encounters themselves—patterns of subjugation, resistance, readjustment, and accommodation—reveal much that is of value about the idea and the practice of modern imperialism. They not only help us to understand something of the conditions, thoughts, and actions of those who lived in different times and in different cultures from our own, but also to better appreciate the considerable legacy of modern imperialism on the nations, cultures, and peoples of today. Western intrusions were transformative all along the periphery.

Imperialism fostered change in a number of ways. It was tied to the creation of a global mesh of financial, investment, and service networks. It extended the reach of industrialism outward from its European source by providing Westerners with the ability to enter and control African, Asian, and Oceanic sites and by provisioning them with at least the semblance of a modern transportation-communications infrastructure. It also sponsored overseas capitalism by encouraging market-oriented production, creating export sector enclaves, and developing monocultural colonial economies (such as in Hawaii and the Congo where sugar and rubber were respectively dominant).

At the same time, social customs that evolved in an urbanizing, industrializing, and bourgeois European environment were transported to very different social settings by imperialism. With Westerners as the ruling elite, the cultural values and artifacts of the new masters (dress, tools, household possessions, and the like) became the aspired norm for some of the colonized. Lastly and most obviously, imperialism introduced new political ideas, institutions, and processes—not to mention new boundaries that remain one of imperialism's sturdiest legacies—that established new systems of governance, law, and order on the one hand and new forms of political identity, loyalty, and resistance on the other.

In other words, territorial imperialism was an integral part of a broader diffusion of Western peoples and Western civilization across the globe. It was the most visible form of Western dominance. But it was not,

157

as some have said, a mere interlude in the drama of conquering capitalism or the tip of the iceberg of a devouring Western culture.

Although the era of colonial development (when the colonizers targeted the colonial economies for systematic growth and expropriation) came after 1914, the pre-World War I period was hardly bereft of ideas regarding colonial governance. One of the most widespread and pragmatic involved placing Europeans atop existing indigenous structures of rule (known variously in colonial Africa as indirect rule, association, *politique de grands turbans*, *politique indigène*, and *politique des races*) which was not as noninterfering in native society as it might at first glance appear. Yet colonial rule usually had fairly limited aims: to reap a respectable profit wherever possible, enhance European power, and maintain order.

Colonial rule incorporated both modern and traditional practices. On the one hand, colonial regimes propped up and often expanded the powers of customary hereditary rulers. They mostly refrained from engaging in social engineering, frequently conserved existing economic structures, and concentrated formal power in the hands of autocratic proconsuls who were not accountable to democratic electorates or discretionary legislatures. On the other hand, the impact of modern Europe was evident in the colonial bureaucracies staffed by persons who were admitted and promoted by merit and who operated in accordance with "scientific principles." Novel technologies and a modern web of roads, rails, ports, and telegraphs that well served the interests of capitalist enterprise (and military subjugation) were introduced. And legal systems that enshrined individual rights and in theory provided equal, certain, and fair applications of the law were imposed. In the 1930s the art critic, Léandre Vaillat, praised the colonized hybrid of modern traditionalism by citing French Morocco as a "laboratory" for occidental experimentations and a "conservatory" for oriental customs.

As we have seen, colonial encounters fell across a broad experiential spectrum. Some places, like Hawaii, were undone by colonialism while others, such as India, were less radically transformed. However uneven or contradictory colonialism's impact, it was everywhere significant. The socioeconomic milieu created by colonial rule in turn spawned new conditions and new social relationships and formations (such as the Bengali *bhadralok*). In all places, it produced opportunities that certain segments of the indigenous populations more or less successfully exploited.

In the process, the colonizers and those indigenes most intimately tied to them forged bonds of mutual dependency. For their part, the colonizers—a small caste of overlords in most colonies—could not have exercised power and privileges without the support of native soldiers, compradors, servants, commercial allies and partners, local rulers, and lower level officials. Thus, native collaboration and a politics of tacit deference were indispensable to European rule. On the other side of the colonial divide, certain of the colonized were powerfully altered by their relationships with the colonizers and typically became materially and psychologically wedded to them. Obviously, the nature of those dependencies differed markedly and in no sense could they be said to have been equal within the asymmetrical framework of colonialism. But their existence helps us to understand better how imperialism managed to sustain itself.

Thus colonialism was a world etched in shades of gray. Identities were often either in flux or became somewhat blurred. Roles were less than crystal clear. Missionaries, for example, often occupied a somewhat ambiguous position because they forged relations with the indigenes that were often more sympathetic, sometimes more knowledgeable, and almost always more intimate than was customarily the case. The European communities also had their own social lepers—vagrants, the insane, and the infirm—who occupied a sort of colonial limbo. Among the colonized, various layers of collaborators and traditional elites often mediated between the foreign rulers and the masses of the ruled. As the case of Miss Bryan and the Maharaja of Patiala showed, there were different hierarchies of dominance and subordination (in this case one based on gender) that could either fortify or cut against the grain of overarching racial hierarchies that colonialism institutionalized.

Through all this, many indigenes preserved their cultural inheritance and retained some autonomy. They both passed along and built on patterns of thought and life bequeathed by prior generations, and drew on their intellectual and social heritage in order to confront the new realities of colonialism. A few indulged in indiscriminate Westernization. Others became cultural creoles. Some selectively synthesized alien and indigenous elements, fabricating new habitats and communities in the process. Some emphatically rejected the new order and held tenaciously to established ways. But whatever the circumstance, the process of acculturation was seldom total and the native identity, however much it had been exposed to foreign influences, was never eradicated, as persistent Hawaiian anxieties during the late 1800s attest.

By combining familiar and alien practices and threading together indigenous thought and Western beliefs, the colonized fashioned diverse reactions, initiatives, and forms of resistance. Among the last was colonial nationalism—itself the offspring of a Western creation (the nation) but tailored to meet local requirements. In India, at the very summit of Western expansionism, nationalists constructed a politics along Western lines that eventually became capable of successfully challenging the *raj*. At the same time, it enabled an indigenous elite that had become partially alienated from its own cultural base (as a result of Westernization) to forge links with the general population by identifying itself with popular and potent socioreligious traditions.

Of course, all of this stresses conscious responses to imperialism and it is important to note that not every African or Asian took much notice of the "lords of human kind." Many never laid eyes on a white man, as a joke about two Indian peasants affirms. On meeting in 1967 after a long separation, one supposedly said to the other, "Did you hear that the

British have left!" (this, some twenty years after the British had departed India). To this, the friend, puzzled, retorted: "Who are the British?" Whether based in fact or fantasy, the story is a useful reminder that in many places the Western impact, however important and enduring, was not boundless.

What intensified the impact of the those colonial encounters we have surveyed was the tenor of the particular historical moment in which they took place. The era of high imperialism (1870–1914) was a distinctive moment in the even larger historical development of modern imperialism. It was a time when Western empires were on the offensive, when the global scales of harnessed power were tilted most decisively in favor of the West. Then the great European powers—and, more spasmodically, the United States—were focused on territorial occupation, economic gain, resource extraction, and strategic advantage. And so great was Europe's lead over the rest of the world, that it was able to undertake all this while diverting relatively little of its wealth, matériel, and manpower to its African, Asian, and Pacific dependencies.

There was the odd spurt of concentrated exertion and the occasional gigantic surge of patriotic adrenaline such as when Britain struggled to overcome South Africa's Boers (1899–1902) and when the Russian imperial steamroller was halted in its tracks in Korea by another expanding empire, the Japanese (1904–1905). There was also the relatively rare moment—such as the Agadir (Second Moroccan) crisis of 1911 and Britain's conquest of the Sudan in the late 1890s—when Europeans veered dangerously close to fighting each other. The latter in particular threatened to embroil European powers in a conflict entirely centered on African concerns. The dramatic climax occurred in 1898 when, after eliminating the Mahdist state in the Sudan, British forces commanded by General Sir Herbert Kitchener were confronted by a small but defiant French contingent led by Captain Jean-Baptiste Marchand at the town of Fashoda in southern Sudan. The French, like Leopold and the British themselves, had rushed in to exploit the "void" in Northeastern Africa occasioned by the decline of the Mahdists. As the British and French squared off, war seemed imminent when, at nearly the last minute, Paris climbed down and instructed its forces to retire. In the final analysis, therefore, imperialism did not provoke a cataclysmic contest: Europe did not hemorrhage itself overseas in the era of high imperialism but in its own heartland during the First and Second World Wars.

Another aspect that made this era unique was a waxing, confident colonizing ethos. Throughout much of Europe and even in the United States, the idea of empire, of ruling over other large groups of very different people, had acquired a viable currency between the Franco-Prussian War and World War I. It enjoyed a level of acceptance, if not of uncritical support, that it did not have before or since (it did not fully survive World War I). This acceptability was largely based on various ideologies of superiority. European cultural pride and racial prejudice fortified the imperialists' will and sometimes blinded them to the numerous inequities of the imperial system. Equipped with a host of justifications—divine dispensation, survival of the fittest, avid patriotism, civilizing mission—Westerners occupied and ruled over an unprecedented portion of the world. So pervasive was the notion that European rule was an agent of Afro-Asian uplift that even the no-nonsense socialist, Karl Marx, saw colonialism as a necessary and beneficial (if nasty) stage in the forced march of "backward" societies towards modernization.

With their transparent arrogance and single-minded covetousness, their assumption that the world was naturally divided into civilized and primitive camps, and their conviction that they were performing an admirable and necessary good for themselves and others, the empires of the late nineteenth century may appear to us as hulking geopolitical dinosaurs. Cumbersome and overextended, they seem to have expired in a rapidly changing global environment that they had in part shaped but that was no longer capable of nourishing them. But, as we know, the imperial record was far more complicated and inconsistent than that image presents. Certainties were softened by doubts, administrative policies were subject to internal criticism and periodic reorientations, and hubris was occasionally tempered by humility. Neither colonizer nor the colonized was a monolithic entity. But if the European behemoths no longer stride the planet at their pleasure, can we be certain that the habits of mind and the material circumstances that breathed life into them are entirely or irrevocably gone? Or is it possible that a new imperial species can arise—or has arisen—in their place?

Acknowledgments

The following works, from which substantial portions are quoted in this book, are protected by the copyright law of the United States and international copyright laws.

Clark, Leon E., *Through African Eyes: Cultures in Change* (New York: Praeger–Greenwood Publishing, 1971), page 333.

de Bary, William Theodore, Ed., *Sources of Indian Tradition*, Volume II (New York: Columbia University Press, 1958), pages 100, 120–121, 159.

Franklin, John Hope, *George Washington Williams: A Biography* (Chicago: University of Chicago Press, 1985), Appendix 1.

Grimshaw, Patricia, *Paths of Duty* (Honolulu: University of Hawaii Press, 1989), page 100.

Hinde, Sidney L., *The Fall of the Congo Arabs* (London: Methuen & Company, 1897), pages 183–185, 187–188, 200–201.

Hirschmann, Edwin, *White Mutiny* (Columbia, Mo.: South Asia Books, 1980), pages 70–71, 299.

Kuykendall, Ralph S., *The Hawaiian Kingdom, 1778–1854,* Volume I (Honolulu: University of Hawaii Press, 1938), pages 68, 31, 134, 153,194, 258–259, 361, 384, 386.

Kuykendall, Ralph S., *The Hawaiian Kingdom, 1874–1893, The Kalakaua Dynasty,* Volume III (Honolulu: University of Hawaii Press, 1967), pages 141, 242, 247, 278, 503, 633.

Liliuokalani, *Hawaii's Story by Hawaii's Queen* (Boston: Lathrop, Lee & Shepard Company, 1898), page 373.

Linnekin, Jocelyn, *Sacred Queens and Women of Consequence* (Ann Arbor: The University of Michigan Press, 1990), pages 25, 62.

Martelli, George, *Leopold to Lumumba: A History of the Belgian Congo, 1877–1960* (London: Chapman & Hall, Ltd., 1962), pages 15–16, 76–77.

Philips, C. H., Ed., *The Evolution of India and Pakistan 1858–1947 Select Documents* (London: Oxford University Press, 1962), pages 10–11. Reprinted by permission.

Russ, William Adam, Jr., *The Hawaiian Republic 1894–1898* (Selinsgrove: Susquehanna University Press, 1961), pages 311, 318.

Samarin, William J., *The Black Man's Burden* (Boulder, Colo.: Westview Press, 1989), pages 184, 239–240.

Schiffers, Heinrich, *The Quest for Africa* (New York: G. P. Putnam's Sons, 1957), pages 196–197.

Slade, Ruth, *King Leopold's Congo* (London: Oxford University Press, 1962).

Woodruff, Philip, *The Men Who Ruled India, Vol. 2: The Guardians* (New York: Schocken Books, 1964), page 48.

Glossary

Afrikaners   *see* Boers

AIA   International African Association

AIC   *Association Internationale du Congo*

Anglo-Indians   the resident British community in India; *see also:* Eurasian

askaris   European-commanded African troops

babu ("baboo")   clerk; used derisively by British to describe Westernized (especially Bengali) Indians

Bantu   largest linguistic group of Central, South, East, and West sub-Saharan Africa

bhadralok   "respectable folk"; Bengali intellectuals

biological racism   a bias confirmed by "scientifically" established differences among "racial" types supposedly based on inherited and immutable character and intelligence traits that are made visible by one's "racial" appearance

Boers/Afrikaners   South African descendants of seventeenth and eighteenth century Dutch, French Huguenot, and German settlers

Brahmo Samaj   a nineteenth and twentieth century Hindu reform society

cantonment   British military quarters in India, often adjacent to British civilian lines (called civil stations)

cassava   tropical plants from whose starchy roots bread and other foods are made

chicotte   a corkscrew-shaped whip made from hippopotamus hide

civilizing mission   imperialism viewed as the vehicle for the material and moral uplift of the colonized

comprador   agent or middleman of a foreign power

Congress   *see* Indian National Congress

copal   resin used in varnishes

cultural chauvinism   a bias in favor of one's own culture and cultural attributes (language, religion, customs)

DOAG   *Deutsche-Ostafrika Gesellschaft*, German East Africa Company

emigrationist colonialism   private or state-sponsored schemes to settle Europeans in overseas colonies

ethnocentrism   a general bias in favor of one's own group, however defined

Eurasian   of mixed European (Portuguese or British) and Indian lineage; *see also* Anglo-Indian

excentric   outside of; refers to theories of imperialism that focus on non-European or peripheral factors

fin de siècle   end of the century; circa 1880–1900

Force Publique   the para-military police force of the Congo Free State

formal (territorial) empire   consisting of political dependencies

Great *Mahele*   "Great Division": major Hawaiian land tenure reform that took place during the 1840s

haoles   white persons in Hawaii

hula   a Hawaiian dance

ICS   Indian Civil Service; the elite corps of officials, nearly all of whom were British

Indian National Congress   the foremost all-India nationalist organization; founded, 1885

indigenes   original inhabitants; "natives"

indigenous   of or pertaining to something or someone native to a particular place

informal empire   noncolonial areas under the strong influence (especially economic) of a Western power

Jain   minor but influential ancient Indian religion

kahuna   a Hawaiian priest

kahuna nui   a Hawaiian high priest

kapus   A Hawaiian system of tabus and prescribed behaviors

liwali **or** *wali*   governor under the sultan of Zanzibar

luau   Hawaiian feast

Mahdist   pertaining to the Islamic Sudanese state created by the Mahdi ("the chosen one") Muhammad Ahmad

maidan   parade ground

mana   divine force or quality

matrilineal   descended or inherited through the female line

memsahib   Englishwoman in India

metropole, metropolitan   the imperial powers; Europe and America

mission civilisatrice   *see* civilizing mission

monocultural economy   an economy based solely or mostly on the cultivation of a single crop

new/high imperialism epoch of rapid Western expansion, circa 1870–1914

"New Europes" areas beyond Europe largely peopled by Europeans (e.g., the United States, Australia, Argentina)

Nilotic of the Nile river

officiers soudanais French military officers posted to the interior Sudanic belt of West Africa

Pax Belgica/Pax Britannica "the Belgian/British peace" or "pacification"; includes the elimination and/or suppression of armed resistance to the colonial regime

periphery the colonies and informal extensions of empire; Africa, Asia, Pacific, South America

petit-blanc white settlers in French colonies of working class or peasant origins

Plasmodium falciparum the organism that causes a deadly sub-Saharan strain of malaria

proconsul high-ranking colonial official

protectionism economic policy of high tariffs to shield national industries from foreign competition

quinine anti-malarial prophylaxis derived from the bark of the cinchona tree

Qur'an (Koran) Muslim holy book conveying the revealed word of Allah (God)

raj rule; British *raj* means the British-run Government of India

ras Ethiopian nobleman, usually translated as "duke"

sahib Englishman in India

sati "true one"; faithful wife; widow self-immolation

sub-imperialism colonial expansion driven by Westerners and Western interests located along the periphery

Swahili-Arab Swahili-speaking people of mixed African (Bantu) and Arabian descent dwelling in Eastern Africa

tabu (taboo) a proscribed or prohibited act or practice

Torschlusspanik "fear of the closing door"; anxiety about dwindling global opportunities (German)

Travail et Progrès "Work and Progress," motto of Congo Free State

Uitlanders "outsiders"; non-Boer (mostly British) white immigrants to the Transvaal in late nineteenth century

Index

Bankim. *See* Chatterjee, Bankimchandra
Bannerjee, K. C., 129
Bantus
  in Central Africa, 35–36, 38–40
  in East Africa, 36
  in South Africa, 14–16
Baratieri, Oreste, 17, 18
Bartellot, Edmund, 47
Bateke, 9
Batetela, 58
Baudouinville, 46
Beames, John, 126, 130
Bechuanaland (Botswana), 15, 16
Belgian Congo (1908–1960)
  forced labor in, 62
Belgium, 1, 2, 9, 36, 40, 41, 62
  improvements in paid for by the
    Congo, 63
Bemba, 152
Bengal
  partition of 1905, 136
Bengali, 130, 137
Bengali *bhadralok,* 122, 123, 133, 134–135,
    136–137, 142
  and indigenous women, 153
Benin, 7
Besant, Annie, 149
Beveridge, Annette Akroyd, 121–122, 149
Bhagavad Gita, 139
Bismarck, Otto von, 4, 9, 21
  and colonialism, 19, 21, 24
Blaine, James G., 88
Boers, 14–16, 27
  commandos, 21
Boma, 50
Bonded labor
  abolition within British empire, 108
  global patterns, 107–109
  motivations and conditions of, 108–109
Borgnis–Desbordes, Gustave, 11
Bornu, 7
Brahmo Samaj, 134
Branson, James, 122
Brazil
  European immigration and, 106
Brindian, 129
Britain, xii, xv, 1, 2, 44, 91, 95, 98
  emigrationist colonialism, 106
  ex–colonial communities in, 111
Britain in Egypt, 9, 11, 18, 24, 47
Britain in South Africa, 14–16
British army in India, 116, 125
British community in India (Anglo–
    Indians), 106, 114, 120, 124–126

assessment of, 132
  lifestyles and rituals of, 129–132
  responses to Ilbert Bill, 119–124
British economic activity in and control of
    India, 116–117
British imperialism, 14–16
  in Africa, 25, 26
  in India, 68, 113–145, 159–160
  in the Sudan, 68. *See also* Sudan
British influence in Hawaii, 74, 76, 79, 97,
    99
British South Africa Company, 26
British views
  of Indians, 117–118, 120, 121, 123, 124,
    130–132, 142–143
  of their role in India, 115, 117, 123–124,
    142–143
British Women's Emigration Association,
    148
Brussels Treaty (1890), 28
Bryan, Miss Florry, 128, 159
Buddhists
  in India, 115, 139
Buganda, 7, 26
Burkina Faso, 11, 12
Burma, 109

Cadbury, William, 60
California gold rush, 85
Cameroon (Kamerun), 9, 24
Canada, 15, 94
  European immigration and, 104, 105, 106
  Indians in, 107
  and Native Americans, 109
Cape Colony, 14–15
Cape to Cairo scheme, 26
Carnarvon, Lord, 15, 26
Casablanca, xi
Casement, Sir Roger
  career of, 50–51, 59
  indictment of the Congo Free State by,
    51, 53, 59–60, 61
Cassava, 35
Catholic Missionaries in the Congo, 55, 56
Cayor state, 12
Central Africa, 9, 66. *See also* Congo
Chad, 68
Chagga, 21
Chamberlain, Joseph, 15, 26
Chatterjee, Bankimchandra, 136–137, 138,
    139, 141, 143
China, xi, 41, 91
  concessionary imperialism in, 91
  trade, 82, 91, 93, 94–95